AFRICAN CULTURAL KNOWLEDGE

Themes and Embedded Beliefs

Compiled and Edited by
Michael C. Kirwen

Nairobi, Kenya

Compilations and text copyright © 2005 Maryknoll Institute of African Studies.
Art work by a variety of African artists.
Published in Nairobi Kenya, 2005.

Queries regarding rights and permissions should be addressed to:
Maryknoll Institute of African Studies,
P.O. Box 15199
00509, Lang'ata
Kenya.

Cover and text design by Maryknoll Institute of African Studies.
Library of Congress cataloging-in-Publication Data
Library of Congress Control Number: 2006306154
ISBN 9966-7126-0-7

AFRICAN CULTURAL KNOWLEDGE

Themes and Embedded Beliefs

Editor
Michael C. Kirwen
Assisted By
Denis Odinga Okiya   Edith Kayeli Chamwama
Production Editor
Edith Kayeli Chamwama

HISTORY AND PURPOSE

The Maryknoll Institute of African Studies (MIAS) is a post-graduate Institute offering courses and programs on-site in Nairobi. The Institute is academically affiliated to Saint Mary's University, MN/USA and Tangaza College, Nairobi, Kenya. Through Saint Mary's University, the Institute offers a Master of Arts (MA) in African Studies and a Master of African Studies (MAS), a professionally focused degree. Through Tangaza College, a constituent college of the Catholic University of Eastern Africa, it offers a joint Tangaza College/Saint Mary's University Certificate in African Studies and a Tangaza College Diploma in African Studies. The Institute's courses are of a participatory type in which students do one hour of professional-quality field research for every hour of class. Courses are offered on both a twelve week Semester basis and a three week Immersion basis. The field research is facilitated by Kenyan university graduates, trained as field assistants, who work with students on a one-to-one basis. Students are required to write a paper for each course in which they show their ability to integrate field research data with the material of the class lectures and bibliographic readings.

Copies are available at the following address
P. O. Box 15199, Lang'ata , 00509, Kenya. Ph. (254-20) 890-765
Fax (254-20) 891-145 Email: miasmu@tangaza.org
Website: http://www.mias.edu

DEDICATION

To the memory of the late Professors Katama Mkangi of
United States International University-Kenya,
Osaga Odak and Odera Oruka of University of Nairobi
and Cuthbert Omari of University of Dar Es Salaam.
Their wisdom and knowledge of African culture
were an inspiration to the content of this book.

TABLE OF CONTENTS

PROLOGUE

African Cultural Knowledge is a magnificent effort at a pedagogical facilitation of a serious and, if you like, a realistic engagement with the anthropological complexities and psychological intricacies of the colorful tapestry of the African culture. In seeking and actually succeeding in plumbing the sub-structural depths of the cultural life of the African societies, it brings to the surface a sharp and bewildering outline of the foundational substance, spiritual underpinnings and commonalities of the African cultural experience and practices. It is a masterpiece of archaeology of cultural phenomena that ends up producing a grammar of culture. It achieves this by exploring, with extraordinary insight, the mystifying superstructures of the African cultural life and by articulating a theoretical narrative that enjoys a near-universal application across ethnic, racial and social delimitations.

The fifteen-theme structure of cultural knowledge suggests, in reductionist manner, how culture can be studied, understood and appreciated in its phenomenological relationship with its essential character. It illuminates the ambiguous relativism of cultural expressions and practices as variously captured in philosophical and sociological texts and traditions. The result is a unique contribution to the methodology of and practical engagement with African cultural reality. In this particular way it breaks new ground in its field.

Prof. Edward Oyugi
Department of Psychology
Kenyatta University,
Nairobi, Kenya, November 2005

FOREWORD

THE MAJOR IMPLICATIONS OF THIS BOOK REGARDING CULTURAL KNOWLEDGE

The African cultural themes presented in this book are located in the very structure of the unconscious, the vast neural network of the mind and memory that interprets experiences and promotes behavior in an automatic mode. The material of this book presents cultural knowledge as an ensemble of fifteen foundational themes. Awareness of these themes allows persons to understand their pervasiveness in their cultural lives, to own and possess them as adults, to be freed from their manipulations, and to teach them systematically.

The hypothesis is that the **theme** of each chapter will resonate and have meaning in all African cultures. Thus, it is the shared cultural knowledge that is the fundamental source of the cosmic and spiritual unity of more than half a billion African people.

The explanation of the themes can also be read as an expression of the beliefs of African spirituality, that is, its underpinning symbols, lived values and ideas, objectified and expressed in a written medium. Also by way of comparison, these beliefs coincide with the underpinning lived values, ideals and beliefs of many spiritualities worldwide, including those of Christianity and Islam.

The delineation of culture into universal themes is not unique to the Maryknoll Institute of African Studies (MIAS). Universals have been part of the conceptual framework of anthropology for many years. Brown (1991) in the third chapter of his book *Human Universals,* discusses the contribution of scholars such as E.B. Tylor (1891), L. Kroeber (1917), Clark Wissler (1923), Franz Boas (1963), and George Stocking (1968), all wrote extensively on the status, role and function of universals, ranging from extreme cultural relativism to monolithic cultural unity.

Furthermore, Brown (1991) describes culture as divisible into "traits" (single items) and "complexes" (more or less integrated collections of traits) (p.40). The "traits" are referred to in MIAS as **domains** (activities), while the "complexes" are the **themes** (values, symbols and ideas). Moreover, as demonstrated by responses from non-African MIAS participants, the fifteen-theme model is not exclusive to African cultures but can be applied to other cultures worldwide. This makes the MIAS cultural model **universal**, a term defined by Brown (1991) as a trait or complex present in all individuals, . . . all societies, all cultures, or all languages – provided that the trait or complex is not too obviously anatomical or physiological or too remote from the higher mental functions (p. 42). Indeed, the fifteen-theme structure of cultural knowledge can be understood as a paradigm of the very nature of human cultures, and as an explanation of socio-cultural integration and development.

The analysis of the field research data into thematic structures follows closely the model presented by Spradley (1980) in his book *Participant Observation* -- the MIAS text book for teaching professional field research techniques and analysis of data.

In this book MIAS presents a new methodology for cultural studies by means of which one can systematically explain, demonstrate and teach African cultural knowledge in a holistic way. This method enables students to see the interrelation of the various themes and how they furnish a comprehensive and consistent interpretation and response to the daily flow of one's cultural life.

Prof. Michael C. Kirwen, PhD, MM
Director: MIAS
Associate Dean: Saint Mary's Un/Mn.
Nairobi, Kenya, November 2005

PREFACE

Since 1989, the MIAS staff and lecturers have presented and discussed the various themes of African cultural knowledge, but did so in a piecemeal manner, without seeing their inner connection or recognizing that together they comprise the basic structure of African cultural knowledge. It is as if they were walking among the trees i.e., the themes but unable to see the forest i.e., the interconnection that creates and sustains the themes. As editing of the material on the fifteen themes from students' worksheets progressed, it dawned on the editors that they had come upon a major breakthrough in understanding the very structure of African cultural knowledge in a comprehensive way. As a result, there is now a holistic understanding and explanation of how African cultural knowledge promotes behavior and interprets the experiences of the ordinary African person from birth to death and beyond. Furthermore, this knowledge, through the fifteen-theme structure presented in this book can now be taught systematically and comprehensively.

As far as is known, the pinpointing of fifteen foundational themes of cultural knowledge is something no other program does or has done. This approach, therefore, represents a major advance in the field of cultural studies. **African cultural knowledge as presented in this publication is the case study** for this type of thematic analysis.

The issue of there being fifteen themes is not set in stone, as other cultures might have extra themes, or a theme like adulthood and elderhood could be presented as two separate themes. Moreover, the material of this book could be organized following a different model or paradigm. However, foundational themes, like grammatical structures of languages, are always limited in number. Indeed, just as speech is possible because of shared grammatical structures that automatically give meaning to sounds according to their pitch and order, so also cultural communication and interaction is possible because of shared internalized thematic structures that automatically create the "normal" interpretation of experiences and patterns of behavior. Cultural themes therefore are actively present in the subconscious minds of members of a culture, and are accessed as needed just like internalized language structures.

The challenges for both African and non-African students when reading this book is to contextualize the themes within their own cultural knowledge and activities. For **African students** the process entails recognizing and understanding the themes as the roots and foundation of the cultural knowledge which is theirs by reason of birth. For **non-African students** the process is to apply these themes to their own cultural knowledge, seeing the African expression of these themes as the stepping stones to understanding and appreciating the way their own cultures are structured, made holistic, and underpinned by similar themes.

ACKNOWLEDGMENTS

Sincere gratitude is expressed to the faculty, students and field research assistants of the Maryknoll Institute of African Studies who made this book a reality through their written responses to the themes forming the fifteen chapters of this book.

Gratitude is also expressed to Missio Munich and the Maryknoll Fathers and Brothers for funds that enabled this work to be published.

INTRODUCTION

Based on field research data collected and analyzed over the past seventeen years, the Maryknoll Institute of African Studies has categorized cultural knowledge into fifteen themes and thirty-five domains*. The themes are the major values, symbols and ideas that bring wholeness and coherence to a culture. The themes explain the nature of life, the nature of creation, the nature of evil, etc. Underneath and within these themes are thirty-five cultural domains, that is, specific activities, rituals, attitudes and happenings that make up the ordinary events in the lives of human beings, from birth to death and beyond.

Themes and domains can be imagined as a thirty-five room mansion with the themes being the foundations, doors, archways, roofs, etc. and the domains being the rooms e.g., the room of marriage, of sickness, of initiation into adulthood, of birth, of political leadership, etc. In an African context, the imagery is that of a rural homestead with thirty-five grass-roofed houses. The themes are the hedge around the homestead, the main gate, the grass roofs, mud walls, the doors, kraals, etc. whereas each grass-roofed house represents one of the cultural events in the life of an individual such as marriage, birth, adolescence, mourning, work, sacrifice, etc. Or the themes can also be imagined as a fifteen piece orchestra playing constantly but subconsciously in one's mind and memory.

MIAS, a post-graduate program, specializes in transforming participants into articulate adults of African cultural knowledge. To facilitate this, each class day, **one** cultural theme and **two** domains are presented. Students are asked to reflect on and briefly write out their meanings within their personal lives and that of the cultures from which they come. The data on the cultural themes presented in the book has been collated from worksheets written between January and August, 2003. The data therefore, are the spontaneous writings of field assistants and students, all of whom are university graduates, the majority being Africans. The ethnic identity of African respondents and the nationality of foreign respondents is indicated in order to illustrate the point that these cultural patterns are shared across ethnic boundaries not only in Africa but elsewhere throughout the world. The responses of the Africans are clear evidence that African cultural knowledge is still the dominant paradigm that directs the lives of ordinary African people, interprets their experiences and creates their artifacts.

The book is divided into fifteen chapters, one for each foundational theme. It begins with the theme *Creator God* (Chapter 1). The arrangement of the chapters is such that spiritual themes come first followed by foundational themes of human community and its preservation, and finally themes undermining the welfare of human communities ending in death. Note that the total number of responses **(R)** listed in the categories is often greater than the total number of respondents **(N)**. This is because many of the respondents included several different categories in their responses.

* There is an intention to publish a book based on the Domains and following the same format.

CHAPTER I
Theme: **CREATOR GOD**

A West African stool in which the Creator God, symbolized by the sun and moon, is supporting all that exists.

CREATOR GOD

Introduction

   All humanity stands in awe and reverence when contemplating both the vastness and intricacies of the world in which humanity finds itself. The questions that are inescapable are: where did this world come from, who made it and where is it going?

God in Africa

   For the more than 500 million Africans South of the Sahara there is only one answer, namely, a creator God who is pure spirit, the source of all life and reality. To deny the existence of the creator God is seen by Africans to be an untenable position. Anyone taking an atheistic position is seen to be not only immature but spiritually without wisdom.

God Elsewhere

   In other cultures the question of creation has many and varied answers ranging from a principle of novelty (a prime mover), a creator God (Christianity and Islam), an unanswerable question (Buddhism and agnosticism) to outright denial (atheism). However every living mature person will have some kind of an answer to the meaning of the cosmos, relationships and the transcendent.

QUESTION

In terms of African cultural knowledge, what is your understanding of the theme of CREATOR GOD? N = 58 [39 Africans, 19 non-Africans]

RESPONSES COLLATED BY FOUR CATEGORIES

[Note that the italicized words in each category illustrate the major ideas and beliefs regarding God's nature and humanity's interaction with God.]

   1. *Attributes of God R=143*
   2. *How God is Known R=31*
   3. *The Responsibilities of Humanity towards God R=13*
   4. *How God is Approached R=18*

AFRICAN RESPONDENTS   N = 39

Attributes of God   (R = 95)

God is a ***creator***, as God is seen as the source of all that exists both living and non-living (24), God is a ***supernatural being*** and a ***controller;*** God is ***higher than any other beings*** that exist on earth and in heaven (15), God is a ***provider*** of resources to all in need in form of land, livestock and children (12), God is ***omnipresent*** because God is present everywhere and in everything that exists

(11), God is *omnipotent* as God is all-powerful and also a vital force (11), God is *pure spirit* therefore invisible to the naked eye and is neither man nor woman (4), God is *beyond comprehension*, as no one can *understand God* nor the *unexplainable phenomenon* that God causes, thus there are *no images of God* in Africa (4), God is a *sustainer* as God prolongs life through lineages and maintains all that is living through forces of nature like light and air (4), *protector* as God takes care of cosmic justice and defends the people (3), has *ownership* of everything on earth and beyond (3), God is *eternal* as God has no beginning nor ending (2), God is *all-knowing,* for God knows all that happens to us (2).

How God is Known   (R=23)

God is known by *blessings* to people through provisions of food, the birth of a child and rewards (8), through *punishments* meted out in form of calamities such as famine, drought, barrenness, floods and lack of sons (7), by *manifestation* in the wonders of creation such as fertility of families, rainfall, abundant food, produce, and livestock (4), by *names* given to God such as *Ngai* for the Agikuyu connoting one who apportions, *Nyakalaga* for the Luo meaning one who is everywhere, *Obong'o* a Luo word denoting the only one and *Amusaba* meaning the Maker in Teso language (4).

The Responsibilities of Humanity towards God   (R=13)

It is the responsibility of man to *revere* and *respect* God (3), to *continue God's* work of c*reation* through reproduction (2), man is *not to call upon God unnecessarily*, lest it brings out God's wrath (2), to *fear* God (2), *not to question* God (1), to *obey* God without failure (1), to live a *God centered life* (1), *not to say bad things about God* (1).

How God is Approached   (R=16)

God is approached through *worship and prayer* at any time and place (6), by going to God's *sacred dwelling* places found in mountains, trees and lakes (5), *sacrifices*, *offerings* and *rituals* as means of appeasing God when God is discontented with us (4), through *intermediaries* such as ancestors (1).

NON-AFRICAN RESPONDENTS N=19
[The respondents answered according to both their own cultures and their understanding of African culture.]

Attributes of God   (R = 48)

God is *omnipresent* as God is everywhere (12), God is *creator* as God is the source of life (11), God is the *sustainer* of life through light and air and the continuation of the lineage (5), God is *beyond comprehension* thus the reason there is no image depicting possible interpretation (5), God is *pure spirit* (5), God is *omnipotent* as God is all-powerful (4), God is a *Unifier* as God unites all of creation (2), God is a *caregiver* and takes care of all creation (2), God is a *protector* (1), God is *immortal* (1).

How God is Known (R=8)
God is known by *manifestation* through wonders of creation such as the sun, moon, harvest, rain and fertility of families (5), God is experienced through *nature,* and *key moments of life* such as fertility, transformation and transition in life (2), through *names* given to God e.g., in the Cameroon country God is known as a question "Who Is This?" (1).

How God is Approached (R=2)
God is approached through *worship and prayer* (1), through *intermediaries* such as spirits, diviners, Jesus and the Bible (1).

SUMMARY
Beliefs expressed regarding the nature of Creator God

God is: the *creator*, a *supernatural being, provider, controller, protector, owner of everything, all knowing* and *eternal*. God is a *unifier, caregiver, omnipresent, omnipotent,* a *pure spirit, sustainer, immortal and beyond comprehension.*

God is Known by: *blessings to people, punishment meted out, key moments of life, manifestation* through nature and the *names* given to God.

Human Being's Responsibilities towards God: *revering, respecting, obeying,* and *fearing God.* They are to continue *God's work of creation through reproduction,* live a *God-centered life, not to question nor call upon God unnecessarily.*

God is Approached through: *worship* and *prayer, sacrifices, offerings, rituals, intermediaries,* and by going to God's *sacred dwelling places.*

RESPONSES FROM WORKSHEETS

[Note that the Creator God is pure spirit, the supreme non-human Being who is the ultimate source and controller of all aspects of life. Furthermore, note that these ideas are shared across African ethnic boundaries.]

❑　　**In terms of African cultural knowledge, what is your understanding of the theme of CREATOR GOD?**

AFRICAN RESPONDENTS　N = 39

[There were ten ethnic groups of Africa represented: Luo (14), Agikuyu (9), Abaluyia (4), Akamba (3), Abagusii (2), Aembu (2), Teso (2), Kipsigis (1), Akan (1), and Bemba (1). The respondents were university graduates; eight women and thirty-one men.]

- Creator is a power from above and it is a must that we keep on praying and uphold the creator on the highest level. You are not allowed to say bad things about the creator. (Abaluyia)
- Creator God means God is the originator of all that exists. God made or created the world and all the living beings in it. God is the provider, protector and originator of everything. (Akan)
- My understanding of the theme of creator God in terms of African cultural knowledge is that God is a supreme being who ought to be feared and respected. God is viewed as the provider and the cause of all phenomena over those that cannot be explained factually. (Luo)
- God is life and life is God. There is no way you can separate these two. Whatever you do determines your life presently and thereafter. (Abagusii)
- God is the giver of life, the protector, and the almighty. God is said to be all-powerful and all-present like light and air. God is experienced in the wonders of creation, the fertility of families, the harvest, and the livestock. (Luo)
- God is the one provider, present everywhere and the one who brought and brings all into being. (Luo)
- Creator God is the provider, sustainer and the maintainer of life. He is everywhere at all times and expects us to obey him without failure. He is all-powerful, invisible, neither man nor woman. He is a spirit that watches over all of us. (Agikuyu)
- Creator God is depicted as the creator of all things in existence according to African cultural knowledge. Since most African societies were patriarchal, He is depicted as the creator of man, and later created a woman. In Aembu culture, God created the man and then gave him a wife, whom He cautioned not to ask where she had come from. (Aembu)

- God is perceived to be the origin of life. He is the arch-elder, the source of life and vital force. (Aembu)
- God is supreme. He is the creator and sustainer of life. Nothing happens to us that He does not allow. When He is pleased with us, things go well. The birth of a child is a sign that God wishes to bless the couple. This is why prayers are made to Him at all times. (Abaluyia)
- In African culture it was believed that God existed. This can be manifested in the way Africans were notoriously religious, offering sacrifices to appease God and living lives that were generally centered on God. The theme creator God means that the origin of all things including knowledge and attitudes can be traced back to God who is our maker. (Luo)
- The creator is everywhere *(Nyakalaga)* and the only one *(Obong'o)*. (Luo)
- In African cultural knowledge there are a number of gods, for example the harvest god, the god of the underworld and so on. However the chief God is the creator God, and this whole collectivity of gods is seen as a "government" with different gods having different "ministries." However these gods are not visible to the human being but know all and see all as they live in heavens. (Teso)
- God the creator is supreme and the one whom the Iteso call *Amusaba* (Maker). The only one who can make. He is worshipped, respected and feared. He cannot be mentioned anyhow. He is always referred to as mighty and no one can do without him. He is always with us at home, in the garden, at school, and when traveling etc. He listens. (Teso)
- God blesses people through many actions that we see e.g., rain, food harvest, etc. and He can equally curse them through droughts, barrenness, daughters and no sons, floods, etc. God is the overall creator through whom ancestors bless or curse us. God has to be worshipped and appeased in case He is angry, and He is revered in the society. (Abagusii)
- The creator God is founder and giver of life, the sustainer of life and reality. In Akamba He is referred to as *Ngai Mumbi, Mwatuangi,* which basically means the creator, sustainer and almighty and He is all present in the whole life. (Akamba)
- In our Kalenjin community, which is further narrowed to Kipsigis, the theme creator God mainly applies to a supernatural being who controls everything and a provider of things like rain. This Being is worshipped by the community and in case of a calamity, people gather in one place, normally a holy place such as a mountain. This should have olive trees. This is where they present their sacrifice to this supernatural being that was only imagined but not seen. (Kipsigis)
- According to African culture, the creator God is a supernatural being who has power over every creature. He possesses super natural power over every

creature here on earth and in heaven. He is a supernatural being and is omnipresent i.e., He exists everywhere. (Agikuyu)

- My understanding of the theme of creator God is that God is creator of the universe and the author of life. Africans believe that God is not only a creator but also a provider and protector hence the different names given to Him. In my own tribe, God is called *Kabumba* which means supreme being, almighty, creator of all things that are seen such as rivers, human life, animals, trees, the sky, moon, and sun just to mention a few. (Bemba)

- In the hierarchy of supernatural beings, God is the highest being. He is creator of the universe. (Luo)

- Creator God among the Agikuyu culture is the father and provider for all the Agikuyu people. He gave them *Githaka* i.e., land around Mount Kenya. The name of God *Ngai* is from the root *Mugai* i.e., He who apportions resources to those in need. So, God, *Ngai,* is the one who apportions natural resources, animals (domestic) and fertile soil to his children. (Agikuyu)

- God, whose name denotes one who spreads like Lake Victoria, is beyond comprehension. He gives life to people and has a listening ear for all. God is love but can be judgmental. People living immorally are already condemned. (Luo)

- According to my cultural knowledge, God is the one who brings rainfall and has all the power to give and get. (Akamba)

- God is source of life and this is experienced in the mystery of creation. God is spirit and we are all continuing with God's creative act of creation. (Luo)

- In my culture, men and women believe God was at the mountain, which was considered a very high point. Later they changed and believed He lived at a tree called *Mugumo*. It was believed that if one went around the tree several times your problems would be solved. The tree is still respected today, and if it fell down due to rains, a ritual has to be performed before it is removed from there (even if it has blocked the road). God was the most powerful of all the supernatural beings for them. (Agikuyu)

- The theme creator God in African culture is in everything: their daily lives, and even in activities, in the harvests, the rains and in the new born. All the things that they do have a base and a meaning in God. The presence of God is felt everywhere and all the time. All things on earth belong to Him. When annoyed He brings drought, famine and even diseases. Rituals are performed to please God and the ancestors. (Luo)

- I understand God as a giver of life, a provider and preserver of human life. God continues the process of creation every time we see a child born or when we see plants sprout. (Abaluyia)

- The supreme creator or *Jachwech* in Luo and it is He who punishes, rewards and exonerates. He is [unique] *Obong'o* and all over *Nyakalaga*. (Luo)

- The theme creator God refers to God as the core of all creation. Nothing happens that He does not know or have control of. He is represented in nature through the sun, rain, wind, harvests and water forms, etc. For this reason, one does not need to pray at a formal time; invoking God while at work, etc. is seen as praying, since He is all over. However, being Holy, His name is not to be taken in vain by being called out without any reason or it will bring out His wrath. (Luo)

- God is everywhere, in everything, and He controls all activities. He is the author of life and the giver of everything. (Luo)

- Creator God is the source of all the things. Literally, the creator God is giver of all things from rain to life. All forms of good things are viewed as blessings from creator God and all evils/calamities are viewed as discontentment from God (the creator). (Akamba)

- God is regarded as the creator and maker of everything in life. His dwelling place was regarded as a Holy place usually in the mountain. People usually appease God so that evil things do not happen to them. (Agikuyu)

- God is the source of life. The theme underpins all other domains in African culture. God rewards and punishes the people depending on their way of life. The theme of creator God makes religion so profound in its diverse beliefs and practices. (Agikuyu)

- The owner of all that is and the provider for all that is. He is the super provider and controller of the universe. He takes care of cosmic justice. (Luo)

- God is the source of life. (Luo)

- From my cultural background, God is owner of the universe, the Supreme Being and the giver i.e., *Mugai*. (Agikuyu)

- He is an all-knowing and omnipotent God, who manifests Himself in different ways. He is transcendent and has to be approached with respect. He has a reason for creating all that exists on earth. He is the source of all that is to be found on earth, except for evil, which is the consequence of man's failure. (Abaluyia)

- In Agikuyu, creator is *Mumbi*. Therefore, in all creation, God is the author of life. (Agikuyu)

- God is omnipresent, lives eternally and He is present or lives on higher grounds-peak of Mount Kenya where no one can reach. God created our first ancestors and gave them livestock and land. All children and things are gifts from God. He gives according to His will. (Agikuyu)

NON-AFRICAN RESPONDENTS N = 19
[The respondents answered both according to their own cultures and their understanding of African culture.]

[There were six non-African countries represented: America (11), Norway (4), Spain (1), Poland (1), Ireland (1), and Indonesia (1). The respondents were university graduates, twelve women and seven men.]

- Perhaps my assistant said it best; "God is everywhere in Africa" as we stood in *Uchumi* and I commented on praise music sounding over the P.A. system. It is critical to understand that God is the "source and foundation of life and reality." It is important to know God as "light and air"-- substances that sustain life and growth. (American)
- Creator God is the one who brought the world into being and maintains it. Creator God does not have an image depicting possible interpretation. Africans do not deny God, to do that is to deny one's existence. Creator God cannot be limited to words but instead appreciated and immortalized through creation. (American)
- I understand that God is very much present in an African's thoughts, actions, etc. on a daily if not moment-by-moment basis. But I also get the sense that God is removed, that is, the ancestors take a more active/pivotal role in one's daily life, and that the supreme being is somehow 'secondary.' (American)
- In terms of African cultural knowledge, my understanding of the theme creator God is as the source and foundation of all life and reality. (Indonesian)
- I understand the creator God to be absolutely foundational and central to African cultural knowledge. All life and reality flows from God. Thus God is all pervasive, all present and inextricably part of all experience. God is particularly experienced in the cycles and vitality of the natural world, and in the key moments of life and death, decay and renewal, fertility, transition and transformation. (American)
- God is present everywhere in the African culture. The wonders of nature are all signs of His presence. It is not possible to think, to live or to love without relating it to God. God is spirit that is why there are no images of God in African culture. (Spaniard)
- The theme of creator God in African cultural knowledge is very important. We can find it in the African story in the [African] religion. (Norwegian)
- God is said to be all-powerful and all-present like light and air. God is experienced in the wonders of creation, the sun and moon, the harvests, the rain, fertility of families and livestock. (Norwegian)

- From what I can understand, creator God is an omni-present being who can only be experienced through His creation, including other people. Since the African spirit world is so prevalent, I believe that this influences and supports their connection to the Holy Spirit. This supports the idea that the Holy Spirit is always with us. (American)

- Creator God brings life from death and re-creates the world with every birth. Each birth carries on ancestral lives and traits created by God. Names are symbolic of the ancestors living in the newly born. The creator God initiates the process by which humanity carries on with ancient traits throughout eternity. (American)

- God is giver and sustainer of life and as such all beings depend on Him. For the African, God cannot be expressed in an image. In Cameroon, God is called "who is this?" a question not a noun. God is a vital force present in all creation. My question: is God a personal God to the Africans? (American)

- Creator God is present in all of creation--uniting all of creation. There is a sense of unity in all of life and no dualism. God is pure spirit and enters all aspects of life at all times and all places, so there is no need to set special times and places for prayer and worship--sense and presence of God is profound and brings a unity of spirit with all of life. (American)

- God the creator is the one who creates everything, sustains everything and takes care of all. (Polish)

- God is pure spirit. God is known through the wonders of creation like the sun and the moon. God is the source of all life and is seen in the fertility of families, in the growth of crops and the protection of each one, the wonders of new life in all its forms. (American)

- I have seen a great deal of symbiosis with creation, and a dependence upon all of creation together for survival. (American)

- God has created everything. His spirit is present in all of His creation. (Norwegian)

- From the history written what I understand is that the Creator started everything and this is explained in several different aspects. (Norwegian)

- God is transcendent and all-powerful. God is known by many through intermediaries such as spirits or diviners or Jesus Christ and the Bible. (American)

- Creator God is a life giving power. Like the sun giving light, creator God is giving life to everything alive on earth. He started it all and is still taking care. (Irish)

EDITOR'S REFLECTIONS

Missionaries in Africa towards the end of the nineteenth century assumed that Africans did not have a concept of a monotheistic creator God. Many of the earlier writings indicate their concern that Africans were polytheistic rather than monotheistic, a theory that was later disapproved. From time immemorial, Africans have conceived of God as one Supreme non-human being who is the creator of all. However, Africans preferred to address their problems to beings such as ancestors who are closer to them. In some of the traditions it is said that small human problems should be solved by ancestors. God should only be approached in case of a major problem.

For Africans, God should be approached in reverence as the source of all life and reality. Moreover, it should be recognized that there are major differences between the God of Christianity and the God of African religion.

DISCUSSION QUESTIONS

1. Where would you place God's abode in this earthly world?
2. Do the ancestors act as intermediaries between God and people in your community?
3. Is the God of Africa involved in human affairs like the God of Christianity?
4. What is your personal understanding of the idea of a creator God?

AFRICAN ILLUSTRATION

GOD'S PRESENCE AND POWER

A Burundian Catholic seminarian on his visits home would say prayers with his mother and siblings, while his father looked on. This puzzled him, and in a book he wrote:

> One day I was so bold as to ask him why he didn't join us for evening prayers. Actually, when mother gathered us to pray before meals or before going to bed, my father said nothing. He remained in his place. Seated. He watched us, we the children, and mother, his wife. It remained an enigma to me. That is why I questioned him. "My son, you are under delusion. You think we have to use formulas in order to pray to Imana our God. When I contemplate the work Imana has accomplished in my house I have no need to tell him about it. Before him I keep silence, and I offer him in silence the house over which he had made me head." (Kayoya, M.(1973) *My Father's Footprints: A Search for Values*. Nairobi: East African Publishing House, p. 35)

RECOMMENDED READINGS

Mbiti, J.S. (1975). *Concepts of God in Africa.* Southampton: The Camelot Press Ltd.

Olupona, J.K. (Ed.) (1991). Major Issues in the Study of African Traditional Religion. In *African Traditional Religions in Contemporary Society.* (pp. 25-23). New York: Paragon House.

Paris, P.J. (1995). *The Spirituality of African Peoples: The Search for a Common Moral Discourse.* (pp. 27-33). Minneapolis: Fortress Press.

NON-AFRICAN ILLUSTRATION

THE CHRISTIAN BELIEF IN GOD AS TRIUNE AS EXPRESSED IN THE NICENE CREED

We believe in one God,
the father, the Almighty,
maker of heaven and earth,
Of all that is seen and unseen.

We believe in one Lord, Jesus Christ,
the only son of God,
Eternally begotten of the Father,
God from God, Light from Light,
true God from true God . . .

For us men and for our salvation
he came down from heaven:
by the power of the Holy Spirit
he was born of the Virgin Mary, and became man . . .

We believe in the Holy Spirit, the Lord, the giver of life,
who proceeds from the Father and the Son.
With the Father and the Son he is worshipped and glorified . . .

CHAPTER II
Theme: ANCESTORS

ANCESTORS
WAHENGA/MAHOKA

The abstract carving by a Makonde artist represents the ancestors, who are spiritual in appearance and closer to God. The image shows the features of a human being such as the hand, foot, nose, ear, teeth, breast and eyes, indicating that the ancestors still able to participate in human activities.

ANCESTORS

Introduction

The question asked worldwide is what happens to a person after physical death. Humanity, in general, does not accept that death is the end of a person's conscious life. The question is where do the people go and what is their role?

African Ancestors

For Africans, physical death is the beginning of the process of dying as one enters into the ancestral community. In fact, Africans do not die in a western sense; they merely transit into another community and then return in the persons of the newly born babies that carry their names. Furthermore, the ancestors being close to God the creator are seen as the owners of life and the protectors of the living and can order, control and affect the lives of the living for better or worse. The fact that they appear in dreams, is proof positive that they are still alive and interested in their friends and families that are still on the earth.

Ancestors Elsewhere

The Christian churches celebrate their ancestors by rituals of sainthood. The secular societies do a similar thing by building monuments and naming streets and buildings after those who were seen to be very important in developing and protecting their societies. Families worldwide remember their dead by elaborate funeral rituals, cemetery headstones at the place of burial, and expensive mausoleums. The Koreans store the ashes of their dead in urns which are placed in a small shrine within their homes, and every year there are special rituals to commemorate their dead. Christian people often pray to (and for) their dead loved one. However, the influence of the dead on the living is only by way of conjecture as there is no sense that they have any power of their own, and can only intercede for the petitioner by taking the appeal to God directly. The belief is that those who die in virtue live on in the presence of God in a place called heaven, while those who die in vice live in the presence of the devil in a place called hell. There is no society anywhere in the world that does not respond ritually and have beliefs regarding the fate of the deceased.

QUESTION

Kindly explain in detail your understanding of the theme of ANCESTORS. Does it have any meaning in your personal, social and community life? N = 60 (47 Africans, 13 non-Africans).

RESPONSES COLLATED BY EIGHT CATEGORIES
1. *Role of Ancestors in the Community R = 72*
2. *Relevance of the Theme of Ancestors R = 38*
3. *Definition of Ancestors R = 41*
4. *Responsibility of People to Ancestors R = 22*
5. *Characteristics of Ancestors R = 19*
6. *Where Ancestors Reside R = 8*
7. *Ancestors and Christianity R = 6*
8. *Communication Between Ancestors and the Living R = 3*

Other Comments R = 18

AFRICAN RESPONDENTS N = 47

Role of Ancestors in the Community (R = 56)
Protect the living (6), are *moral guardians* (6), give people their *identity* (4), give *blessings* (4), are *intermediaries* between people, God and other spiritual beings (4), are *community guides* (4), *owners of land* (3), *owners of livestock* (3), *source of life* (3), set up *laws that govern* people in different aspects and areas of the community (3), owners of *vital resources* (2), *punish offenders* (2), act as *role models* (2), *warn* people *of misfortunes* (2), developed *customs and values* (2), are *custodians of culture* (2), maintain *communication* with the living whenever there is an event, *assisting them where necessary* (1), are *care givers* (1), *give* people *wisdom* (1), *pray* for the community (1).

Relevance of the Theme of Ancestors (R = 28)
We still use *ancestors names*, hence *reflect their personality* (6), do not have any relevance (3), *personality and character* of the living resembles that of the *ancestors they are named after* (3), the living are *a reincarnation* of the ancestors (3), since *life is recycled,* I am part and parcel of the ancestral reality (2), ancestors can influence one's life either *positively or negatively* (2), they are *forefathers* of the community (2), *regarded affectionately* as they still have a *stake in the physical world* (1), we *inherited most of the skills and arts* from them (1), helps people accept the fact that *physical death is a passage* to another form of life (1), skills they developed form the *basis of our economic and social development* (1), ancestors *point to our history* in time (1), are *guides for sexual relations* (1), way to *honor* the people who *lived tirelessly* for their community, and *contributed good things to all* (1).

Definition of Ancestors (R = 29)
Lineage members who *died long ago though they are still remembered* (4), our *great-grandfathers* from whom *we are descended* (4), our *forefathers who physically departed long ago* (3), all *dead people* (3), relatives who *lived long before we were born* (3), departed members of the family who *lived*

exemplary lives when they were on earth (3), *spirits* of our forefathers that live among us and watch over us (2), *departed souls* who live in the world *through nominal reincarnation* (1), those who *lived good ethical lives and died at a mature age* (1), fellow *believers who have gone before us* and whom we shall *meet when Christ returns* (1), the *forefathers and mothers* of the community who have *long ago passed on to the spirit world* (1), those who died in the community but *are still remembered* in *form of re-naming* someone or something (1), *spirits of people who died long time ago* and the *living cannot remember their names* or *how they looked* (1), *venerated patriarchs* of the community (1).

Responsibility of People to Ancestors (R = 14)
Appease them through *sacrifices, offerings and libations* (4), live according to *customs and moral standards* they set (4), *respect* them (2), *name children* after them (2), meet their *demands and expectations* (1), hold *memorials to honor* them (1).

Characteristics of Ancestors (R = 12)
Closer to *God in the hierarchy of power* (3), lived *good lives while on earth* (1), died at *a mature age* (1), *omnipresence* (1), can either be *male or female* (1), *libation for male ancestors* is poured from the *right hand, while for the female is from the left hand* (1), must have *sired children* (1), must have been *respectable* people (1), *holy* (1), demand *attention from the living* (1).

Where Ancestors Reside (R = 6)
They live in *us through the process of reincarnation* (4), ever *present in society* with the living (2).

Ancestors and Christianity (R = 6)
Christian faith has *discouraged* some people from knowing more about the theme of ancestors with the teaching that *they were dangerous beings* to be avoided (1), *Catholic church teaching* on the *communion of saints* draws one closer to *ancestors* (1), African ancestors have a *greater and profound* meaning to some people *in comparison to European saints* (1), it is *easier to identify with one's ancestors than with Christian saints* (1), ancestors and saints can *be equated* (1), ancestors *function in the same way as Christian angels and saints* (1).

Communication Between Ancestors and the Living (R = 3)
Through *dreams* (1), *diviners* (1), *young children* (1).

Other Comments (R = 10)

Ancestors are *not mediators between God and me* (1), [I] still wrestle with the *idea of how the living named after particular dead people have traits of these people* (1), we know the *names of ancestors though we do not know* their physical appearance because they lived before we were born (1), Africans have *rituals and ceremonies* to remember their dead (1), ancestors are dead and should be forgotten *except in naming* the newborn after them (1), in some cultures, *conscious efforts are made to forget the dead after the funeral* (1), ancestors are *not supposed to be interacting with the living* unless there is a serious reason for it (1), my lineage is considered *progressive, hospitable, accommodating and creative* -- positive ideals I can only attribute to my ancestors (1), as a Christian I believe in *talking directly to God* (1), those who do *not acknowledge ancestors suffer* (1).

NON-AFRICAN RESPONDENTS   N = 13
[The respondents answered according to their understanding of African culture]

Role of Ancestors in the Community   (R = 16)

Protect the living (5), are *owners of land* (3), *moral guardians* (2), are *the source of life* (2), *give wisdom* (1), keep people *responsible* (1), *mediate* between people and God (1), keep people *faithful* to their roles in society (1).

Definition of Ancestors   (R = 12)

Our *dead grandparents* (2), *all dead people* (2), a person who *died physically* long ago *and has a meaning in my life* (1), someone who *lived an exemplary life* in his/her life time (1), *respected members of our lineage* who have died (1), someone who has lived *long enough to teach the living* (1), *relatives from past generations who are in the spirit world* but may be *invited or invoked* to unite with the newborn in the family (1), who died long ago but *their spirits are still living together with the living* (1), *spirits of dead relatives* (1), good men and women *who died and passed on to be near creator God* (1).

Relevance of the Theme of Ancestors   (R = 10)

Has *no relevance* (2), influences people to *live peacefully* (1), ancestors are seen as *present and supporting us in our earthly pilgrimage* (1), life stories of ancestors have *shaped an individual's opinion of life* in many respects (1), the ancestor is part of one's life because *he/she descended from him* (1), [my] parents always refer to ancestors when *talking of work, leisure, weather and catastrophes* (1), *when one does the will of ancestors* he/she gains respect in the community (1), ancestors continue to influence some individuals in areas of their life *through their word and example* (1), *echoes the belief in communion of saints* in the sense that they are part of the church of God's people (1).

Responsibility of People to Ancestors   (R = 8)
Respect them (2), *revere* them in different ceremonies (1), *imitate* them by *adopting most of their attitudes and characters* (1), *speak well* of them (1), *carry on* what the ancestors have established (1), *carry on their good name* (1), *bestow their names* on children (1).

Characteristics of Ancestors   (R = 7)
Closer to God in the hierarchy of power (2), their *names and spirit continue to live* on in their descendants (2), *immortal* (1), one must *have lived a good life* (1), must have *led a saintly life* (1).

Where Ancestors Reside   (R = 2)
Within people (1), in *special places* (1).

Other Comments   (R = 8)
Ancestors *choose specific individuals* to whom they bestow unique duties which they carried on while on earth (1), to find out *more about my ancestors I ask the elderly members of my family* (1), in my community we refer to ancestors as *veci-elders* (1), the history of one's family *influences patterns of attitude and actions* that are difficult to break (1), most people are only able to *trace their genealogy as far as their grandfathers* (1), the theme of ancestors is *foreign to my culture* (1), in my culture we do acknowledge that *the deceased have some presence among us* but are not so embodied (1), I think of my parents as people who *lived good lives, are close to God and I talk to them* when I need their *intercession* with God (1).

SUMMARY
Beliefs expressed regarding Ancestors

Ancestors are: *great-grandparents* from whom we *are descended* who *physically departed long ago*, we *cannot remember their physical appearance* though they are *still present in spirit form* and we *remember them through naming* the *newborn* after them, *departed lineage members, spirits of our forefathers* who lived *good and ethical lives*, and were *respected members* of the society who passed on to be near the *creator God*.

Role of Ancestors in the Community: to *protect* the living, give *identity*, *bless* people, are *moral guardians, intermediaries between God, people and other spiritual beings, owners of land, property and vital resources, source of life, role models* and *custodians of culture*.

Relevance of the Theme of Ancestors: *influence* people's lives, are the *source of life* in the community, still have a *stake* in the physical world, help people understand that *physical death* is only a transition to the next world, that life is *recycled,* and echoes the *belief in the communion of saints* in the sense that they are part of the church of God's people. People still use their *names, get their personality and character* from them.

People's Responsibilities towards Ancestors: *appease* them through *sacrifices, offerings,* and *libations,* live according to the *customs* and *moral standards* set by the ancestors, *respect them, name newborn children* after them, hold *memorials* to *honor* them, *revere* and *include* them in ceremonies and to *speak well* of them.

Characteristics of Ancestors: they are *closer to God* in the hierarchy of power, lived *good lives* while on earth, *died at a mature age, must have sired children, respectable, holy, demand attention* from the living, their *names and spirits* continue to live on in their descendants, and are *immortal.*

Where Ancestors Reside: in people through *nominal reincarnation,* are *ever present* in the society, and in *special places.*

Ancestors and Christianity: the *Catholic church's* teaching on the *communion of saints* draws one closer to ancestors, *ancestors* have a *greater and profound meaning* as opposed to *European saints* as it is easier for Africans to *identify with* their ancestors than with *Christian angels and saints,* some *denominations of Christian faith* discourage people from knowing more about the theme of ancestors with the *teaching that they are dangerous beings.*

Communication Between Ancestors and the Living: through *dreams, diviners* and *young children.*

RESPONSES FROM WORKSHEETS

[Note that in African cultures, the moral quality of one's life on earth determines one's place in the ancestral world. Those with a bad reputation are quickly forgotten, their names are lost forever, and effectively they go out of existence.]

❑ **Kindly explain in detail your understanding of the theme of ANCESTORS. Does it have any meaning in your personal, social and community life?**

AFRICAN RESPONDENTS   N = 47

[There were eleven ethnic groups represented: Agikuyu (13), Luo (12), Abaluyia (8), Abagusii (3), Tutsi (3), Teso (2), Akamba (2), Aembu (1), Kipsigis (1), Tigrinya (1), and Akan (1). The respondents were university graduates, twenty women and twenty-seven men.]

- The ancestors are our forefathers who physically departed long ago. We regard them affectionately as they still have a stake in the physical world. They can demand attention from the living. Most of the times, they communicate through dreams and diviners. They live in us through the process of reincarnation. Stories abound of children as young as three days old demanding to be accorded [proper] treatment and actually asserting that he is so or so who departed long time ago. In fact, I have been told several times that I acted and behaved like our great-grandfather. He was a respected man among the elders and was always involved in solving land disputes, etc. Our ancestors are the owners of land and livestock, which they left to us. Their wise sayings and modalities of good behavior that they developed and nurtured is what has seen us through life, be it personal, social, or community life. (Agikuyu)
- These are our great-great-grandfathers of whom we are the descendants. They have a lot of influence in our lives. How we behave and act is greatly influenced by the behavioral etiquette they bequeathed us. (Agikuyu)
- The term "ancestor" refers to the dead great-grandparents. Though we know their names, we cannot remember their physical appearance since they lived before we were born. Yes, the theme of ancestors has meaning in my life because I ask for assistance from them when I need to do a difficult task. (Agikuyu)
- The concept of ancestors has meaning in my life because during ceremonies, we engage in pouring libation, which then gives men

assurance that nothing they do could possibly go wrong. The libation pouring ceremony maintains harmony between the ancestors   and us. (Akamba)

- Ancestors are the departed souls who live in the physical world through reincarnation. Actually, we carry their names and hence reflect their personality in our daily lives. (Abaluyia)

- To me, the ancestors are the ones I have descended from and they maintain communication with those in their lineage whenever there is an event. If the ancestors' wishes are violated, punishment is to be expected from them although this can be reversed through sacrificial rituals to pacify them. (Luo)

- Ancestors are lineage members who died long ago although they remain unforgotten. They are closer to God than the living dead and the living. (Agikuyu)

- Are those who died long time ago and I am related to them by blood i.e., I can trace my genealogy to them. The theme has a lot of meaning in my life and the pattern of my growth in the community. (Luo)

- Ancestors are those who have departed from us whom we cannot remember because they lived many years ago, long before we came into being. They influence our lives because we live according to the customs they developed. We share in their beliefs. Most of the skills and works of art that we partake in was inherited from them. Through the process of naming they are reincarnated in us. (Abaluyia)

- Ancestors are the spirits of our forefathers influencing my personal life for good [better] or worse. Sometimes I associate my failure or successes with the ancestral powers/spirits. (Agikuyu)

- They are those members of our lineage who departed from physical life long time ago i.e., they lived in another lifetime long before we came into this life. They give me identity for I can tell from which clan I descended from and more specific which family. They are the owners of property e.g., land and cattle, and we inherited these vital resources from them. They are the ones who laid down laws and regulations governing interactions in the community. This regulation covered spiritual life, economic life, social life and political life. Thus the cohesiveness of our community can be wholly attributed to them. Of most importance are the rituals and laws governing interactions within the family. This includes how to marry, when to marry, how to co-exist within the family structure, the relationship between co-wives and between children and the parents, also about role differentiation on the lines of gender and age. (Agikuyu)

- Ancestors are those who lived good (ethical) lives and died at a mature age. Also of importance is the fact that they must have had children to remember them as ancestors. It has meaning in my personal, social and community life in that we have a lot of beliefs, which were handed down to us by our ancestors and which influence our lives a lot. Some of these beliefs deal with property management and inheritance; death and what to do about it i.e., how to mourn, where to bury the remains and how to bury them; rituals to be performed and how to co-exist with the reality that the physical life is a passage to another form of life. (Abaluyia)

- Ancestors are the dispensers of morality and venerated patriarchs of the community. They influence the behavior of the living because they are custodians of our culture. The theme has a deep meaning given that I bear the name of an ancestor. (Aembu)

- The theme of ancestors is a living reality. The West celebrates memorials of loved ones i.e., saints and heroes. Africans remember their dead in ceremonies like *rapar* which means remembrance, and during the naming of the newborn. (Luo)

- An ancestor is my relative who died long time ago before I was born. My Christian faith has discouraged me from trying to understand this theme. I was taught that they are dangerous beings to get interested in. They are dead and they should be forgotten except when naming newborns after them. The only connection I have with my ancestors is fond memories of them but I wouldn't like them to appear to me. I would rather they rest in peace. In my culture, after a burial, conscious effort is made to forget them. They are not supposed to be interacting with the living unless there is a serious reason for it. (Abaluyia)

- Our ancestors act as models in our lives. We are to act and behave by the standards they set for us. The skills that they developed form the basis of our economic and social development. (Abaluyia)

- Ancestors are the forefathers of my lineage. They gave me life through nominal reincarnation, a fact supported by a mark I bear on the upper left eyelid similar to my grandfather's. Thus I believe that life is recycled and therefore I am part and parcel of the ancestral reality. (Luo)

- Ancestors are the founding fathers of my family lineage and ethnic community. I am proud of them for they gave me identity. My lineage is considered hospitable, accommodating and creative. We are considered progressive, open to new ideas and possible changes I can only attribute this positive ideals to my ancestors. (Abagusii)

- I got my identity from my ancestors. Without them I would not be in the world today. Their blessings and prayers support the whole community and me. Everything that we possess came from them. (Akamba)

- Those who lived long time ago. My community refers to them as *ndemi* and *matathi*. They were the first to clear land and rear livestock. From them came *Agui, Maina,* etc. They were the forefathers of the community. They do not have much meaning in my life but there are others of my community who attach a lot of importance to them and who interpret many daily happenings to the influence of the ancestors. My grandfather used to pour libation as a way of pleasing them. Though of importance is the fact that those of our ancestors who were males received libation from the right hand while the female received through the left hand. This happened before any beer could be taken by those present. (Agikuyu)

- In the hierarchy of power, ancestors are closer to God and can influence occurrences in our lives. They are omnipresent. If I don't live according to the society's expectations I will offend the ancestors e.g., if I break the taboos. (Abagusii)

- Ancestors have a lot of meaning in my personal life. Their beliefs and values have been passed down to me in different ways e.g., through naming. I am an ancestor myself since my great grandmother lives on through me. (Agikuyu)

- Ancestors are very important in my life. When the Catholic faith teaches on communion of saints, this radically draws me to my Gikuyu ancestors. For me, these (Agikuyu ancestors) have greater and profound meaning in my worldview than European saints. I could easily identify with my ancestral spirits than Christian saints. The name Kariuki is of my ancestors. I feel blessed by him and struggle to live according to his ideals. Thus I feel blessed and empowered to go on in life and in death to join them in the community of the living dead. (Agikuyu)

- My idea of ancestors is that of people who have lived good exemplary lives that should be emulated. I do not however believe they are go-betweens between God and me. As a Christian, I believe in talking directly to God. Ancestors are fellow believers who have gone before us and whom we shall meet when Christ returns. They are resting now and they do not influence life. But I still wrestle with the reality of how the living named after particular dead people have traits of these people. (Abaluyia)

- Ancestors are those who are dead. Personally, I believe these people live within us and should be respected and offered for sacrifices. In my community life, these people are greatly recognized and the few who do not acknowledge them end up paying so much to make them clean [be cleansed] and ask for forgiveness. (Agikuyu)

- Ancestors are the departed members of the family lineage who lived exemplary lives when on earth. In my community life, ancestors influence people's lives by warning them of misfortunes and preparing them for blessings. Ancestors do not influence my personal or social life. (Luo)

- Ancestors are members of my lineage who died long time ago. They influence my personal life either positively or negatively. (Abagusii)

- These are the forefathers and mothers of the community who have long ago passed on to the spirit world. The living are a reincarnation of the ancestors.

This can be seen through their behavior that tends to have a similarity. Only good ancestors are remembered. (Abaluyia)

- Ancestors are our great, great, great - grandmothers and grandfathers, some of whom we still remember, some not. They watch over us and want the best for us. I am named after my maternal grandmother in whose footsteps I try to follow. (Luo)

- The ancestors are the forefathers of the community. They guide us through life and warn us if there is harm coming our way or if we are doing wrong. I believe this is so and it is why we still hold memorials to remember their passing. (Teso)

- By ancestors we mean those who have died in the community but are still remembered either in form of naming someone or something [after them]. The ancestors are spirits that live among us and watch over us. In the community, they are our protectors whom we cannot see. (Luo)

- They are the moral guardians, protectors, and care-givers of the living. They are vital since they are the source and protectors of the living. (Luo)

- Ancestors are spirits of people who died a long time ago and the living cannot remember their names or what they looked like. However, they are believed to be present in the world of the living and influence their lives in one way or another. Ancestors are appeased through libation and sacrifices. (Agikuyu)

- Ancestors are respected. They help the living, especially members of their families. They are holier than us and therefore cannot sin. They are our intermediaries. They help us daily in our prayers to God. They are very active in our daily lives. (Teso)

- Ancestors is a general concept. It is honoring people who lived tirelessly for their community, and people who contributed good to all. They can be equated to saints as they play the same role. Ancestors point to our history in time. (Abaluyia)

- The ancestors are an important component of life in my community. They are the link between the living, the divine spirits and God the creator. The ancestors are living and with us everyday. My sister called Aringo is the reincarnation of my grandmother who died fifteen years ago. (Luo)

- Ancestors are the people who have died and are seen to be the guide, and protectors of the living. They take part in blessing people, punishing evildoers, giving out names and dictating the life span of a person on earth. This is still meaningful in my community life. (Kipsigis)

- Ancestors are those who lived before us -- our forefathers. In my personal life, I still use my ancestor's name. In my social life, I cannot have a sexual relationship with people from the same ancestral background. In my community life, everybody respects the ancestors. (Luo)

- Ancestors are important in my life. They bless people and give them wisdom. (Agikuyu)
- Just as saints and angels act, so do ancestors. They are good people who have died. They assist the living. (Luo)
- In my personal, social and community life, ancestors mean the parents who are in my lineage. The old ones now dead represent us in the other world. (Tutsi)
- Ancestors are our forefathers who still watch over us in the land of the living. I am named after one of my ancestors that means they are relevant. (Luo)
- Ancestors are members of my family who belong to the past generations who belong to my family tree. They are always remembered and referred to since the living have been named after them, and it is claimed that there is physical remembrance and even have a character/personality similarity. The family is always referred to as the family of so and so who died many years ago, yet the community will always refer or associate one with that individual. (Agikuyu)
- The theme of the ancestor does have a meaning for me personally. Frequently, I do ask the elderly members of my family about my ancestors. I have much respect and admiration for them. I try to imitate them by adopting most of their attitudes and characters. I believe their life stories have shaped my opinion of life in many respects. (Tigrinya)
- An ancestor is someone who lived an exemplary life in his/her lifetime. To become an ancestor one is called upon to live a good life by relating well with others inside and outside his community. (Akan)
- The ancestors passed on their lives to us, thus their life continues through us. They choose specific individuals to whom they bestow unique duties, which they carried out during their time on earth. They attain immortality through nominal reincarnation. (Tutsi)
- An ancestor refers to a person who died physically a long time ago and has a meaning in my life e.g., my great great grandparents. The theme has a great meaning in my personal, social and community life. This is seen through the reverence accorded to them in different ceremonies e.g., naming, initiation, paying of bridewealth, death and mourning. (Tutsi)

NON-AFRICAN RESPONDENTS   N = 13
[The respondents answered according to their
understanding of African culture.]

[There were five non-African countries represented; America (8), Norway
(2), Italy (1), Ireland (1), and Indonesia (1). The respondents were
university graduates, eight women and five men.]

- Ancestors are those respected members of our lineage who have died. We speak well of some of them. They can give us a sense of pride as members of their family or lineage for the good deeds done while they were alive. (American)
- The quality that I can easily associate with the ancestors is wisdom. Therefore an ancestor is a person who had lived long enough to teach the living. One who was able to influence the others to live peacefully. He is part of my life because I descended from him. In my community we refer to the ancestor by the use of the word *Veci* which means elder. My parents often refer to them when they talk about work, leisure, weather and catastrophes. Often *Veci* are grandfathers and we are only able to go down the genealogy to as far as our grandfathers. (Italian)
- Ancestors are those relatives from past generations who are in the spirit world but who may be invited/invoked to unite with a newborn in the family. This is mostly foreign to my culture. In my culture we do acknowledge that the deceased have some presence among us but are not so embodied. (American)
- Ancestors are those who have lived before. It is necessary to respect them and carry on what they have established and their good name. Ancestors do not have meaning in my culture group. (American)
- The history of one's family influences patterns of attitude and actions that are difficult to break. (American)
- Ancestors are those who have died. They are in a domain closer to God and can influence Him. In my community, ancestors are simply those in your family who have died. (American)
- We have two categories of ancestors. Those whose names we have forgotten and those who are still remembered. The ancestor has a certain meaning in my community. (Norwegian)
- To be an ancestor, one would have to live a saintly life and after death, this person would be considered close to God. In my personal life, I would think of my parents as people who lived good lives and must have been close to God. I talk to my parents sometimes when I need them to intercede for me with God. (American)

- Ancestors are those who died long ago but their spirits are still living together with the living. They are meaningful in my life, socially and communally because they are the guardians of my life and the society. (Indonesian)
- Ancestors are the spirits of dead relatives. They are the owners of the land, the source and protectors of life of the living and their moral guardians. Doing my ancestors' will is doing good and traditional things, that gives me respect in social and community life. (Irish)
- It depends upon where one begins looking at the life cycle. Ancestors are the guardians of life and land. Their names and spirit continue to live on in their descendants. They are the ones who keep the people responsible and faithful to their roles in society. My ancestors, at least my parents, continue to influence me in areas of my life through their word and example. This is very much alive in me when I reflect on my behavior. (American)
- No particular meaning in my life personally or not in my social community. Parents are not dead. (Norwegian)
- Ancestors are those good men and women who have died and passed on to be near the creator God. They are the owners of the land, which is the possession of the whole community. They are the caretakers and protectors of the living, and moral guardians of the community. They live in special places, but also in those descendants who are named after them. The theme of ancestors echoes my belief in the communion of saints i.e., are part of the whole community of the church of God's people. Whether as official saints or not, they are invoked in prayer as intermediaries before God. Their names are bestowed on children. They are seen as present to us living here and supporting us in our earthly pilgrimage. (American)

EDITOR'S REFLECTIONS

For Africans, the state of ancestorhood is a very important goal desired by all. While on earth, people strive to live moral lives in order to secure a place among the ancestral community. Ancestorhood is the path to nominal reincarnation, as babies are named after the ancestors. Furthermore, ancestors are seen as the owners of both life and land, and also protectors of the living. By way of contrast, in many non-African cultures, ancestors are seen as remote beings who may or may not influence the lives of the living. An example of this is the status of saints in the Christian churches.

DISCUSSION QUESTIONS

1. Is the veneration and respect for Christian saints akin to that accorded to ancestors in Africa? Explain.
2. Discuss the statement that ancestors are the owners of the land and control the events and lives of the African people.

3. What is the role and function of ancestors in recycling life?
4. In your personal life, are there any ancestor-like people who care for and watch over you?

AFRICAN ILLUSTRATION

TRADITIONAL PRAYERS EXPRESSING THE ROLE AND FUNCTION OF ANCESTORS AS OWNERS OF THE LAND WITH POWER OVER EVIL
(Offered at a Luo sacrificial ceremony)

Onyango, an Elder, prayed:

"We are standing before you, yes, our ancestors. We are setting for you a bull-- we are coming so that you help us. You drive away for us the evil thing that is destroying us, so that it go out from us. Aa, owners of the land, rescue us all -- accept one and all this our thing we are giving you."

"Yaye, Ojode, father of the land, Onyando father of Ogalo -- what are you afraid of in this your land -- why are you letting the death finish us off -- chase away this enemy -- let it go far away."

"Eat one and all -- you are the owners of this land -- this is your sacrifice -- you chase away for us evils."

Another elder prayed:

"Our ancestors and fathers -- you brought us into this land and death now is killing us finishing us, yaye -- why don't you eat -- this is your sacrifice -- open for us the land -- chase away for us this terrible thing."

The respected elder Okebe finished the prayers saying:

"We have already eaten together with you our grandfathers and fathers -- you are the ones who found for us this land -- let each person return with peace to his house -- don't let him return to more troubles. All evil we are placing in this reed basket -- may they withdraw and go far away."

RECOMMENDED READINGS

Idowu. E.B. (1975). *African Traditional Religion: A Definition.* (pp. 178-189). New York: Orbis Books.

Ray, B.C. (1976). *African Religions: Symbol, Ritual and Community.* (pp. 131-153). Englewood Cliffs, New Jersey: Prentice-Hall Inc.

Gyekye, K. (1996). *African Cultural Values: An Introduction.* (pp. 13-14). Accra: Sankofa Publishing Company.

NON-AFRICAN ILLUSTRATION

ANCESTORS/FOREBEARERS IN THE WESTERN WORLD

At the time of the burial of a person, he/she is effectively cut off socially, politically and economically from that of the living. However, those who have shown exemplary skills and ability and have been of great value to the society whether religiously, socially or politically are often celebrated through statues and endowments, buildings that carry their names, or are given honorific titles such as the "founder of the country" or the "person who has restored the integrity of a community."

Family members who have passed away and were very important in the lives of the living are often remembered in celebration of their goodness and deeds. Moreover, people will at times pray to their parents or grandparents when in need or even in times of celebrations. The major difference between African and Western ancestors is that the Western ancestors do not have the kind of power and presence in the land of the living as they do within African cultural reality.

CHAPTER III
Theme: LIVING DEAD

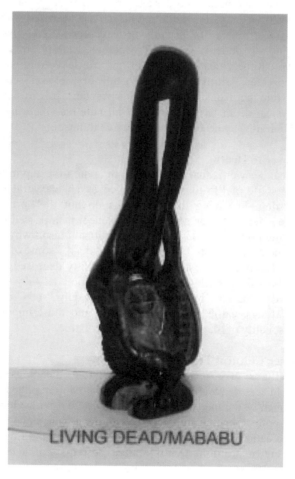

LIVING DEAD/MABABU

The stylistic carving shows distinct human features such as the eyes, nose, hand, teeth and the leg of a person. This represents the people who have recently died but their human features are still grounded in the earth while their spirits are soaring upward. It is as if they are upside-down.

LIVING DEAD

Introduction

One of the big lies of cultures is that once a person attains adulthood, he/she will remain in that state forever. However, the reality is that living adults walk on a razor's edge between order and chaos. A twenty-four hour fever can debilitate a healthy person to a point that he/she has to be fed with a spoon. An accident can cut off one's life instantly or leave one severely handicapped. A fire or drought can suddenly leave a prosperous, healthy adult in poverty or starvation. An untimely death of a loved one can leave one emotionally and spiritually depressed. Ultimately, in the game of life everyone falls off the razor's edge into permanent chaos, and surrenders to physical death. The reality of physical death has been part of all cultures since the beginning of time, and all cultures, by necessity, seek to give it meaning.

African Answer to Death

The African answer is that physical death is the first step in the process of recycling one's life, a life that was received as an ancestral gift. There is, therefore, wisdom in saying that "Africans do not die" precisely because human life does not cease or go out of existence; it is passed on to the new generation being born. This idea is the foundational reason why Africans have a category of persons who are called "the living dead," some of whom are still living -- the wise moral elders -- and others recently deceased i.e., those who are passing their lives back to the new generation as they move into the ancestral world. Thus a living dead person is not only "seen" in terms of his/her children, things, cattle, property, but also, and most importantly, in the faces and personality of those who carry his/her name.

Death in Other Cultural Traditions

Other cultures give physical death different meanings. The western Christian world sees death as a transformation into a new stage of being where one is permanently damned to hell or saved to live with God in perpetual happiness. In both cases human life goes with the person since life is seen as a unique, new creation that remains with one forever. At the time of death, the deceased are cut off from the living totally, and remain alive on earth only in the memories of those who loved (or hated) them. Other cultures e.g., Hindus, understand death to be a type of migration of the soul/spirit into other life forms e.g., a cow, as one undergoes rites of purification until the cycle is broken. The ancient Egyptians understood death to be a passage into another world that mirrored that of the living. Hence they created elaborate funeral rites, mummified the bodies of the dead, buried them together with the household goods, slaughtered animals and sacrificed slaves so they could carry on their lives in the world on the other side of the grave.

QUESTION ASKED

Kindly explain in detail your understanding of the theme of LIVING DEAD. Does it have any meaning in your personal, social or community life? N = 77 (57 Africans, 20 non-Africans)

RESPONSES COLLATED BY NINE CATEGORIES

1. *Responsibilities of Humanity towards Living Dead   R = 39*
2. *Definition of the Living Dead   R = 33*
3. *Role of Living Dead in the Society   R = 33*
4. *Characteristics of Living Dead   R = 31*
5. *Significance of the Theme of Living Dead   R = 23*
6. *Impact of the Theme of Living Dead on the Living   R = 15*
7. *Communication Between the Living and Living Dead   R = 13*
8. *Where Living Dead are Found   R = 14*
9. *Relevance of the Theme of Living Dead   R = 7*

Other Comments   R = 10

AFRICAN RESPONDENTS   N = 57

Responsibilities of Humanity towards Living Dead   (R = 29)

To *name their children* after them (8), to *respect* them (3), to *do things that please them* (3), to do *what the living dead demand* (3), to *emulate the living dead one is named after* (2), to *revere* them (2), to *offer sacrifices* to appease them (2), *not to talk about the living dead negatively* (1), to *redress wrongs and evils* to *restore social order* (1), to *consult* the living dead *on important issues* (1), to *avoid what the living dead do not like*, to *prevent their wrath against the community* (1), to *pour libations* (1), to *share food with them* (1).

Definition of Living Dead   (R = 23)

Are people who *died in recent times* and *their memories are still fresh in people's minds* (9), *lineage members who died recently* and their *memories are still in relatives' minds* (4), those *who lived in the community and died recently* (3), are members of *one's extended family and clan who died recently* and *have not been named* (1), is *the one that exists between the spirit and the ancestors* at all times (1), the *dead yet the memories of their good works and qualities* still *remain with the living* (1), have *died but their spirits are still among us* (1), people who *died in our life time*, whom *we knew and related with* when they were alive (1), the *remembered dead* who are part and parcel of the community (1), died recently and *their children and properties are still around us* (1).

Role of Living Dead in the Society (R = 29)

Have *positive* and *negative influences* on the *individual and the community* (4), *intercede* for people (4), *apportion blessings and prosperity* (4), are *role models* (2), *occupy a position* in society (2), are the *link between humanity and the spiritual world* (2), *link* between the *living* and the *dead* (2), *guardians* and *protectors* of the living (2), cause *losses and misfortunes* when their *demands are not met* (1), *nourish* people to *go on with life* (1), are *guardians* of a *society's culture* (1), *influence social order and disorder* (1), give *solutions to crises in life* (1), *can curse* (1), *control personal, social and communal life* (1).

Characteristics of Living Dead (R = 24)

Are *still remembered* by the living (8), are in *spirit form* (4), *know what is happening* in the society (3), are *respectable* (2), have *children and property* (2), are *similar to Christian saints* (1), *benevolent* (1), *buried with respect unless the death was unnatural* like in the case of suicide (1), make *demands such as a newborn should be named after them* (1), while *alive he/she was pious*, had *reputable moral standards* and *outstanding leadership qualities* (1).

Significance of the Theme of Living Dead (R = 9)

There is a *link* between *the past and the present through naming*, hence a continuation of life (2), death *is a passage leading to the life beyond* (1), *spirits of the living dead are alive within humans* (1), *signifies* the *immediate stage after the living* (1), *symbolizes* the *beginning of a new life* (1), are *sort of saints* to the living (1), are *a link between the living and the dead* (1), are the *source of life* (1).

Impact of the Theme of Living Dead on the Living (R = 10)

Makes people *ensure that correct burial rites and rituals are carried out according to traditions* of the clan or community (2), makes us *aware of our duties towards the dead* (1), helps *individuals have an easier understanding of life after the earthly life* (1), makes people understand that *though the dead are departed from them in body, they are still with them in spirit* (1), the *living treat the dead with respect* (1), *inspires good living* (1), that *physical death makes it possible for the integration of the living dead into the spirit world* (1), shows *how we relate with the dead* (1), children *named after the living dead portray their qualities and mannerisms* (1).

Communication Between the Living and Living Dead (R = 8)

The living dead communicate with the living through *dreams* (4), the living *speak to* the living dead and ask for their advice or help (3), the living dead can communicate through *thoughts* (1).

Where Living Dead are Found   (R = 14)
Their *presence is felt around us* (7), are *still with the living in the society* (6), *co-exist* with *the living* and the *yet to be born* (1).

Other Comments   (R = 4)
Have *no effect on present lives* (2), *Christianity has overwhelmed ancestral belief* (1), there are *some dead members* of the community *whose names are still remembered* but they *are yet to join the living dead* (referred to as *chisokoro*) (1).

NON-AFRICAN RESPONDENTS   N = 20
[The respondents answered both according to their
own cultures and their understanding of African culture.]

Responsibilities of Humanity towards Living Dead   (R = 10)
Respect the living dead (2), *pray* for them (1), we *cherish their memories* through tombstones and photos (1), remember *dates of death* by taking flowers to the gravesite (1), should be *aware of them* (1), are *remembered by most Christians* (1), *remember the dead* (1), can *influence the transition of the dead into the ancestral community* through the *correct burial rites* (1), *honor* them by showering flowers on their graves (1).

Definition of Living Dead   (R = 10)
Those who *died recently* (2), all *dead people* (1), is the whole *idea of saints and the souls of the departed* (1), those who *died recently and are constantly around us* (1), have *died and yet their absence still leaves a void* in daily activities and *are remembered for what they did* (1), a *person living without any contact with the living God* (1), one who *died and the spirit is still around the family* (1), what is *mentioned, recollected or remembered* after a person has died (1), the *people who died and we were attached to in our daily life* (1).

Role of Living Dead in the Society   (R = 4)
Influence the lives of the living (3), influence the living in *memory* (1).

Characteristics of Living Dead   (R = 7)
Are in *spirit form* (2), are *remembered* (2), *honored* (1), have *power* (1), make their *presence known through various sightings* requiring appropriate response (1).

Significance of the Theme of Living Dead (R = 14)

Is a *transition from earthly life to spiritual life* with the ancestral community and the creator God (2), helps individuals to *believe that we will meet the departed in the future life* (1), supports the belief that the *departed are taking care of us* (1), naturally *a part of us in heaven* (1), to know that *burial procedures are very important* to *enable a person [to] enter the world of ancestors* (1), one has to *be buried in his/her ancestral land in order to join the ancestors* (1), *rites and rituals* have to be performed in order *to make the dead a part of the lineage* (1), the *recently deceased* is *added to the ancestral line* (1), *signifies the integration of the spirit of the deceased into the living ancestral community* (1), we have to *respect the dying*, the *recently dead,* the *memory of the life of the recently deceased and their family* (1), should *have respect for creator God, life and death* (1), the *end of physical/earthly life is not the end of existence* (1), the *soul of the deceased goes to heaven* (1).

Impact of Living Dead on the Living   (R = 5)

The living *ensure the dead are accorded the correct burial rites* because the *ancestors still have power over them and their land* (1), *ancestors* serve as the *guardians of human life* (1), they are the *source of life* (1), care is taken to *keep peace with them* (1), people *avoid mentioning death for the fear of inviting it* (1).

Communication Between the Living and Living Dead (R = 5)

By the *living talking to them* (2), through *prayer* (2), there is a belief that *rituals and prayers* [to the living dead] *keep all in balance* (1).

Relevance of the Theme of Living Dead   (R = 7)

That *Jesus Christ* is an *example of the living dead* (2), has no relevance (2), *similar to Christian belief in the communion of saints* (1), the *dead are still with us and still meaningful in our lives* (1), is a *continuation of life* (1).

Other Comments   (R = 6)

Bad people or *those not buried properly turn into ghosts* (1), *good people become ancestors* (1), concept of the *living dead is not accepted in America* (1), once a person dies, he/she is dead (1), *some families tend to believe in communication beyond the grave* (1), the *period* of the *living dead lasts as long as the problems that the person caused are not solved* and/or someone else *has carried on the good work he/she started* (1).

SUMMARY
Beliefs expressed regarding the Living Dead

<u>Living Dead are</u>: *people who died recently* whom we were attached to in life and *their memories are still fresh in people's minds.* They are *members of the lineal family* who *died recently* and *children have not been named after them, memories of their good works and qualities still remain with the living,* and *their children and property are still around us.*

<u>Characteristics of Living Dead</u>: are *in spirit form, respectable, benevolent, have children and property,* are *similar to Christian saints,* were *pious* while alive, of *reputable moral standards, outstanding leadership qualities,* and were *buried with respect.* They can demand that the *newborn be named* after them. They can *cause loss and misfortunes* when their demands are not met, can *curse* the living, and influence *social order and disorder.*

<u>Role of Living Dead in the Society</u>: to *intercede* for the living, *influence the decisions* of the living, apportion *blessings and property,* acts as a *link* between the *living, the dead and the spiritual world.* They are the *guardians* and *protectors* of the living, and the *cultural guardians.* They give *solutions to* crises in life, *control personal, social and communal* life.

<u>Responsibilities of Humanity towards Living Dead</u>: to *name the newborn* after them, *respect, emulate, honor and revere* them, offer them *sacrifices* and *pour for them libations to appease* them. People are to *consult them, avoid* what they do not like, *redress wrongs and evils* to restore *social order, pray* for them and *cherish their memories.*

<u>Significance of the Theme of Living Dead</u>: it shows *the link between* the *past, and present through naming,* shows that *death is a passage leading* to the *life beyond,* shows that *the spirit of the dead are still living,* and *symbolizes* the beginning of a *new life.* The theme helps *individuals believe that they will meet the departed in a future life,* signifies the *integration of the spirit of the deceased* into the living ancestral community, and shows that *the end of physical life is not the end of existence.*

<u>Impact of the Theme of Living Dead on the Living</u>: makes people a*ware of their duty* towards the dead, *ensure* that *correct burial rites and rituals* are carried out in accordance with the traditions. It *inspires good living,* helps people have an easier *understanding of the after life.*

<u>Communication Between the Living and Living Dead</u>: *dreams, thoughts, prayer,* and through *direct speech* when the living ask for help or advice.

RESPONSES FROM WORKSHEETS

[Note that in African cultures, since human life is recycled, death is not the ultimate state, rather it is a transition into ancestorhood with a return to the land of the living through the newborn. It is said that Africans will only die when God dies.]

❑ Kindly explain in detail your understanding of the theme of LIVING DEAD. Does it have any meaning in your personal, social or community life?

AFRICAN RESPONDENTS   N = 57

[There were thirteen ethnic groups of Africa represented: Luo(17), Agikuyu (15), Abaluyia (7), Abagusii (4), Kategi (2), Akamba (2), Teso (2), Aembu (2), Tutsi (2), Kipsigis (1), Bemba (1), Tigrinya (1), Akan (1). The respondents were university graduates, nineteen women and thirty-eight men.]

- The living dead are the ancestors, those who have died in the past and occupy social position [in the community]. Ancestors are vital key points who are benevolent and co-existing with the born and the unborn members. I feel that the respect accorded to the elders/aged should continue even after death. (Agikuyu)
- Living dead are members of my family, ancestral line who have died. Members of my family carry the names of those ancestors and they are still remembered. I will have children bearing names of my family members so though they die they continue being reborn. This ensures the continuity of families and the society as a whole. (Agikuyu)
- The living dead among my community are the *Jachien* [spirits] who visit the living at night in dreams *(lek)*. The dreamer identifies it as a departed relative and invariably is asked to do something. When the request is not met, then the *jachien* causes loss or misfortune. Sacrifice *(misango, liswa)* is critical to restoring normalcy in the community and individual life. (Luo)
- Living dead are those people from my kin who have died recently. They have a strong influence in my personal, social and community life. Thus the living dead can influence my present behavior/actions, success, and security. (Abagusii)
- The living dead is the one that exists between the living and the ancestors all the times. It is also the beginning of a new life. (Kategi)
- The living dead are the brothers, sisters, aunts, parents, uncles and members of one's clan who have died recently and they have not been named. They have a great meaning because naming them will then channel us into the ancestors who are acting as our guides and protectors. (Kipsigis)

- The living dead have meaning in my life in that the spirits of those who are living dead live within me. If I am doing something that would for instance anger my dead grandfather, I find myself not doing it because I feel he is around and not happy with me. In community life we tend to do those things that please these people. (Agikuyu)
- The living dead have meaning in my life. They give my life meaning from its radical unity with the source of it. The ancestral spirits bless the living by giving us life, wealth and power-vitality. (Agikuyu)
- The living dead are people who lived in the community and died recently. Personally the living dead are sort of saints to me. In the community they are seen as people who intercede for us. (Luo)
- The living dead are the source of reference to the African. It is the continuity and hence through naming a link to the present and the past. (Akamba)
- The theme of the living dead is evident in my community. My elder brother was named after my paternal grandfather who was an elder in my clan. So my brother is expected to act as an elder in my clan, the way my grandfather did. (Abagusii)
- The living dead are people who have died recently. They are remembered by conducting some services once in a while. (Agikuyu)
- The living dead show the link between the living and the dead. It also shows unbroken relationship through the living drawing their life from them. It shows how I am attached and relate with the living dead. It also shows how the family relates and is linked to their living dead as the source of life. Community life is linked to the living dead. (Luo)
- The theme of the living dead refers to those who are dead but once lived in the community (ancestors). The living dead are highly respected in my community. This is seen right from the time one dies. They are buried with respect unless their death was unnatural like in the case of suicide. The living dead are never talked about negatively and are honored in case they come back, for example in a dream or thought of someone in the community, whatever they say will be. (Luo)
- The theme of the living dead is similar to Christian saints. They intercede for us in good and bad times. They nourish us to go on with life and support our cries to God. (Abaluyia)
- The living dead are those who have died but their spirits are still among us. They influence us positively and negatively. They appear in dreams. Sometimes the wishes of the living dead have to be fulfilled. In my personal life, the living dead have to be respected. This also applies to my community life. (Luo)
- The living dead are the people who are dead yet their memories of good works and qualities still remain with the living. It has a meaning because

these people are seen as our intermediaries and through renaming them we feel that they are still living with us. (Bemba)

- Living dead implies that death is a passage leading to the life beyond. In Africa we believe one who dies goes home (called by God). He/she is called by the ancestors and joins the spirit world. Thus we offer them some food [drink] through libation. The dead share this food he used to share while on earth. This makes him/her active in sharing in the family activities, thus reliving his/her life in fullness. It has meaning in my personal life as it makes me very much aware of my duties towards the dead and have an easier understanding about the life after my earthly living. (Teso)

- The living dead means that though the dead are departed in body, they are still with us in their souls. It does not have any relevance in my personal life but in the life of the community it has great relevance in that the dead are treated with great respect and burial ceremonies held honorably. (Luo)

- The living dead are people who died in the recent times and their memories are still fresh in people's minds. They influence people's lives even in death. They are the guardians of a society's culture. (Agikuyu)

- These are people of the lineage who have recently passed away and their memory is still in their relatives' minds. As a Christian I believe that once people die, they go away and are not directly involved in the affairs of the living. They are supposed to be resting. Even though I bear the name of my ancestor and we name children after our dead that is as far as it goes. I do not expect these departed to be actively involved in the social and community life I lead. (Abaluyia)

- My community strongly believes in the living dead. They are part and parcel of us and they contribute to our ancestral lineage. Socially, the community depends on them for blessings and prosperity. (Luo)

- The living dead are those who died in our lifetime. We know them and we related with them when they were living. It has meaning in our personal, social and community life because how we act needs to be pleasing to the living dead. (Luo)

- The living dead are immediate relatives or people who have recently died, and they are very fresh in the living people's memories. It has meaning in my personal life and community life because we keep remembering and talking about them. (Abaluyia)

- These are the remembered dead, who are part and parcel of the community. They influence the social order, and any social disorder is understood as coming from their influence. As such, any wrongs (or evils) must be redressed to restore the social order. (Aembu)

- The living dead are those who have passed on/away before us from our lineage. In my community and social life, Christianity has overwhelmed the ancestral belief but the dead are remembered in memorial ceremonies. My personal life reflects this social and communal belief. (Teso)

- The living dead are those whose memories are still fresh in the minds of the living. These people are significant since they inspire good life through the fond memories of them. They also link us with the spiritual world. (Luo)
- The living dead are our forefathers and due respect should be accorded to them. We are because they were. (Agikuyu)
- It has a lot of meaning. The living are bound together with the dead. [Through them] respect for life is promoted since the dead can still unite with the living. (Luo)
- The living dead are important and are seen as the immediate stage after the living. They are seen to be the guardians and protectors of the living and link the living and the ancestors. They are consulted in important issues by the living. (Akamba)
- The living dead are part and parcel of our daily lives. Although they are dead, they affect our lives e.g., when eating we pour food in remembrance of the dead. The African community consists of the unborn, the living dead and the living. (Luo)
- Those who have died are not fully dead but they are living because though they are dead they still influence those who are living. They are still remembered and they still have their children and property. (Agikuyu)
- The living dead are those who died recently. My dad died when I was only eleven, eighteen years ago. I still miss him and ask for his advice in my daily life. I use his name to keep his memories alive. Children in my clan who were named after him portray his qualities and mannerisms. (Luo)
- The living dead are those who have died recently and gone on to join our ancestors. Their spirits are still with us if the correct burial rites and rituals were carried out according to the traditions of the clan/community. It has an important meaning in our life because when they communicate it shows a practical picture of their presence and guides us in our lives. They give us solutions to crises in our lives. (Luo)
- Both my parents have passed away and they are in the realm of the living dead because we can still remember them. Sometimes they appear to me in a dream when I am asleep, and the good behavior of respect for others has and is helping me in my inter-personal relationships. The living dead are still affecting the living in a very practical way. They can even demand to be named through a child. There have been occasions when I believed that my departed parents were with me and they continue to encourage me whenever I am in problems and discouraged. (Luo)
- The living dead are those who have died recently and we can still clearly remember them; because they have died recently their pictures are still

very clear in our minds. Therefore we would always want to relate well with them. (Luo)

- As a member of the Roman Catholic Church, and a religious, yes, indeed, the theme of life after death does shape all activities of my life. However, I cannot say that the theme of living dead, particularly the belief that ancestors are the owners of land, has any significant meaning in my personal, social and community life. (Tigrinya)

- The living dead are people who have recently left this world on their journey to join the ancestors. It has a lot to do with my personal, social and community life. (Tutsi)

- The living dead are the immediate relatives that have just passed away. They are therefore still in our families through the names that we give them. Their relevance to me is that they are sources of blessings and protection. (Abaluyia)

- The living dead were part of the society, just like the living and the unborn. They were part of the continuous life cycle and were revered by the other members of the society. (Agikuyu)

- The living dead are the category of people who are recently deceased. The process of physical death makes it possible for their integration into the spirit world. We are at direct contact with the living dead spiritually as their names are given to our children. Socially and communally, anything they don't like is seriously avoided to prevent their anger. This is held as true/possible because of their properties, their children, livestock and land through which they are remembered. (Agikuyu)

- The recently departed are referred to as the living dead. They influence the living as their spirits are still said to be with us. This theme started having a deeper meaning in my life/family after the death of my father whose spirit and memories are still very fresh in us. He died three years ago and I believe he knows what is happening in the family/clan. (Agikuyu)

- I believe that once people die, they go to a place of rest to wait judgment day. The dead do not and are not supposed to make the life of the living difficult. We name [children] after the living dead in order to remember them. So even if they do not come back to trouble us or give messages, their memory lives with us in those we name after them. (Abaluyia)

- The living dead are still connected to the society and are to be always appeased. (Luo)

- The living dead are those members of the community/clan who have just died and whose memories are still fresh in our minds. Yes it has some meaning in my personal life because I feel that we still maintain a certain relation with them. I would not do anything against their wishes. (Agikuyu)

- The living dead are the deceased who died recently especially those whose children and properties are still around. They are unhappy when their children are mistreated or their property is misused. (Akan)
- The living dead in the ascendancy towards becoming ancestors are crucial in a person's or society's development as they can bestow blessings or curses and at times act as intercessors. Through naming, good people are seen to have come back to life through children. Their great and good deeds are remembered and emulated. It thus becomes easy to lead a good and moral life as role models are to be remembered. (Agikuyu)
- The living dead are the departed members of the community who led a respectable and fruitful life. (Aembu)
- Those who have passed away before us. They control the social, personal and communal life in an African context. (Agikuyu)
- The living dead have an influence on the living e.g., I was named after the dead mother of my father. We meet once a year to celebrate her life though she is dead. (Kategi)
- The living dead to me is a real phenomena. A pious man is revered and acknowledged for years/centuries. To be remembered is to be a man of reputable moral standards, outstanding leadership qualities. We need to respect the living dead and to continue their memory. (Abaluyia)
- A term used to refer to the collective members of the family who have died recently is *chisokoro*. Many grandparents together are also called *chisokoro*. It must be then that these are the dead members whose names are still remembered and are near to join the living dead. It gives me a sense of pride to be associated with people whose lives and behavior are known. I can shape my life to live in a positive way as per their example. (Abagusii)
- The living dead are those who have recently died and I believe their spirits are hovering around and watching carefully how their remains are being treated. The theme has meaning in my personal, social and community life in that I am keen to see to it that the living dead's biddings are followed to ensure they pass all the levels towards ancestorship. (Luo)
- The living dead refers to relatives who have died in the recent past and are remembered. I feel strongly bonded to those of the living dead in that I was close to them during their lifetime. My maternal grandmother, and a priest friend whom I am related to as an older brother are among the living dead whom I often speak to and I am sure they hear and respond. (Agikuyu)
- The living dead are individuals who died recently and we vividly can remember them. If accorded proper rites and respect, they have a positive influence in my social and community life. They enhance protection and prosperity. (Abagusii)

- The living dead watch over our lives as saints do in the Catholic Church. (Abaluyia)
- The living dead are people who died and those who we were attached to in our daily life. (Tutsi)

NON-AFRICAN RESPONDENTS   N = 20
[The respondents answered both according to their own culture and their understanding of African culture.]

[There were seven non-African countries represented: America (11), Norway (4), Poland (1), Spain (1), Indonesia (1), Ireland (1), and Italy (1). The respondents were university graduates, fourteen women and six men.]

African Perspective
- The living dead are all dead people. Thieves, bad people or those not being buried properly turn into ghosts. The good people become ideal and are called ancestors. It has no meaning to me. (Norwegian)
- When a person dies, he/she has not completed the process of dying. Only the body is dead. There is a process that enables the person to enter the world of the ancestors, in which the burial procedures are very important. One comes back to the land that the ancestors own, that's why being buried in the land of the ancestors and not in Lang'ata is so important. (Spaniard)
- The living dead are those who have recently died. Death is a process and the rituals and rites must be performed in order to make the dead a part of the lineage. The recently deceased will be added to the line of ancestors. (American)
- The stage of living dead seems to me a transition from this life into the ancestral community. It assumes that the living can influence that transition through the correct burial rites. The incentive for the living to do this is that the ancestors still have power over the living and their land serving as guardians and as a source of future life. (American)
- There is always communion between the living and the ancestors. They are remembered and honored. They make their presence known through various sightings, which require an appropriate response. Ancestors have power and so care is taken to keep peace. Rituals and prayers keep all in balance. I often talk to and about my mother and lately realize more and more how much of an influence she has on my life. (American)
- The living dead concept recognizes that physical or earthly life is not the end of existence, or of one's life journey. It is a transition from earthly life to spiritual life with the ancestral community (and the creator God). Though not identical, it has similarities to the Christian belief in a communion of

saints, i.e., that those who have died have moved on to a "spirit life" in God. They are still with us, and still meaningful and present in our lives. (American)

Non-African Perspective

- The living dead while not named as such in our culture, are definitely remembered by most Christian people. The recently deceased are mourned, prayed for and to, and their memory cherished through tombstones or photos. (American)
- The main influence of the living dead would be Jesus Christ who is risen and is with us. Christians would be guided by the gospel of Jesus. Sunday Mass would be a community celebration and a social gathering in rural areas. (American)
- According to my culture, the living dead is the whole idea of saints and souls of our departed. There is a possibility of communicating with them through prayer. We offer prayers for them; remember dates of death and by taking flowers to the gravesite. My father died a year ago so the living dead helps me to believe that we are going to meet each other in the future life, that he still takes care of us, that naturally a part of me is already there in heaven. (Polish)
- I understand it as those who have recently died and are constantly around us and we should be aware of them and respect them. (American)
- In some ways the living dead is still staying with the living family. It is meaningful because life is a circle. (Indonesian)
- The living dead is the integration of the spirit of the deceased into the living ancestral community. Personally this gives meaning to me when I make Jesus this "door opener" in social life with those who believe in the same. Has meaning in community life in form of respect. Respect to those who are close to die or those who have recently died, the memory of their life and therefore also their family. Respect for death, to creator God and to life. (Irish)
- Most people do not think of the living dead as having influence in present events. They only influence us in memory. (American)
- The living dead are those who have died, yet their absence still leaves a void in daily activities and they are remembered for what they did. After a point the person is still remembered but the void, especially in the job situation is filled and life continues. (American)
- While surviving relatives remember the departed, the spirit more or less leads a personal continuation of life. People regard it, as being much like a human being though it is dead. I will also remember a dead person but not as a human being. (Norwegian)

- The (concept of the) living dead in America is not accepted. We believe once you are dead you are dead. But there are latent superstitions in some families that lean towards communication beyond the grave and we yearn in our grief of loss to keep in touch with the deceased loved ones. Family systems theories interpret the influence of the living and dead ancestors on each human being. (American)
- The living dead according to me is a person who never died. The spirit is still around the family. It has no meaning in my personal life. (Norwegian)
- The living dead to me in my culture is what is mentioned, recollected or remembered after a person has died. When the person is dead you honor them by showering flowers over his grave. From earth [back] to earth with his body and the soul goes to heaven. (Norwegian)
- I look at every human being as a certain amount of energy (sort of summary of education formation -- both formal and informal, and experiences gotten), and when someone dies, this energy does not disappear but is still around us. It is possible to see and feel it through people's memories and through the activities that he or she has done during his or her lifetime. I also think that the period of the living dead lasts as long as the problems that the person has caused are not solved and/ or someone else has carried on the good work he or she started. Death in general scares people more so nowadays when new diseases are killing many people. So people prefer not to mention it to avoid inviting it. (Italian)
- The living dead are those who have recently died. My own parents have died within the past five years. I think of them often and talk to them occasionally. I have even asked them to help me understand why I am here in Nairobi! They still impact all facets of my life. (American)

EDITOR'S REFLECTIONS

In Africa when a person dies, it does not mark the end of his/her life but is a fulfillment of one of the rites of passage that a human being has to go through in life. A recently deceased person is still in touch with what is happening on earth and is even believed to be influential in social and community life. For instance, among the Abaluyia of Western Kenya, when the husband/father dies, he is buried in front of his house so that he can see who are coming into the compound and also, at the same time continue his role as the protector of the family. Whenever a person dies, his/her life does not cease as it is passed on to a newborn baby. The deceased's life is recycled through nominal reincarnation. The living dead visit and communicate with the living through dreams, often asking that a child be named after them.

DISCUSSION QUESTIONS

1. As an African who has been named after a living-dead person, are you in fact, now that person. Explain.
2. What are the similarities and differences between the living-dead of Africa and the Christian saints?
3. Are the wise elderly living persons, after whom children are being named, considered to belong to the community of the living-dead even though they are still physically alive? Explain.
4. What is your personal understanding of what will happen to your life once you have died?

AFRICAN ILLUSTRATION

RITES DONE AT THE DEATH OF A PERSON

During my grandmother's funeral, I observed that she was always surrounded by relatives telling stories, enquiring from one another of their well-being and that of their families. I even saw some relatives eating their food close to the body and occasionally one of them would adjust her clothing and covers. The daughters and wives of the deceased's sons spread their beddings to sleep near the body at night. They were relating with the deceased as if she were still living. The idea was that even though she was dead, she was still being included in the activities going on in the lives of her living relatives. **[verbatim report of a field assistant].**

RECOMMENDED READINGS

Mbiti, J.S. (1991). *Introduction to African Religion.* (pp. 125-126). Nairobi: East African Educational Publishers.

Idowu, B.E. (1973). *African Traditional Religion: A Definition.* (pp. 173, 175-189). New York: Orbis Books.

Zahan, D. (1979). *The Religion, Spirituality and Thought of Traditional Africa.* (pp. 36-52). Chicago: The University of Chicago Press.

NON-AFRICAN ILLUSTRATION

A WESTERN ILLUSTRATION OF LIMINAL EXISTENCE BETWEEN DEATH AND BURIAL

At the death of a person in North America, the body is usually taken to a funeral home where it is embalmed, dressed in new clothes, made to look alive by the liberal application of cosmetics, laid in an expensive box-like casket and then brought out for viewing for several days before burial. The mourners often remark how the person looks so peaceful, and they interact with each other and the deceased as if the person were still alive.

CHAPTER IV
Theme: NOMINAL REINCARNATION

NOMINAL REINCARNATION
UZIMA WA MILELE

The stylistic carving shows a woman embraced by a man giving birth to a snake. The snake is a symbol of everlasting life as it is said to continue to shed its skin and never dies. The meaning is everlasting life, *Uzima wa Milele,* through procreation.

NOMINAL REINCARNATION

Introduction

Naming of newly born children is a mandatory and common feature of all cultures. In some Western cultures children are named after their parents, grandparents or famous people as an honor to them. In African cultures naming is very important as it gives a person an identity as a human being and a permanent place in a lineal family.

Naming of Children in Africa

This theme is tied in with the understanding of the nature of human life. As life is recycled, the mechanism by which this takes place is that of procreation. Since life comes to a person as a gift, it must be passed on to continue the cycle. The way this is done is by naming a newborn baby after a highly respected elder who may be living or recently deceased, or an ancestor. The naming ceremony is both ritual and reality as it effectively makes a child a human being linked to ancestral blood through the person whose name it carries. Indeed it is commonly believed that the child has the looks, characteristics, attitudes and personality of that person. If a child dies after being named, it is considered a full human being and is buried accordingly. And, if the child is male, it is possible that later on a young woman would be married in his name (known as a ghost marriage) in order to give birth to children to carry on his name and life. Everyone, therefore, must marry and procreate. Consequently, if a married couple is infertile, the feeling is that their life has been stopped up, and frustrated. This is expressed saying "without children one's house falls down or one's life is incomplete." Marital institutions like polygamy and widow inheritance arose to ensure the fertility of all families. If, for example, the first wife is childless, the second wife brings children into the homestead. In a survey done a number of years ago, women were asked if it were better to be a junior wife or unmarried. The overwhelming response was a junior wife, with the comment that one begets children no matter what one's status is in the marriage. In Africa, many ethnic groups continue to measure a person's social status and wealth in children. Thus to be childless is a state of abject and complete poverty.

Naming of Children and the Understanding of Life Elsewhere

Most cultures worldwide that are outside of contemporary western influences still value children for at least social and economic purposes. Whether there is the idea of nominal reincarnation is not clear - this idea might be peculiar to Africa. Parents, however, often name their children after their grandparents, but this is seen as more honorific than an essential passing on of life. More recently, in westernized cultures where birth control is practiced, and life itself is seen to be a personal possession in a linear mode, procreation is no longer seen by many as an essential element of marriage relationships; procreation has become optional and depends on the needs and objectives of the couple. The result has been a declining birth rate to a point that some societies are no longer replacing those who die. This has resulted in a dramatic increase in the population of the elderly and calls into serious question the stability and viability of the societies.

Human Life: Recycled or Linear

In real time a person's biological and cultural life has a certain African dimension to it, that is "looking back" to its source in the fertility of one's parents and the socializing community, both of which are givens and pre-exist one's present life and existence. Biologically and even socially all living people are inter-related and carry the same set of genes, similar cultural themes i.e., ideas, values and symbols and similar human activities from birth to death and beyond called domains. To argue that one's personal biological life is a new creation experienced in a linear mode is as much a cultural, learned statement as an African saying that biological life is recycled and entails the essential personal return of ancestors to the living human community through the newly born who carry their names - nominal reincarnation.

QUESTION

Kindly explain in detail your understanding of the theme of NOMINAL REINCARNATION. Does it have any meaning in your personal, social and community life? N = 50 (32 Africans, 18 non-African).

RESPONSES COLLATED BY THREE CATEGORIES
1. *Relevance of the Theme of Nominal Reincarnation   R = 64*
2. *Impact of the Theme of Nominal Reincarnation   R = 38*
3. *Definition of Nominal Reincarnation   R = 22*
Other Comments   R = 17

AFRICAN RESPONDENTS   N = 32

Relevance of the Theme of Nominal Reincarnation   (R = 39)
Some communities *name [the newborn]* after the dead members of the community (6), emphasizes on the individual level that there is *need to recycle life* (4), is a reminder that *one will live on after death* (3), strengthens the *belief of life after death* (3), implies that *life is cyclical in African cultures* (3), life is *continuous* (3), when one *dies he/she is replaced by a newly born* child (3), through *reincarnation life is passed on* from one generation to another (2), some communities *name [the newborn] after both the living and the dead* (2), people still value *nominal reincarnation* especially *when a child*

falls sick (1), *life given to a newborn child is a gift from the ancestral community* (1), it *signals* to the community the *coming back of its members* (1), the *naming custom unites* the *living with the ancestors* (1), *ancestors come back to life through the newborn* (1), the *newborns are our refuge of hope* of *living again* in this world (1), makes *dead people present* by naming new members after them to *acknowledge their contribution to the community* (1), through it *life is rejuvenated* (1), to *honor, respect and let the spirit of the ancestors continue to live among us* (1), death is the *beginning/entry into another phase* of life (1).

Impact of Nominal Reincarnation   (R = 27)

Explains the *resemblance* of people to their ancestors (13), *affects one's social life* because of the *society expecting a person to resemble the one he/she is named after in personality, character and roles* (4), when a *member of the community dies, a child born immediately after is named after the deceased* (2), many times the *actions of an individual* are compared to those of the person he/she is named after (2), makes people *strive to leave behind a good memory* (1), a person *owes his/her survival* to the community (1), an *individual's existence* is *dependent on* the *existence of the community* (1), makes people *relate well* in the community (1), gives one *motivation to remain strong in character* like the person he/she is named after (1), the community tends to see the *image of the dead person in the one who is named after him/her* rather than that person as an individual (1).

Definition of Nominal Reincarnation   (R = 14)

Giving the *name of a deceased person/ancestor* to the *newborn* (3), being *born again* (2), the *coming back of an ancestor through the naming of a child after the dead ancestor* (1), when *human life is recycled and given to a newborn child* (1), the *belief that life is a cycle* (1), *continuity of the life* of an individual even after *death through rebirth in the naming system* (1), the *birth and ritual transmission* of life from one stage of development to another (1), process in which a person who is *living dies and it is believed that his/her spirit is transferred to a newborn,* thus making *him/her a living dead* (1), process of *recycling human character* (1), *rebirth of an individual* either in *name or form* but not in reality (1), *naming of the newborn to occupy a place in the lineage* (1).

Other Comments   (R = 6)

Is a *change of life* similar to the *Christian belief of being born again* (1), everyone wishes to be *remembered through naming* (1), how an individual *relates with others affects the quality of life for generations* to come (1), a person's name is *cut off from the life cycle if he/she does not procreate* (1), a *name confers identity* and *character* and even at times *determines the fate* of an individual (1), when *married in a different culture*, at times *one is not sure whether they will be remembered* because of the *difference in naming systems* (1).

NON-AFRICAN RESPONDENTS N = 18
[The respondents answered both according to their
own cultures and their understanding of African culture.]

Relevance of the Theme of Nominal Reincarnation (R = 25)
Does *not* have any *relevance for me or my community* (6), *procreation is necessary for continuity of life* (4), implies that *life is recycled* (3), there is *no death in African culture* (1), one *continues to live through* one of his/her descendants *that is named after him/her* (1), death is *not the end of life* (1), life is *given to a newborn* from a *pre-existing source of ancestral life* (1), life is *continuous* (1), people live on by *using the names of ancestors* (1), ensures *one's life will continue through memory* (1), a *child is seen to carry on the family line* (1), signifies that *someone has come back* to the community (1), the *hope to return to the land of the living* is through a *baby carrying one's name* (1), associated with the *cycle of life from birth to death* (1), a *newborn is the reincarnation of an ancestor* (1).

Impact of Nominal Reincarnation (R = 11)
There is some *resemblance between the newborn and an ancestor* (2), a newborn is *named after the ancestor embodied* in the child (1), when an *ancestor dies his/her name is given to a child born in the same clan* (1), one is expected to *live on the land of ancestors and do what they did* (1), when a child is born it *gets its name from the family* (1), children are thought to have a *part of their ancestral heritage in them* (1), confers *respect on family elders* (1), one must *live a good life so as to be named* (1), *traits of elders* become known when *they join the ancestors* (1), a *child is named after an ancestor* (1).

Definition of Nominal Reincarnation (R = 8)
In *African thought it is when a newborn embodies the spirit of the ancestor* after whom it has been named (1), is the *remembrance of dead ancestors* by giving their *names to the next generation* (1), naming after *a relative and somehow embodying his qualities* (1), *making ancestors out of other people* (1), the way in which *one's name is carried on by descendants after death* (1), the continuous process of *continuing the family lineage* (1), is the *living dead coming back to life* in a newborn child (1), the cycle of life from *conception to ancestry* (1).

Other Comments (R = 11)

In our culture *each baby born is a new life created by God* (1), life is *a gift from God* and *people must take care of it* (1), *names* are *not important* in my culture (1), most people in our society do *not believe in reincarnation* (1), this theme is *best explained by the theme of the living dead* (1), we believe that certain *biological and emotional traits* may be passed down from *parent to child* (1), as *a woman religious I am not* physically renewing life and sometimes this realization of *no personal lineage leaves an empty feeling* (1), the *living dead* can be part of the family even up to five generations (1), *naming after the dead seems to be akin to nominal reincarnation* (1), ancestors generally *do not mean* anything to me (1), sometimes *a family name will be given to a child in my culture* (1).

SUMMARY
Beliefs expressed regarding Nominal Reincarnation

Nominal Reincarnation is: the *ritual transmission* of life from the dead to the living. It is the *belief that the spirit* and *personality of a dead person* lives on through a *newborn.* It is the *remembrance of the dead ancestors* by giving their names to the next generation, the dead coming back to life through the newborn, is when a *newborn embodies* the spirit of the ancestor after whom it has been named, the *coming back to life of an ancestor* through naming a child after him/her, *recycling of human life* and giving it to a newborn child, the *birth and ritual transmission of life* from one stage of development to another, the *process in which the life and spirit of a highly respected elderly person whether living or recently dead is transferred to a newborn,* is the process of *recycling human character,* and the naming of a newborn *to occupy a place in the lineage.*

Impact of the theme of nominal reincarnation: *explains the resemblance of people* to their ancestors, affects the way people *live socially,* a *newborn gets to be named after a recently deceased person,* makes people *strive to leave behind a good memory after their death,* and it gives a person the *motivation* to *remain strong in character* like the person he/she is named after.

Relevance of the theme of nominal reincarnation: emphasizes the need to *recycle life,* is a *reminder* that there is *life after death,* implies that *life is cyclical,* through nominal reincarnation life is *passed on from one generation to another,* life is given to a newborn child as *a gift from the ancestral community,* it is the *naming custom* that unites *the living* with the *ancestors,* it is to *honor, respect, and to let the spirits of the ancestors* continue living among us.

RESPONSES FROM WORKSHEETS

[Note that naming is very important in African cultures as a name gives a person access and a permanent place in the community that gives the name. For example, a Christian name makes one part of the Christian community. In like manner the biological and social life of ancestors are passed on and recycled by their names being given to the newly born.]

❑ Kindly explain in detail your understanding of the theme of NOMINAL REINCARNATION. Does it have any meaning in your personal, social and community life?

AFRICAN RESPONDENTS N = 32

[There were eleven ethnics groups represented: Luo (11), Agikuyu (7), Akamba (3), Abaluyia (3), Teso (2), Abagusii (1), Kipsigis (1), Bemba (1), Tutsi (1), Kategi (1) and Aembu (1). The respondents were university graduates, fourteen women and eighteen men.]

- It is real and traits appear in both. It does have a meaning and in the community people still value it especially when the child becomes sick. (Luo)
- The coming back of a dead ancestor to life through naming of a child after the dead ancestor. (Teso)
- It is through [nominal] reincarnation that a life is lived from one generation to another, and a person is a person because the community is there and (is alive) living. No man is an island. A person exists because the other people exist. John Mbiti says, "I am because we are." (Akamba)
- Nominal reincarnation is when a human life is recycled and given to a newborn child as a gift from the ancestral community. It has meaning, as there is need for recycling life, which makes us relate well in the community. (Luo)
- It is the belief that life is a cycle and that the implication is that of continuity of life. To the community, it is a sign of "repetition" or coming back of the members. (Akamba)
- Nominal reincarnation is just what a certain group in the community believes. This has meaning in my personal, social and community life in that I resemble the person I was named after and possesses his characteristics. (Agikuyu)
- Nominal reincarnation is the giving of the name of an ancestor or a deceased person to a newborn. I appreciate this naming custom. It unites me with the ancestral spirit of my "namesake" ancestor and gives me motivation to remain strong in character like him. (Agikuyu)

- It has a meaning to me because it makes me believe that there is life after death because we believe that when a person dies he/she comes back in another person within the clan or the family. (Bemba)
- We believe that when a member of the community dies, then any baby born immediately after must be named after the deceased thereby making him or her become the living dead. (Luo)
- This is the act of naming a newborn after dead friends and relatives. People normally tend to take the characters of those they are named after. (Luo)
- Nominal reincarnation is the continuity of life of an individual even after death through rebirth in the naming system. A dead ancestor comes back to life in the form of a newborn child. I am named after my paternal grandmother who is still alive and is sure I carry on her name. So even after death she continues to live. So people in the society call me the mother of my father. (Agikuyu)
- This theme means taking flesh in another person through naming. He who is named after an ancestor will have his traits. Though not hundred percent true, there are some similarities or resemblance in the traits, as I said. (Luo)
- Nominal reincarnation means rebirth and the ritual transition from one stage of development to the other. This can also imply re-naming of the newborn to occupy a place in the lineage. (Agikuyu)
- Implies that persons never die in vain. They change state of life similar to Christianity. They become our refuge of hope. People are made present by naming new members to acknowledge him or her. (Abaluyia)
- Nominal reincarnation means being reborn anew. This is what underpins being renamed after a deceased father, mother, grandparents or any other member of the community. (Luo)
- Nominal reincarnation denotes coming back to life through another person. Having been named after a dead relative, it affects my social life. The community often expects a lot from me as they keep on referring to me as their long gone cousin. Many times my actions are related to hers among many other things. (Luo)
- Reincarnation is the process in which people that are living die and it is believed that their spirit is transferred to a newborn and then he/she comes to live again. (Akamba)
- Nominal reincarnation means when one dies another comes to replace him/her by being born. My paternal grandfather died before my parents got married. After my first-born brother was born, he was named after my grandfather who was a clan elder. He is supposed to act as an elder in my clan. My father died, so my elder brother handles the family affairs and he is supposed to act as an elder (together) with my uncles in the community. (Abagusii)

- Nominal reincarnation is the process of recycling the human character. For example if among the ancestors there were lazy, industrious people or even wrestlers, then the children given these various names will eventually posses the exact characters. (Kipsigis)
- Nominal reincarnation is the coming back of life. That is when one dies someone is born to replace his/her life. The one who replaces the gone life is expected to behave and act like that person. For instance, I am named after my grandmother and I am told I behave like her. (Agikuyu)
- I was born when Kategi died. Kategi thus remains in me socially and in the community too. (Kategi)
- The theme reminds me that I will live longer when I die. (Agikuyu)
- Through nominal reincarnation, the life of the ancestors is continued in the newborn. This makes life re-cycled within African cultures. The newborn is expected to have the same traits like the ancestors and also behave and act in the same way. That is why life never ends. (Agikuyu)
- Nominal reincarnation is actually the rebirth of somebody either in the name or form but usually not in reality. In my personal life it has meaning because it is common in our community to be named after someone dead or alive and you tend to be associated with that person. (Luo)
- The theme means rebirth of the ancestors through procreation. It has meaning in my community life since children are mostly named after their ancestors. (Abaluyia)
- The theme underpins the cyclical principle of human life. Human life resembles nature, which is governed by periodicity i.e., period of upward movement/growth, inertia, etc. Through nominal reincarnation, life continues and is rejuvenated. (Aembu)
- To me this means leaving behind a good memory. I may or may not be named because the culture I am married into names in a way [that] I might not be named. But yes, I do feel it would be nice to be remembered. I hope I am doing something that will be worth remembering. (Abaluyia)
- Nominal reincarnation means coming back to life of the ancestors through the rebirth of children who resemble them. It has meaning in my community life in that it helps explain the resemblance of ancestors to their grandchildren. (Luo)
- I believe that even with my physical demise, life continues and how I relate with others and myself will affect the quality of life for generations to come. (Luo)
- Life is a cycle and death is the beginning/entry into another phase of life. One's name is cut off from the cycle if he does not procreate. The name confers identity, character and even determines the fate of the person. (Luo)

- Nominal reincarnation is the naming of children after their ancestors mainly their parents and grandparents. It has meaning for it helps us honor, respect and let the spirit of our ancestors continue living. (Teso)
- The theme of nominal reincarnation means from my point of view someone who died and is reborn as someone else's child that looks like the deceased. (Tutsi)

NON-AFRICAN RESPONDENTS N = 18
[The respondents answered both according to their own cultures and their understanding of African culture.]

[There were six non-African countries represented; America (12), Norway (2), Ireland (1), Poland (1), Spain (1), and Indonesia (1). The respondents were university graduates, eleven women and seven men.]

- In an African context, where there is no death, we continue to live in different ways. It is still nominal that you are still alive in the person of one of your descendants who is named after you. (Spanish)
- It is something that is very important in African culture. Life is recycled it means [that it] does not end with death. When a child is born it gets a name from the family and this means that life is continuous. Someone was born again. Life is a gift from God so people have a responsibility to take care of it and to procreate. (Polish)
- In nominal reincarnation, life is given at birth from a pre-existing source of ancestral life. The baby is not a new life but rather the essence of the ancestor for whom the child is named. In my culture, each baby born is a new life created by God. (American)
- A newborn child is named after the ancestor that is embodied in the child. This is part of the life recycling process. People also live on through using their names. Names are not important and most people do not believe in reincarnation in my society. (American)
- Nominal reincarnation in African thought is when a newborn child embodies the spirit and life of the ancestor after whom it has been named. I don't think this theme has very much relevance in my culture. (Irish)
- I have studied it and come across it in different religions but it does not influence anything in my life. (Norwegian)
- What I understand by nominal reincarnation is that when an ancestor dies, his/her name is given to a newborn baby in the clan. That baby is then said to reincarnate the dead ancestor. This theme does not apply in my personal/ community life. (American)

- Nominal reincarnation is the remembrance of the dead ancestors by the giving of the name to the next generation e.g., naming the child after the dead grandfather, etc. (American)
- Being named after a relative and somehow embodying his good qualities and it ensures my life (via memory) will continue. Yes in a way as through baptism we "take on" Christ and become his brother or sister. In so doing we perpetuate his life (words and deeds) and we share in it too. We speak in much the same way although there is a great difference in meaning and intention. (American)
- Nominal reincarnation is meaningful for my life and also the community. It is so as I face so many experiences and discover new values that are meaningful for my life. (Indonesian)
- One seems to be expected to live on in the land of their ancestors and do what their ancestors did keeping the lineage alive throughout. Also the naming after one recently deceased seems to be akin to reincarnation. (American)
- A child is seen as carrying on the family line. [It is] making ancestors out of other people. It is a negative thing not to reproduce. Children are thought to have a part of their ancestral heritage in them and are therefore named after an ancestor. Family elders are respected. However, ancestors generally do not have meaning in my life. Sometimes a family name will be given to a child but other than that, there is no relation to everyday life. (American)
- Nominal reincarnation means the way in which one's name is not lost but is carried on by a descendant after one's death. For this to happen, one must be seen to have lived a good life, especially in bringing children into the world to continue the cycle of life. When one dies and passes on to the living dead, one's name will be given to a new child. I do not see any direct meaning for my life, but it resembles my hope for sharing in the resurrection after I die and pass into the communion of saints. (American)
- My understanding of nominal reincarnation is explained as "the living dead." The living dead can be a part of the family up to four or even five generations. It is possible for something of the features, characteristics and personality of such a spirit (the living dead) to be noticed in a newborn child. Then people would say that so and so has come back, has returned or has been reborn. (Norwegian)
- Nominal reincarnation is the continuous process of continuing family lineage. It does not have any meaning in my life. (American)
- Nominal reincarnation is the living dead or ancestor coming back in a newborn child. My culture does not believe in this. The closest we come to it is believing that certain biological and emotional traits may be passed down from parent to child. (American)

- Hope to return to the land of the living is through a baby carrying one's name. (American)
- The cycle of life from conception to ancestry is associated with nominal reincarnation. Elders' traits become known when they join the ancestors. New life can receive the name if there is a resemblance. No procreation, no continuation of lineage. As a woman religious, I am not physically renewing life, and sometimes this realization of no personal lineage leaves an empty feeling. (American)

EDITOR'S REFLECTIONS

In African cultures human life is recycled, that is, there is only so much life available, and it has to be preserved, protected and passed on to the next generation. Therefore, life comes to a person as an ancestral gift and it is mandatory that this gift be handed on through fertility. If one does not procreate, his/her life is truncated and ends. In light of this, to be childless is a most untenable personal situation and is seen by many as a curse -- it is ultimate poverty.

DISCUSSION QUESTIONS

1. In African cultures, it is believed that life is recycled and thus ancestors continue to live on in the society through the newborn. Explain how this is possible.
2. What factors determine the naming of a child after a living or deceased person? Discuss this in relation to your culture.
3. In some cultural traditions such as the Hindu, the way a person lives now determines the form and status in which he/she will be reborn, called reincarnation. In your opinion does this idea have any relation with the African concept of nominal reincarnation?
4. What do you personally believe about the nature of your life? Is it linear or recycled? Explain.

AFRICAN ILLUSTRATION

THE CASE OF A CHILD BEING MISNAMED

My Aunt's child had first been named after my grandmother. The child refused to suckle the mother's breasts when she was one week old, and would cry for a long time. Medical check ups revealed that the child was fine and not suffering from any ailments. Later on my aunt was advised to take the child to her husband's home to be renamed. The clan elders gathered and performed some rituals. They then started calling out different names; when the paternal grandfather's name was called out, the child stopped crying. She was put on her mother's breast and she begun nursing normally. Thus the child's name was changed from the maternal grandmother's name to the paternal grandfather's name and she lives on happily ever since. **[Verbatim report of a field researcher]**

RECOMMENDED READINGS

Magesa, L. (1998). *African Religion: The Moral Traditions of Abundant Life.* (pp. 81-92). Nairobi: Paulines Publications Africa.

Kirwen, M.C. (1987). *The Missionary and the Diviner.* (pp. 107-131). New York: Orbis Books.

Mbiti, J.S. (1991). *Introduction to African Religion.* (pp. 28, 92-93). Nairobi: East African Education Publishers.

NON-AFRICAN ILLUSTRATION

WESTERN ILLUSTRATION OF THE NAMING OF CHILDREN

In a family of five children, the first born was named after an uncle, the mother's brother, and the last born after the paternal grandmother whose hair was the same color of red. The names were seen as honorific with no sense that they shared or expressed the other person's life or personality. However as they grew up, they were, at times said to be just like their namesakes. Moreover, at the baptism of infant children they are said to have ritually taken on the life and spirit of Jesus Christ. Thus, it was hoped that they would express in their adult lives the love and concern for all like Jesus did, and become "alter Christus" -- a kind of African-style nominal reincarnation of Jesus.

CHAPTER V
Theme: AFRICAN LINEAGE

AFRICAN LINEAGE/UKOO

The carving depicts an African lineage in which all its members, the living, the dead and the unborn are totally entwined sharing all aspects of their lives.

AFRICAN LINEAGE

Introduction

A person can only become a human being if he/she is socialized into a living, viable community organized in terms of family relationships. Without community support, encouragement and education, a baby dies of neglect, or if raised by animals, becomes a feral child exhibiting animal traits and habits.

African Lineage

In Africa the socializing community is organized around the lineal family and it is made up of the living, the dead and the unborn children all of whom are descendents of a recently deceased grandparent. It can be anywhere from five or six people to fifty/sixty or more. It is the heart or liver (the Luo symbol of the seat of the emotions) of human life, the place of birth, love, marriage, sickness, work, death and inheritance. The lineage is not a voluntary grouping of people; it is the essential part of being a human being. If a person is thrown out of his/her lineage, it is like being condemned to the Christian hell, for he/she is cut off from the roots of existence and wanders the earth like a lost sheep, unprotected and culturally dead.

Family Structures Elsewhere

Again, all living culture has special family structures and rituals ensuring that their children attain full adult maturity through their carefully organized socialization. For example, in the urban cultures of the West, the nuclear family consisting of one man, his wife and their children is the norm, with local governments giving a "lineal" kind of support in times of sickness and tragedy e.g., financial subsidies for widows and orphans, a support that is ordinarily provided by the lineal families of Africa. Fragmentation and break up of family structures in many contemporary cultures, including those of Africa, have been disastrous for children as they grow physically into adulthood with an adolescent mentality and worldview.

QUESTION

In terms of African cultural knowledge, what is your understanding of the theme of LINEAGE IDEOLOGY? N = 91 [67 Africans, 24 non-Africans]

RESPONSES COLLATED BY FOUR CATEGORIES

[Note that the lineage structures and rituals link a person
with both the living and ancestral community.]

1. *Significance/Importance of the Lineage R = 100*
2. *Incorporation into the Lineage R = 45*
3. *Definition of Lineage Ideology R = 36*
4. *Duties and Responsibilities of an Individual in the Lineage R = 23*

AFRICAN RESPONDENTS N = 67

Significance/Importance of the Lineage (R = 67)
Links a person to a *family, clan and community* (13), gives an individual his/her *identity* (11), gives one *a sense of belonging* (11), *connects* one to *the past through the dead, the present through the living, and to the future through the yet to be born* (6), *determines the values, rituals* and *behavior* of the members (6), is the *basis of the family* and by extension the *community* (5), *accords* one certain *rights* in the *community* such as *respect and security* (3), gives *life* and *existence* to the individual (3), *determines the rites of passage* (2), helps in the *distribution of wealth* through *inheritance* (2), *legalizes woman-to-woman marriage* for the *continuation of the family name* (2), is the *basis of recycling of life* (2), *creates oneness with the creator God* (1).

Incorporation into the Lineage (R = 33)
Through *naming* (13), *patrilineal descent* (8), *marriage* (3), going through *all rites of passage* (3), *blood ties* (3), *clan membership* (2), *matrilineal descent* (1).

Definition of Lineage Ideology (R = 29)
A *continuity of life* (9), *tracing* one's *origins* to the *great forefathers* (9), the *interconnection between* the *dead*, the *living* and the *yet to be born* (4), the *enhancement of life through procreation* (3), *preparation* for going through *critical stages in life* (3), *cultural understanding* that holds together a given lineage (1).

Duties and Responsibilities of an Individual in the Lineage (R=18)
Bearing children to continue the lineage (9), must *know his/her family line/tree* (5), *marry or get married* (3), to see *forefathers* as the *guides* and *models* of the *present life* (1).

NON-AFRICAN RESPONDENTS N = 24
[The respondents answered according to
their understanding of African culture.]

Significance/Importance of the Lineage (R = 33)
Symbolizes the *recycling of life* (6), *gives a person a sense of belonging* (5), *legitimizes the family* (4), gives an individual his/her *identity* (3), the *individual gets* his/her *existence* from the *lineage* (3), is the *continuity of life* (3), *incorporates one* into the *community* (3), maintains *cohesion and harmony* in the community (2), *carries* on the *name* of an individual *after death* through *naming a newborn after the dead*, thus *sustaining* the *memory*

of the departed (2), is *significant* in times of *deciding* the *inheritance* (1), *guarantees good administration of common property* (1).

Incorporation into the Lineage   (R = 12)
Through *naming* (11), *blood ties* (1).

Definition of Lineage Ideology   (R = 7)
Is the *continuation of the family line/tree* (2), the *lifeblood* of a person (2), it is a *way of seeing the relationship* of *humans* to their *ancestors* (1), is the *life energy* or *vital force* of a person (1), it is the *family that has passed on, the family the person lives with and the family that is yet to be born* (1).

Duties and Responsibilities of an Individual in the Lineage   (R = 5)
Bearing children to continue the lineage (2), *emulate the person* he/she is *named after* (1), owes *loyalty and obligations* to the *family* (1), should *marry from a respectable family* in order to continue the lineage (1).

SUMMARY
Beliefs expressed regarding the nature of the African Lineage

<u>The Lineage is</u>: *the continuity of life, tracing one's origin to the great forefathers, enhancement of life thro ugh procreation,* and represents *the interconnection between the dead, the living and the yet to be born.* It is the *lifeblood* of a person, the *continuation* of the *family line,* and the *life* energy of a person.

<u>A Person's Responsibilities in the Lineage Includes</u>: *bearing children* to continue the lineage, *knowing his/her family tree,* to *marry,* and to see the *forefathers as the guides and models* of the present life.

<u>The Lineage Gives a Person</u>: an *identity, legitimacy, links him/her to the living and ancestral community, determines values, rituals and behavior of the members,* through *naming, initiation, and marriage.*

<u>A Person is Incorporated into the Lineage through</u>: *naming, patrilineal descent, marriage, blood ties, clan membership, matrilineal descent* and by *going through all rites of passage.*

RESPONSES FROM WORKSHEETS

[Note that the lineal family in Africa -- all who are descended from a recently deceased grandparent -- includes the unborn, the living youth and adults, the highly respected elders and those who have died recently, called the "living dead," together with the ancestors, i.e., those who have died in the past. Everyone in Africa owes his/her life and human socialization to membership in a lineal family -- the root of one's human existence.]

❑ In terms of African cultural knowledge, what is your understanding of the theme of LINEAGE IDEOLOGY?

AFRICAN RESPONDENTS N = 67

[There were thirteen ethnic groups of Africa represented: Luo (19), Agikuyu (18), Abaluyia (9), Akamba (6), Abagusii (3), Akan (2), Aembu (2), Teso (2), Tutsi (2), Kipsigis (1), Bemba (1),   Tigrinya (1), and Nubian (1). The respondents were university graduates, twenty-six women and forty-one men.]

- It is an obligation that occupies an important position in an African to desire to marry so as to build up his own family group and prolong his father's clan. In other words, lineage is a unilineal descent group whereby all members trace their genealogical relationship back to a family ancestor. (Bemba)
- My understanding and knowledge about lineage is that it is a continuation of life. For example naming after ancestors to make life a continuing process. In Africa, cultural lineage is practiced. A baby is named after an elderly person and the death of this person does not end his memories since he is remembered by the mention of the living, i.e., the one named after him/her. (Agikuyu)
- The communities in Africa believe in the past. The attachment and reference to the past is more significant and a guide to their lives. In this respect the notion of ideology is vital in the sense that the forefathers are the guides and models of the present. (Akamba)
- Lineage ideology is the process in which a family or families stretch, by way of giving birth to children, to the next generation. This means that a person can trace his/her origin back to several generations following his lineage. (Akamba)
- The lineage is patriarchal among the Agikuyu. It retraces the ancestral background of the living members of the community via the clan and ends with the nine daughters of Gikuyu and Mumbi the progenitor couple of the Agikuyu people. Each must belong to a particular clan. Each clan has its stereotype ascriptions and attributes like, the witches, the "evil eye," the

clans that provide good girls for wives, the clan that provides bad girls for wives. (Agikuyu)

- Lineage ideology refers to the human cycle. This supports the idea that there is no new life created at the birth of a baby. This is because when a baby is born, it is given the name of a living dead, that is, ancestors who died recently. This mainly signifies that they are not dead but are now living within us. (Kipsigis)

- My understanding is that continuation of the family and clan lineage is very important. Especially the male sex is more important in the sense that the males are the ones that continue the family name in the Abagusii community. If one does not have a male child or if one is childless, then she can take another woman as her "wife." The woman would be having sons who have no fathers -- in essence a single mother whose children will take over the barren woman's names and inherit her property. If one dies without a child, then during the burial a chick is placed on the grave to "mourn her," which means that it is a curse to die without leaving someone behind to continue the lineage. (Abagusii)

- As an African it is important for us to know our family tree, which is traced from the father's lineage. This helps us understand where we come from and it also gives us a sense of identity and belonging. (Luo)

- Lineage concept is a typical form of society, which grows and brings forth life. People pulled together and did much in relation to work, celebrations and social cohesiveness. People needed each other to effectively manage occurrences such as calamities and harvesting large portions of cultivated land. The communal dimension was well defined. (Abaluyia)

- The lineage is very important because it enables the individual to trace his origin. There is union with the dead e.g., I am named after my grandmother and her name continues within the clan. That is why among the Agikuyu some names are strictly known to have come from a certain place. (Agikuyu)

- Lineage ideology is the ideological process of enhancing life through procreation. This ultimately determines one's descent, the clan and community one comes from. It gives one a sense of identity and belonging. (Agikuyu)

- Lineage ideology matches the expression "no man is an island" and stresses the dependence of society on community spirit and the fact that an individual is isolated and without identity outside of his lineage. (Luo)

- My understanding of African culture and lineage is the same as represented by the *Makonde* carvings. It is best summed up in J.S. Mbiti's words "I am because we are, and because we are I am." Each individual must keep within the protocol of the society they are born into as this will identify who they are, and influence their values, and behavior. If they do not follow this they become outcasts with no identity at all. (Luo)

- This is an ideology to help people trace their [family] lines. It helps people to be accommodated in their communities, to be taken care of and be helped. Lineage is a form of identity. (Luo)

- In terms of African cultural knowledge, I understand the theme of lineage ideology is important in that it brings about continuity of a family line through birth of children. Luos value children and expect marriage to be followed by the birth of children and hence encourage the aspect of marriage in the society. Children are also seen as a source of wealth. (Luo)

- Lineage is the tie which links you to the family. According to my culture it is believed that the blood of the mother is what gives you your identity as a member of that particular family. So my tribe is matrilineal in nature. (Akan)

- Lineage ideology proves to us that we do not exist on our own but we draw life from our linkage with the community. It shows our originality and roots. It shows how our origin determines our destiny. It is a proof of oneness of God our creator from whom we draw life. As we trace our ancestral lineage we find that it links us to Adam whose origin is God the creator. (Luo)

- Lineage ideology makes a person. You are so much into your ancestors as they are into you. "I am because we are." (Abagusii)

- The theme of lineage ideology means the continuation of a family, the importance and the connection of each member of the family. I am from my father; my father is from my grandfather, and so on. We all are related to a lineage (line of your own family or clan). (Tutsi)

- The lineage gives one his identity and belonging. (Luo)

- Lineage ideology is what makes a person survive in the African culture. Lineage is what connects humanity with the past, present and future. The living dead are experienced in the present through naming, which is a fundamental existence of recycled death. Normally people named after some dead person acquire similar traits and characters. (Luo)

- It is the lineage that gives one life and existence. Without our lineage we are not. (Luo)

- It is my lineage that gives me my identity. It makes me belong to my community. It makes me feel secure. (Luo)

- It reflects the customary law among our community members going back to the first ancestor, Gikuyu (first man). This theme determines the rites of passage from conception to afterlife. One cannot be buried until he is initiated (circumcised) according to the customary law accorded by the lineage. (Agikuyu)

- Lineage ideology explains that the existence of an individual can only be traced through a family tree or family descent, as the family gives an individual life and identity through the naming system/rituals. (Agikuyu)

- This is where one belongs, where the family ties are created and strengthened. Each group of people has specific rituals, ceremonies, taboos, laws and beliefs that bind them, hence creating culture. (Agikuyu)

- It is through the lineage that one gets life in his community. For a person to exist he/she has to belong to a lineage. Lineage gives one life. It is also through the lineage that life is passed on from one generation to another. A person cannot exist outside lineage. (Akamba)

- Lineage in the African culture is given through naming. For instance I was named after my great grandmother whom I hear we have resemblance. (Luo)

- Being in a lineage means you belong somewhere. You are part of that group. Among my people, the Abaluyia, a child has to be given a name by his or her father's family/lineage. That is where he belongs. If the people refuse to give a name, it means that they have not accepted the child and he does not belong there. Such a child will be brought up without belonging to any lineage. The mother and her family will take responsibility but the chances of such a child being mistreated are high. Being accepted into a lineage through being given a name from it is important for a sense of belonging. (Abaluyia)

- Lineage ideology means the family line of a given people where one traces his roots in the past generations especially the father's side in a patrilineal society. (Abaluyia)

- Lineage ideology entails the dead family members of a person, the living and those yet to be born. (Luo)

- Lineage ideology is the principle, which underlines the horizontal and vertical dimensions of relationships within a community. These dimensions are reckoned through blood ties, consanguinity or rites of passage (i.e., the territorial rite of passage). Lineage ideology is the basis of the cultural themes. (Aembu)

- Lineage ideology is a society's way of creating order in the society. Relationships are established in a lineage. Lineage encompasses the ancestors, living dead, the living and the yet to be born. It is very important for all individuals for it gives one an identity and a place to belong. (Agikuyu)

- Lineage ideology means that every person has to pass through all rites of passage from birth, initiation to adulthood and death. (Luo)

- In terms of African cultural knowledge my understanding of the theme of lineage ideology is that bodies may die but one's spirit never dies and continues living in the lineage through the children of a family, and the name of a family is carried on from one generation to the next through its sons, for daughters get married to other families and so belong to the family they marry into. (Teso)

- Lineage ideology is part and parcel of an African. We need to belong and this sense is strong amongst us. To be outside a lineage is to cease to exist. You are dead even if you are still living. By this we acknowledge the unity and importance of life. (Teso)

- This is the line of a people. Ancestors and the living dead are reborn through their children's children. This group has an identity and stick together. They also may have distinctive traits. It is recognition of the male members of the community. (Luo)

- My understanding is that continuation of the family and clan name is very important. Thus every family encourages their child to get married and marry in order for them to bear children. The first boy and girl were named after the male's parents while the next boy and girl were named after the female's parents. Extra children are named after the brothers and sisters of the parents, favor being given to the male side. (Agikuyu)

- The term lineage ideology connotes generation that is through naming, from one's ancestor the generation continues to exist. This is particularly so from the boy's side who always takes the family name. Hence having children was considered important in order to continue with the family lineage. Those who did not have children were seen to have ended their own generation and they would no longer exist in their offspring. (Luo)

- The lineage ideology in terms of African cultural knowledge to my understanding is that each person has a duty and responsibility to make sure that there is continuity in the family and clan through bearing children and the lineage should not be extinct. Hence the Akamba people invented the "iweto" marriage system in order to perpetuate lineage in cases of barrenness or in case of a marriage where only girls are born. (Akamba)

- It is the systematic fulfillment of one's societal expectations and undergoing all rituals pertaining to life. (Abagusii)

- Lineage ideology binds and joins together the living, the dead and the yet to be born in a vast African family that is the source of the individual security and identity. (Agikuyu)

- I understand that to understand an African well, I must understand his marriage, eldership and death entanglements i.e., he gets his status and honors on how he performs [his duties] according to lineage ideology. He also gets his rights of inheritance from his lineage. (Agikuyu)

- This is an African theme that deals with how one passes their name/self to others. This is the continuity of an individual, family and clan that continues even after death. Through children, an individual's name and family name continues and thus does not die with physical death. (Agikuyu)

- It is the inter-connectedness between the living, the living dead and those not yet born. They form one family tree that is linked with the past, the present and the future. (Abaluyia)
- In my view, it is a conception of those activities and events that are related in a fundamental way to the continuity of a clan's existence. (Luo)
- Members of a community are linked through lineage. (Aembu)
- It is the continuation of life in a particular group through birth. It is also the continuation of one's name, his/her parents, grandparents and ancestors. (Akamba)
- In my understanding, it is that one must participate in the procreation process. Once one dies without leaving a child behind, this person will be forgotten and [this] is not positive according to African people. (Tutsi)
- Lineage accords one with a sense of belonging, prestige, character and customary behavior. One is identified with a group of equals and marked boundary against things like incest, marriage, burial, etc. (Agikuyu)
- This is the root of one's being and the attachment to generations to come. (Abaluyia)
- Lineage is continuity from the present back to the great forefathers. The worst punishment is to cut somebody off from the lineage, which is tantamount to killing one (cutting one off) from humanity. When a baby is born, one of the ancestors is believed to be returning back to the world because life is recycled at the time of birth. (Luo)
- From an African point of view, a person does not exist alone, and there is deep value in naming which gives the person the right to belong to the lineage and receive the fullness of life with other members. (Agikuyu)
- People's sense of belonging is bound by their blood relatives to promote peace. People feel as one and prosperity was distributed as set out by community. (Abaluyia)
- Lineage ideology is the school of thought that determines which people are related to a certain generation. (Akamba)
- The theme underlies all the activities and ceremonies associated with procreation and continuity of the clan in particular and the whole community at large. (Agikuyu)
- You must belong to a lineage. It is a must if you want to belong both now and in the future after you physically die. Not to belong to a lineage means that you do not exist, you belong nowhere and this is tragic. (Abaluyia)
- This is the descendent process of life where it is enhanced or recycled through procreation i.e., the "family" tree. (Agikuyu)

- Life is continuous and is transformed from one person to another. For instance, a grandson named after his grandfather who is already dead takes his life. This forms the [family] tree of life. (Agikuyu)
- This is a situation whereby I am party to my community, and all activities that I do should hinge around my community. I also have an obligation to my community. (Abaluyia)
- For Africans, [the] life cycle is not complete without having married and had children. The one who remains barren works against God's divine plans, breaks lineage continuity, and as such cannot claim to have lived a worthy and honorable life. (Tigrinya)
- Lineage ideology demonstrates that a person only lives because the lineage has given the person a name. A foetus is never considered human until named but gets a normal burial ceremony because it possessed a spirit. It is therefore the lineage that gives one a human normalcy. (Nubian)
- Is a culture's way of preparing people to acknowledge and go through the critical changes of life. (Abaluyia)
- Lineage ideology is the continuation of life through naming and all the ceremonies that go with it. (Agikuyu)
- Lineage ideology is the cultural understanding that holds a given lineage together. (Luo)
- It is that which places a person within a context in terms of others, both dead and living. (Agikuyu)
- African culture sees lineage ideology as a way of building a family setting. (Akan)

NON-AFRICAN RESPONDENTS N = 24
[*The respondents answered according to their understanding of African culture*]

[*There were a total of six non-African countries represented: America (14), Norway (6), Indonesia (1), Spain (1), Ireland (1), and Poland (1). The respondents were university graduates, twenty-five women and ten men.*]

- Lineage ideology is the way of seeing the relationship that each human being has to his/her ancestors -- his/her true life. This gives each person a sense of belonging and place. Names are important, especially those that refer to an ancestor. In this way the person carries on the name (life) of the ancestor. (American)
- My understanding of the theme of lineage ideology is for the continuation of family life and also for the purpose of inheritance. (Indonesian)

- From what I understand, lineage ideology is the purpose and identity of a person. The tribe is the person's place of belonging. Without the tribe the person has no identity. Lineage ideology is more than the tribe or clan but even more specifically is the family that has passed on, the family the person lives with, and family that is yet to be born. (American)
- It seems that for the African, one's lineage is of utmost importance. One draws their very identity and sense of pride from their lineage. This may be due in part to passing on of land to one's children, which happens in United States of America but not of an importance related to survival. (American)
- The ideology of the lineage is very important in African cultural knowledge. A human being exists because of the lineage. By naming, a person is given life and is incorporated in the lineage. By naming, a baby is linked forever with the ancestral life. Blood life is recycled. (Norwegian)
- In African culture, there is no life outside of the lineage. African culture sees life as a finite entity. Every newborn baby is seen as an ancestor who returns rather than a new person with its own unique original identity. It is the name of the lineage that gives an African his/her identity. (American)
- It is something very strong and gives sense of belonging to a clan. One carries the name of the clan and in this way has common ancestors. The moment of getting the name is [the] time of getting into the lineage of a given clan. An immoral person may be sent out of the community and even the name can be taken back, and he/she no longer belongs to the lineage of the given clan. (Polish)
- This refers to the "vital force" meaning life energy, harmony with structures: bestowed by God. It gives a person an identity without which one is a "nobody." I get my identity through the "naming ceremony," which connects me with the ancestors of the clan and now the expectation is for me to emulate his virtues. (American)
- A person's identity is first and foremost related to his family and the tribe he is a part of. His loyalty and obligations are tied to the family line. (Norwegian)
- The worst possible punishment is to expel a person from his/her lineage, which effectively cuts him/her from human life. (Norwegian)
- Lineage ideology in African culture teaches that an individual is a person as they are identified through/in their family. All a person is or does is expressed and interpreted through this lens of the family. Thus, an individual is expected to marry into a respectable family and have children to carry out the ancestral lineage. Unmarried and childless people are seen to be unhealthy and somehow cursed by ancestors or evil spirits. This scheme helps to preserve lineage bloodlines through ages and holds the community together. (American)

- Lineage ideology is very important. The birth and naming of a child carries on the family lineage. Being disowned is literally the end of a person being accepted in their family and culture. Having children is important in continuing the family lineage and the family name. (American)
- While we discussed lineage as linked to naming, it seems to me that lineage is linked through bloodlines. The influence of ancestors is very strong and very present not past. The basic unit of the society is family in a straight line from grandparents to parents to children. The "extended" family includes many generations but friends cannot be grafted into it as in my culture. (American)
- Lineage ideology seems to reflect African culture's sense of profound interconnectedness of life that flows from the creator God. We are born not as isolated individuals, but as social beings whose full human existence will come via naming and incorporation into the life of the community. The newborn does not represent a new life, but recycling of life within the family tree, the family line. (American)
- Naming often represents a family's sense of who is coming back in shape of the new child. The person's life as it unfolds will enrich or detract from the family's name. The whole life is lived out within the context of family lineage, family connection and is seen and judged in this way. (American)
- Lineage ideology is the "tree of life" or "family tree," which says that a person exists as a human being only because the lineage has given the person its life through naming, and thereby has incorporated him/her into the lineage. (Norwegian)
- Lineage is basic to life. The family is the primary unit and its forms and functions vary but basically it has social and economic functions. The people of a certain lineage support one another in daily life, performance of rituals and in times of crisis. There are roles and responsibilities within the group and organization of the group keeps life balanced. Reciprocity is an invaluable part of the lineage. (American)
- Family seems very important to Africans who seem to be able to trace their ancestors for generations. Africans are usually named after their grandparents or other relatives. These names are important to sustain the memory of their relative after he/she dies. (American)
- A human being is considered human after he/she is named. Then he is linked to the "tree of life" forever. If he misbehaves seriously he can be de-linked, which is the worst possible punishment. The "tree of life" is the family, the social community and the ancestors (plus potential children). (Irish)
- This is a basic item in African culture. From the moment of their birth, African people belong to a group, although it is the actual moment of naming when one is incorporated into his/her lineage. There is no real life

outside the lineage. The belonging is not chosen; lineage is something given to the person and is the usual link to their ancestors, who live again in that person; there is no death in Africa. (Spaniard)

- I understand that there is no new life being created at the birth of a baby, but it has to be given a name and then connected into the family line. Then the baby is accepted as a human being and has his/her rights and connection to life. The name either comes from the mother's side or the father's side depending on whether it is a patriarchal or matriarchal family naming. (Norwegian)
- [Lineage is] members of a group that can trace their genealogical relationship back to a founding ancestor whether dead or alive. (Norwegian)
- There is no real human life except through membership to a lineage. There is a sense that at birth, it is not a new life, but a returning life. (American)
- That human life is passed/given via the lineage and naming of the person. It involves the incorporation of the person into the society and ancestral family. Lifeblood of the person. To be expelled from a lineage is the worst punishment. (American)

EDITOR'S REFLECTIONS

In African cultures, the lineal family is the main socializing agent. An adult's personality is a reflection of his/her family background. The preference for a Western-style nuclear family in the urban areas has given people a way of opting out of responsibilities for lineal family obligations. As written earlier in the anthropological note, the lineal family includes the yet to be born, the living and the dead descendants of a common ancestor. This lineal reality is still alive and well in contemporary Africa. However, as more and more people migrate to urban areas, the interaction of the lineal families becomes more irregular. Members of the lineage gather together at the home of the parents or the grandparents during the festive Christmas and New Year's season. After this they go their separate ways and may only gather together for a relative's wedding or funeral. This breakdown of the lineal family interactions has left many widows and orphans living in urban areas without a family support system. In turn, this has given rise to street families, an increasing number of child-headed households, and an increase in the level of prostitution.

DISCUSSION QUESTIONS

1. What is the name of your lineage? Write the names of your fore bearers as far back as you can remember.
2. Among some patrilineal ethnic communities, a widow can be dispossessed and thrown out with her children by her brothers-in-law. How is this possible given a lineal family structure?

3.   What are the major reasons for the differences between the nuclear family structure of the western world and the lineal family structure of Africa? Explain.
4.   What is the family structure within which you were born and socialized? Explain.

AFRICAN ILLUSTRATION

AFRICAN LINEAL FAMILY

The birth of a child signifies the entry into the lineage of a new member who is made to be a human being through naming. The child's development is the lineal family's responsibility, such that if a child is doing something wrong, any adult has a right to admonish or even punish him/her. Also the lineal family makes important decisions concerning the individual e.g., who goes to school. Again, the lineal family assists the individual to move from one stage of life to another e.g., initiation into adulthood. The family assists the individual in determining the right partner for marriage, planning the marriage ceremony and fulfilling requirements of the marriage. All resources are held in common and family relationships are expressed in plural form e.g., 'our mother, our brother.'

At death, it is the lineal family members who ensure that the necessary rites and rituals are performed to enable the person to join the ancestral community. Furthermore, the behavior of the individual impacts on the reputation of the family. If a person's actions are destroying the reputation of the family, he is warned to change his behavior. If he does not then he will be ostracized from the lineal family and left without any human identity.

RECOMMENDED READINGS

Gyekye, K. (1996). *African Cultural Values: An Introduction.* (pp. 35-50, 75-92). Accra: Sankofa Publishing Company.

Paris, P.J. (1995). *The Spirituality of African Peoples: The Search for a Common Moral Discourse.* (pp. 77-89). Minneapolis: Fortress Press.

Shorter, A. (1998). Marriage and Family in Africa. In *African Culture, An Overview.* (pp. 83-95). Nairobi: Paulines Publications Africa.

NON-AFRICAN ILLUSTRATION

A DESCRIPTION OF THE WESTERN EXTENDED FAMILY

The lineal family of Africa is often equated with the extended family of the Western world. However the extended family of the Western world is a **voluntary grouping** of people who are the immediate descendants of a grandparent or siblings, and who interact on social and, at times, financial basis due to emotional, social and educational need.

In the Western world, the local governments operate as a safety net for the nuclear families that make up what is called the extended family. For example, if a brother dies leaving children, they are not seen to be the responsibility of his siblings. If a sibling does help them, it will be out of special affection and charity. At the same time the local governments often provide school fees and a certain amount of financial and social help for widows with small children that will continue until the children reach a certain age. Furthermore, at the time of inheritance there are often major conflicts within the extended family resulting in members spending years without speaking to each other over what they consider to be the unjust and unequal distribution of the family's resources...The extended family of the western world, therefore is not the same as the lineal family of Africa.

CHAPTER VI
Theme: LEADERSHIP

LEADER/KIONGOZI

The carving shows an elder seated in a contemplative mood. Leadership is a respected position reserved for those considered to be wise and just in decision making.

LEADERSHIP

Introduction

No society can exist without leadership no matter how minimal or corrupt. To think that persons can exist outside of a structured community is unreal. In fact, the very idea of a community entails shared and designated responsibilities for the sake of the integrity and survival of the group. Human life begins in a most helpless and dependent mode that survives only if there is a pre-existing community that takes responsibility for ushering that life into mature adulthood -- a process that takes upwards of twenty to twenty-five years.

African Leadership

There are a wide variety of leadership positions in African societies -- heads of households, diviners, herbalists, local chiefs, rainmakers, prophets, elders -- all attain their status based on either their meritorious lives, through inheritance or through a deep mystical experience. The political power that they have is sacral and comes from the ancestors. In a special way they are the visible representatives of the ancestral community and are responsible to the local communities. To gainsay a respected leader is not only unwise, but is seen to be a rejection of the supporting community and can result in one being disowned.

The situation in Somalia where there has been no functioning central government since the early 90's highlights the fact that without leadership, even though corrupt, chaos ensues. A medical doctor flying to Baidoa, Somalia every month related how difficult it was to continue the work of the hospital where he was the chief medical officer, since he never knew what to expect, whether he would be received in a friendly manner and even whether there would still be a functioning hospital when the plane landed.

The introduction of democratic elections for national leadership roles in many African countries has often bypassed traditional leadership resulting in young, unacceptable and unstable national leaders who are ineffective and scorned by local elders. Furthermore, since they are not responsible to the local communities, they find it acceptable to use local government facilities for personal benefit and grandeur e.g., the Kenyan 1992 Goldenberg scandal.

Leadership Elsewhere

Worldwide there is a large variety of political systems from democratic governments to religious-style autocracy, military dictatorships, authoritarian dictators, tribal chiefs, elected councils of elders, etc. However, in all cases the families in these societies have their essential family leaders playing the roles of parents, heads of households, grandparents. The paradox is that these family leaders survive no matter which political system surrounds them. For some analysts, the family unit, whether the extended family of the West or the lineal family of Africa and elsewhere, is an essential element of human nature.

QUESTION
Kindly explain in detail your understanding of the theme of LEADERSHIP. Does it have any meaning in your personal, social and community life? N = 70 (52 Africans, 18 non-Africans)

RESPONSES COLLATED BY NINE CATEGORIES
1. *Role of a Leader in the Society R = 56*
2. *Characteristics of a Leader R = 49*
3. *Significance of the Theme of Leadership R = 34*
4. *How One Becomes a Leader R = 23*
5. *Leadership Today R = 20*
6. *Definition of a Leader R = 18*
7. *Definition of Leadership R = 16*
8. *Types of Leaders R = 15*
9. *Responsibility of People towards Leaders R = 6*
Other Comments R = 22

AFRICAN RESPONDENTS N = 52

Role of a Leader in the Society (R = 34)
Guides the community (4), is *a moral guardian* (3), **enhances** community welfare (3), *acts as a judge and arbitrator* in the community (2), *represents* the interests of the people (3), *ensures the community lives in harmony* (2), *promotes unity* in the society (2), *counsels* people (2), *maintains social order* (2), *protects* the community (2), *guides* the community to attain its perceived goals (2), is *the representative* of people in the community (1), *works together* with the community (1), is *an overseer* (1), *helps the group to make the best decisions* (1), *leads* by example (1), *presides over community proceedings* (1), acts as *a spiritual guide* (1).

Characteristics of a Leader (R = 36)
Is *a role model* (5), *morally upright* (4), has *an outstanding/exemplary positive character* (3), *wise* (3), *responsible* (3), *respectable* (2), *charismatic* (2), acts according to *the interests* of the community (1), *respects* other people (1), is *authoritative* (1), an *expert* in various fields (1), a *specialist* e.g., *diviner or rainmaker* (1), must have *gone through all acceptable rites of passage* (1), is *articulate* (1), *understands* the people he/she is leading (1), is *a reconciler* (1), is *development conscious* (1), a *good listener* (1), *advanced in age* (1), *reliable* (1), *allows for dialogue* with others (1).

Significance of the Theme of Leadership   (R = 30)

Helps to *maintain order* in the society (7), implies *a service to all* (4), helps to *control chaos* in the society (2), implies that *leaders are influential* in the community (2), helps to *maintain unity in times of conflicts* (2), *necessitates self discipline* (1), necessitates the *performance of communal activities* (1), makes one to be *a role model* for his/her community (1), a leader *knows all that is happening in the community* (1), helps to *improve people's quality of life* (1), *defines* the *leader's responsibility* to the group (1), is a *demonstration of political organization* (1), *puts an individual above the standards of the common man* (1), is *a sign of good qualities* in a person (1), a leader is the *symbol of authority, unity, good governance and good life* in the society (1), it is *a religious role that is God-given* (1), makes one *have a say* in the community (1), leaders are *representatives of God and ancestors* (1).

How One Becomes a Leader   (R = 19)

By *appointment* (7), as a result of *special characteristics and qualities* (3), through *election* (3), through *training* (2), by *inheritance* (2), by *virtue of having been born into a lineage of leaders* (1), through *grooming* e.g., among the Maasai, a young man was groomed to be a leader from the time he was a warrior (1).

Leadership Today   (R = 15)

Leaders today are *self-seekers* at the expense of the society (1), *African leaders are looting the resources* of their countries leading to the continent facing a lot of *problems such as famine and wars* (1), leaders have *become bosses rather than servants* of the people (1), leaders *do not act in the interests of the community* (1), many leaders are *dictatorial* (1), they *do not exercise justice* for all (1), today's leaders *include priests, teachers and local government officials* (1), *political leadership* has taken over the *center stage* from *cultural leadership* (1), at times *politicians consult other people like community reconcilers* to bring *peace* to their people (1), leadership is *associated with wealth, authority, corruption and other vices* (1), *leaders today do not feel* they have *any religious obligation* to the society unlike the *traditional leaders* (1), the *judiciary* now takes care of *legal matters* (1), *police have the responsibility* to *ensure that law and order are maintained* in the society (1), it means the *power to do and act on behalf* of the people with other *personal motives such as acquiring wealth and fame taking the forefront* (1), every *social, economic and religious institution* has different leaders who help in the *organization and creation of order and harmony in the institution* (1).

Definition of a Leader   (R = 9)

Is *a person chosen* from a group because of *particular outstanding leadership qualities* (2), a person with *ability to execute on behalf* of the people (1), someone who has been given *authority by God* to lead people (1), one *in charge* of a group of people within the community (1), *a caretaker* of the people (1), a *specialist who protects, nourishes and oversees* the people who he/she *is given responsibility for* e.g., *rainmaker or diviner* (1), one who *guides* a community to *its perceived goals, settles disputes and acts as a spokesperson* for the community (1), any person in a social situation *in charge of* making decisions on behalf of others (1).

Definition of Leadership   (R = 11)

Is *a state* which is given or accorded to *an individual due to [his/her] extraordinary or outstanding character* in the society (1), is *a condition through which one has the responsibility of controlling, directing and guiding* certain aspects of life/work situations (1), is *one who is supposed to preside over the affairs of the community* (1), is the *trust bestowed* on one to act on behalf of others with reference to them (1), is *a proven record of the ability* to lead others (1), is an *individual's ability to lead and be an example* to others in the society (1), a process whereby one acts as *a guide, protector, advisor, judge and facilitator* because of *traditional wisdom in organizing and taking control* of *people and activities* in the *society* (1), is *the position* given to a special person within a community to *lead and organize* other people in *different endeavors* (1), is *the process of directing the actions* of individuals or groups of people *towards a common purpose or goal* (1), is the *ability*, on an individual level, to *organize* one's life and *achieve personal set goals* (1), is *to possess some power* over a group of people and be able to control them (1).

Types of Leaders   (R = 10)

Community leaders/elders (2), *heads of families* i.e., men (2), the *eldest son* who takes over leadership of the family after the death of the father (1), *clan leaders* (1), *priests* (1), *teachers* (1), *local government officials* (1), *parents* as leaders and role models for their children (1).

Responsibilities of People towards Leaders   (R = 6)

Respect leaders (4), *obey* them (1), *pray* for them (1).

Other Comments   (R = 15)

For *leadership to succeed there should be mutual respect* among the people (2), *good leadership* leads to *success* in the community *if properly utilized* (2), *dialogue is essential* for all in the society (1), there are *leaders in every aspect of life* (1), *counseling by parents, elders and other community members* helps to *overcome hardships* in the community (1), *any human group needs leaders* and leadership (1), an individual *may or may not* join a group depending on its *type of leadership* (1), leadership *in pre-colonial societies had strong ties in the daily running of the society both socially and religiously* (1), God meant for the world to have leaders in *every human situation* (1), leadership *comes with experience* (1), *cultural* leaders had *good qualities* in comparison to *present leaders* (1), *leadership and wisdom* go hand in hand (1), leadership is *hierarchical* from ancestors to the people (1).

NON-AFRICAN RESPONDENTS N = 18
[The respondents answered according to their own cultures.]

Role of a Leader in the Society (R = 22)
Guide the community (5), *promote unity* (3), *promote peace* (2), *inspire* the people (2), *ensure the continuity* of the group/community (2), to *lead* his/her people to *holistic social development* (1), *supervise* the community (1), *help members* to achieve their goals (1), is *a spokesperson* (1), is the *final arbiter* (1), in charge of *resources* in the community (1), *maintains order* (1), *ensures the success* of the group (1).

Characteristics of a Leader (R = 13)
A good listener (2), *practices good judgment* (2), is *just* to all (2), *patient* (1), *wise* (1), has *life experience* (1), *delegates* work (1), has *qualities of servanthood* (1), should *exemplify* a mode of life worthy of being followed (1), *respects the trust given to him/her* to lead the people in the group (1).

Significance of the Theme of Leadership (R = 4)
Provides visionary means and ways *of solving problems* affecting people in their daily lives (1), a leader is *a symbolic representative* of the group (1), is the *link between human beings and God, spirits and other invisible things* (1), *good leaders bring out the potential* in their followers *by holding the vision before them as a goal that is attractive and life giving* (1).

How One Becomes a Leader (R = 4)
Through *election* (4).

Leadership Today (R = 5)
Leaders are *determined by popularity, wealth and ability to meet certain goals* that are *not necessarily beneficial* to the people (1), leaders *control rather than lead* (1), leaders are *my friends and myself*, as we look up to one another for advice (1), leadership is *an admired personality*, a characteristic a few have (1), it seems that *most leaders are not good role models worthy of being emulated* (1).

Definition of a Leader (R = 9)

Is *a person chosen by the community*, to unite members and help them grow in a sense of a caring community (2), is *someone who has responsibility and makes decisions* (1), is one *who directs, plans and allocates resources* fairly (1), is *one who knows to lead* others in *religious activities* (1), is *one who has followers* (1), a person with *a vision and sees* his/her followers as capable of living that vision (1), is an individual that *has power and serves* the community (1), is the *one who can discern God's call* and has the vision to live and lead others into that call (1).

Definition of Leadership (R = 5)

Is *taking responsibility consciously and willingly* to serve others (1), is *the role* one plays in a given community (1), is *to lead* in a way that everybody in different settings will feel responsible for regulations and decisions (1), is *the quality* needed by those people *who head organizations and institutions* (1), is *an ascribed or earned title* given to members of a group (1).

Types of Leaders (responses refer to African communities) (R = 5)

Diviners (2), *heads of household* (1), *chiefs* (1), *elders* (1).

Other Comments (R = 7)

Many people *do not want* to become leaders because *the position is quite demanding* (1), *every group* of people *must have a leader* (1), I prefer to *promote team leadership that is democratic, inclusive and a form of servant leadership* (1), leaders *receive their power to lead from God and their mandate from the people* (1), *maintaining a leadership position* is determined by *the leader's performance* (1), *elders are worthy leaders in African countries because of their experience and wisdom* (1), each person is to give their best in *a joint project* (1).

SUMMARY
Beliefs expressed regarding Leadership

A Leader is: a person chosen from a group because *of particular outstanding qualities,* a person with the *ability to execute on behalf of the people,* has *authority* from God, a *caretaker, specialist and guide of the people,* a person in charge of making decisions on behalf of others in a *social situation.*

The Characteristics of a Leader are: is a *role model, morally upright,* has *outstanding and exemplary character, wise, responsible, respectable, charismatic, authoritative, an expert in various fields, a specialist, articulate, understanding, reconciler, a good listener, development* *conscious, reliable, just to all, patient, advanced in age* and *allows for dialogue with other people.*

The Role of a Leader in the Society: is a *moral guardian, enhances community welfare,* acts as a *judge* and *arbitrator,* is a *representative of the people, guides, protects, leads and counsels people.* The leader is *an overseer* and *spokesperson* of the people.

The Significance of the Theme of Leadership is: helps to *maintain order, and unity* in the society, and *control chaos* in the society. It is a sign of *good leadership qualities* in a person. A leader is the *symbol of authority, unity, good governance and good life in the society, symbolic representative of the group,* is a *link* between *human beings, spirits and God.*

A Person Becomes a Leader through: *appointment, election, training, inheritance, grooming, being born in a lineage of leaders,* and by *having special characteristics and qualities.*

Leadership is: *a state* given or accorded to an individual as a result of their *outstanding character* in the society. It is the *trust bestowed* on a person to act on behalf of others, a person's ability to *lead others,* act as *a guide, protector, advisor, judge and facilitator* because of his/her wisdom.

Types of Leaders: *community leaders, heads of families, clan leaders, priests, teachers, local government officials, parents, diviners, chiefs and the eldest child in the family.*

Responsibilities of People towards Leaders are: to *respect, obey and pray for leaders.*

Leaders Today are: *self-seekers* at the expense of the society, *looting* the resources of their countries in Africa, *bosses rather than servants* of the people, *dictatorial, and unjust. Political leadership* has taken over the center stage from *cultural* leadership. *Wealth, popularity and the ability to meet certain* goals are the determinants of leadership today.

RESPONSES FROM WORKSHEETS
[Note that leadership in African societies is based on status, wisdom, age, specialization, courage, character and charisma.]

❑ **Kindly explain in detail your understanding of the theme of LEADERSHIP. Does it have any meaning in your personal, social and community life?**

AFRICAN RESPONDENTS   N = 52

[There were thirteen ethnic groups represented: Agikuyu (14), Luo (13), Abaluyia (9), Abagusii (4), Aembu (2), Teso (2), Tutsi (2), Akamba (1), Kategi (1), Nubian (1), Kipsigis (1), Akan (1), and Tigrinya (1). The respondents were university graduates, twenty-two women and thirty men.]

- Leadership is important in any communal affair where people respect each other. I feel that leadership is necessary in self-discipline and communal activities. (Agikuyu)
- Leadership is a good quality in a person. I admire the quality because it makes one to be a role model in his/her community. (Abaluyia)
- Yes, leadership has meaning in my personal, social and community life e.g., I am a leader in my community where I am informed of most of the things that happen or are happening in the community. (Kategi)
- Leadership comes with experience, age or inheritance. Some people learn from the throne if they are heir apparent. As in the case of the Maasai, leaders are groomed from [the stage of] young warriors. (Abaluyia)
- Leadership is a state, which is given/accorded an individual due to their extraordinary or outstanding character in the society. (Aembu)
- Leaders were the community's role models and perpetuated the ideals of the community. They acted according to the communal interest in contrast to today's leaders who are self-seekers at the expense of the society at large. We see African leaders who are looting their countries dry, as the continent remains bogged down by wars and famine. Cultural leaders are certainly people we should have learnt from for good leadership qualities. (Agikuyu)
- Leadership is a condition through which one has responsibility of controlling, directing and guiding certain aspects of life/work situations. It has a practical meaning in my personal, social and community life. (Luo)
- Leaders are respected. I have been brought up to be obedient to leaders. In my personal, social and community life, I do not believe in rebelliousness, but in mutual respect and dialogue. Without leaders, there would be a lot of chaos around us. (Luo)

- Leadership is critical in all human activities and understanding. There is need for leadership to arrest chaos no matter how small an activity people are engaged in. God is a God of order and leadership -- whether earned or inherited -- is necessary for order. (Abaluyia)
- Leadership entails the idea of having a leader who is supposed to preside over the affairs of the community. Without leadership, there would be no proper order in the society. Lack of leadership leads to a state of anarchy. (Luo)
- Leadership maintains order and harmony in the family/community. I consider it to be a very important and vital factor to an individual, community and society at large. (Agikuyu)
- Leadership is creating unity and harmony in any society. Good leaders are identified through positive qualities and respect. Personally I respect leaders. I always pray for good leaders who are role models. A successful community has good leaders. (Abagusii)
- Leadership is the trust bestowed on one to act on behalf of others with reference to them. In any aspect of life, there is a leader. You are either being led or leading. (Abagusii)
- Leadership brings about success in the community/society if properly utilized. Yes, leadership has meaning in my personal, social and community life. It is through leadership that people's lives improve. It is also through counseling by parents, elders, members of a community and leaders that a community/society overcomes hardships in life. (Agikuyu)
- Yes, leadership is a proven record of the ability to lead others. Some people are blessed with the qualities of a leader. (Agikuyu)
- For me, leadership is essential in a community because it brings order in what would otherwise be chaotic. There is need to harmonize, organize, control, coordinate and bring order in all occasions in a society. (Agikuyu)
- Any human group needs some leaders and leadership. A leader should be a person with the ability to execute (dispense) on behalf of the people. (Luo)
- Leadership implies responsibility for the well being of the group. It also carries privileges with it. Yes, in the sense that I may or may not join a group depending on whether or not I like the leadership. (Agikuyu)
- Leadership is an ability to lead and be an example to the society. Leaders are either born or trained. To be a leader, you must have special characteristics like kindness, [be] a role model, etc. The theme means a lot in my personal social and community life because I have to be responsible and be a good role model to others. (Agikuyu)
- Leadership capability was bestowed on people in a particular lineage and it demonstrated political organization. (Nubian)

- A leader is a person chosen from a group, who has particular qualities that are outstanding and he/she is expected to show the other people the way forward. In community life, these people are very respectable in society and more authoritative. In social life, the leaders are expected to work hand in hand with the other members of the society. (Agikuyu)
- Leadership is the process whereby one acts as a guide, protector, advisor, judge, and facilitator because of traditional wisdom in organizing and taking control of people and activities in society. (Kipsigis)
- A leader is someone who has been given authority by God to lead people. They could also be experts in various fields. They could also be rainmakers. In my life, a leader should be respected as the authority comes from above and not below. (Luo)
- A leader is a person who is chosen to lead people e.g., men are heads of families in the Abagusii community thus they are family leaders. My father was the head of my family, but after he passed away, my elder brother is now the leader of my family as he takes care of the family business and he is seen as the legitimate man of the family who is authorized to take care of my father's properties. (Abagusii)
- Leadership is a position that is given to a special person within a community to lead and organize other people in different endeavors. (Akamba)
- It is the process of directing the actions of individuals or groups of people towards a common purpose or goal. (Luo)
- I think that leadership and wisdom go hand in hand. (Luo)
- Leaders are the representatives of God and ancestors in the society. (Luo)
- Individuals are chosen as a result of their abilities to oversee, guide and protect others. A leader is a representative of the people in the community. (Abaluyia)
- A leader is any person, man or woman, who can be given responsibility. You must have gone through acceptable rites of passage. A leader is appointed or elected by people to guide and represent given interest. (Abagusii)
- Leadership in my own understanding is a person in charge of a people within a community. This person should be charismatic, wise and articulate so as to understand the people whom he leads. In my personal life, it means one who takes care of people. In a household, usually it is the husband who is the leader, then community elders right from the village status to that of the nation i.e., from the local sub-chief to the president. (Luo)
- Leadership means service to all. Leadership is supposed to enhance community welfare. It is supposed to bring togetherness and understanding in the community. It should allow for dialogue and leaders should listen to people. Unfortunately these days leaders have become bosses. Their decision is final. There is no justice exercised for all. (Teso)

- Leadership is helping a group of people do what they want to do. Personally, it is the ability to organize my life to achieve my goals. In the community, a member or members are appointed/selected or elected to help the community to attain its goals. (Luo)

- Leadership is having a say over a community. That is possession of some power over a group of people and being in a state to control them. A leader is very important. He controls behavior and brings or ensures the community lives in harmony. (Agikuyu)

- Leadership for me is about service to the community. The leader is the reconciler and builder of the community. He speaks last after all have spoken. He helps the group make the best decisions. He leads by example. In contemporary society, leaders are priests, teachers, and local government officials. Parents particularly are leaders and examples for their children. (Agikuyu)

- Leadership is about service not power and prestige. A wise leader will always bring his people together in time of conflicts as well as guide and counsel them. (Abaluyia)

- Political leadership has taken center stage over the cultural leadership. However, sometimes politicians go back to the community reconcilers, to bring peace to their people. (Abaluyia)

- All community's proceedings are presided over by selected members of the community-leaders. They are selected on the basis of their age, wisdom, and their position in the community. They must be morally upright. (Agikuyu)

- The theme of leadership involves numerous people i.e., the diviners and rainmakers who aim at protecting, nourishing and overseeing the people whom they are given responsibility for. They have the power to judge and promote proper behavior, which is hierarchical from ancestral spirits. (Luo)

- Leadership means the possession of exemplary character. It is above the standard of the common man. A leader is supposed to lead others in all fields of life and he/she is supposed to lead others to be morally, socially and spiritually excellent. (Luo)

- A leader is a person who guides a community to its perceived goals, handles disputes and acts as a spokesperson for the community. In my personal, social and community life, the only added characteristic is that a leader is responsible for his actions. (Teso)

- A leader is a person who is wise and cannot behave badly. He is the person I can trust and who can guide people. (Tutsi)

- The leader is the symbol of authority, good life in the society, unity and good governance. Today, leadership is associated with wealth, authority, corruption and other very bad vices. (Luo)

- Leadership refers to any person(s) in a social situation who is in charge of making decisions on behalf of others. This may be in a family situation, clan or society. Leadership in the contemporary society includes the head of families, elders, church leadership and the political leadership. The leadership in pre-colonial societies had strong ties on the daily running of the society both socially and religiously. In the contemporary society, the political leaders are/do not usually follow any religious obligations towards the society. (Agikuyu)

- Every human institution needs a leader/leaders, as this is how God meant the world to be like. We have chiefs, and government leaders to do this. The judiciary takes care of legal matters while the police keep law and order. We need leaders for the good social order of the community. They are necessary be they appointed or elected. (Abaluyia)

- Leadership office offers directives or guidance to the community. Leaders talk for or on behalf of the masses. Today leadership means power to do and act on behalf of people but with other personal motives like acquiring wealth and fame. (Abaluyia)

- Leadership is a God-given role. It is religious. Leaders are supposed to be morally upright since they serve living members directly and also the non-living indirectly. Contemporary leaders are supposed to be charismatic and morally upright. (Aembu)

- Leadership is important in society for leaders organize and help create harmony within the clan or community. Good leaders were valued and still are in the center in African communities for they influence every member of the community. In present societies, every social, economic, and religious institution has leaders who help to organize, create order and harmony in the institution. (Agikuyu)

- Leadership is a role one plays in a given community. I see a leader as the center of unity in a particular community. A good leader inspires me. (Akan)

- Not many people want to be leaders because of the demands it holds. Every group, association or society must have leadership. At times, people may surrender their lives to the leader. (Abaluyia)

- In a community or society, people choose one among them to guide them, supervise and show them the way to prosperity and peace.(Tutsi)

- I believe the meaning of leadership relates to taking responsibility to consciously and willingly serve others -- to consciously lead them towards holistic social development. (Tigrinya)

NON-AFRICAN RESPONDENTS   N = 18
[The respondents answered according to their own cultures.]

[There were five non-African countries represented: America (12), Norway (3), Poland (1), Indonesia (1), and Spain (1). The respondents were university graduates, twelve women and six men.]

- Leaders are the people who are chosen by the community, whether formally or informally, to keep the members together and to have them grow and nourish one another in a sense of a caring community. (American)
- Leadership/leaders help the members of a community/society and group organizations to achieve their purpose. Leadership provides visionary means and ways of solving problems affecting lives of people in their day-to-day lives. (American)
- My own understanding of leadership has some overlap with African traditional notions, but also some points of tension. The hierarchical and sexist reality of the traditional model is at odds with the style of leadership I have been involved in. I want to promote team leadership, democratic, inclusive, servant leadership. At the same time, I appreciate and affirm the particular role of the designated leader as spokesperson, final arbiter and symbolic representative of the group itself and the wider world. (American)
- Leadership and its contemporary meaning in my personal, social and community life is to lead in a way that everybody in their different settings will feel responsibility for regulations and decisions. (Norwegian)
- A leader is someone who is not young. Someone older, with life experience and wise. Someone who has responsibility and makes decisions. In African tradition, that will be a head of the household, chief or a diviner. In contemporary society, a leader is the one who has power, and really is the one who serves the community. (Polish)
- A leader is someone who directs, plans and allocates resources fairly. He treats people equally. He delegates work. (Norwegian)
- People in leadership have the right and power to uphold morality and values of the group. (Indonesian)
- A person in leadership shall be someone who knows how to lead others in religious activities, and who serves as the link between their fellow human beings on the one hand, and God, spirits and invisible beings on the other. (Norwegian)
- A leader is one who has followers. A leader is one who respects the trust given to him/her to "oversee, protect and nourish" the people he/she leads. In contemporary meaning, I believe a leader can discern God's call and has the vision to live and lead others to that call. (American)

- Leaders receive their power from God and their mandate to lead from the people. How they functioned as leaders, determined if they stayed in that role. Today, leaders are more the type of person who is popular, has money, meets goals not necessarily those of the people and controls more than leads. (American)

- Leadership is given to someone who demonstrates the qualities of servanthood, justice, a listening ear, and can make the best decisions for the community. Normally, the person is elected by the community or organization to maintain order and promote growth. (American)

- The leader in one society is, first of all, the one that brings together the community. They are there to keep peace and to ensure the continuation of the group and its success. Experience is very important to attain wisdom, and that is why elders (often in group) are worthy leaders in the African societies. (Spaniard)

- Leaders are chosen communally, not self-appointed, and people see them as valuable in guiding behavior. Leaders in my personal life are friends who I look to for advice. I also serve as a leader for them. (American)

- Leadership is the quality needed by those people who head up organizations and institutions. The purpose of the leader is to bring harmony and focus to the group to exercise subsidiarity ensuring each person feels welcome and is expected to give of their best to the joint project. The leader must be a listener and practice patience and discernment. (American)

- My understanding of leaders is that they have a vision, and see their followers as capable of living that vision. Good leaders bring out the potential in followers by holding the vision before them as a goal that is attractive and life giving. (American)

- Leadership is an ascribed or earned title given to members. Also, it is an attitude of the person and characteristics of his/her life. (American)

- Leadership positions are composed of elders and diviners. They are the leaders of the community, guiding the members of the group in all they do. In my community, leadership is not an ascribed position but rather an admired personality, a characteristic that few have. (American)

- I feel that leaders should exemplify a mode of life worthy of being followed. However, in my society, it seems that most leaders are quite bad at living a good life. (American)

EDITOR'S REFLECTIONS

In Africa, leaders are respected and popular people in the community. Their mandate comes from the ancestors through the community and they are representatives of the people they lead. Since African societies are sacral in nature, all leadership is fundamentally spiritual. There are also special leaders such as diviners, herbalists, rainmakers and priests, who are specially selected people. Leadership in contemporary African societies is in flux. At times it reflects traditional values and ideals, and at others it reflects a more democratic and equalitarian political, economic and social order.

DISCUSSION QUESTIONS
1. Are contemporary democratic leadership roles and styles in harmony with traditional leadership roles and styles in African countries?
2. Why is political and economic corruption rife in many African countries even though leadership is perceived as fundamentally spiritual and responsible?
3. Should religious leaders be concerned only with spiritual /religious issues and not comment on political issues that affect people in the society? Explain.
4. Who are the leaders in your personal life? Explain.

AFRICAN ILLUSTRATION

TRADITIONAL POLITICAL LEADERSHIP
[CASE OF JOMO KENYATTA IN KENYA]
In 1953, at the beginning of Mau Mau uprising in Kenya, the British colonial masters arrested six leaders of the Kenya African Union (KAU) party hoping to subdue the uprising by depriving the party of leadership. Among those arrested was Jomo Kenyatta. The colonial government hoped that by arresting these leaders the uprising would be curtailed.

In 1961 as the British colonial rule was coming to an end, the colonial administrators planned to hand over power to local leaders. However, since the accepted African leaders were in detention the British had no one with whom they could negotiate. Thus, they released Kenyatta along with others and began to engage them in political dialogue. In the end political power was handed over to Kenyatta as the Prime minister of a newly independent Kenya. Later on he became Kenya's first president. The same events were played out years later in South Africa with Nelson Mandela.

RECOMMENDED READINGS
Magesa, L. (1998). *African Religion: The Moral Tradition of Abundant Life.* (pp. 216-241). Nairobi: Paulines Publications Africa.
Gyekye, K. (1996). *African Cultural Values: An Introduction.* (pp. 109-121). Accra: Sankofa Publication Company.
Ayittey, G.B.N. (1999). *Africa in Chaos.* (pp. 85-118). New York: St. Martin's Griffin.

NON-AFRICAN ILLUSTRATION

ILLUSTRATION OF POLITICAL LEADERSHIP
IN WESTERN EUROPEAN COUNTRIES

Democracy as a political system is a rather recent feature in the worldwide political order. In fact, at the turn of the century, as the monarchies of Europe fell from power, many emerging governments were taken over by military dictators. By 1922 large parts of Europe -- Spain, Italy, Germany and Russia -- were under authoritarian military-style regimes. The result was a tragic loss of life from 1914 to 1945, through military conflicts in Europe that exceeds anything that the world has known since the beginning of time. Eighty million people died in the second part of what is called the Second World War from 1939 to 1945. Presently, western democracies, oblivious to their own recent history, have taken the high moral ground demanding that Africa, the Orient and the Middle East should be ruled by democratic governments. The moral tragedy of Christian Europeans is illustrated as follows:

I arrived at the home of a war widow with two teenage sons. In the living room on the mantelpiece was a picture of their father, a captain in one of the axis armies. The family was Catholic and the father had been an active member of the Parish. When I asked what had happened to him, the answer was that he had gone off to fight on the Russian front where he was captured, and fifteen years later had died of malnutrition in a prisoners of war camp.

If as a Catholic he had resisted the government's orders to invade Russia, he most likely would have been imprisoned and perhaps executed. However, because he didn't resist his inevitable death was of no value either to his family or his country. **[Verbatim report of a visitor to Europe in 1968].**

CHAPTER VII
Theme: ADULTHOOD AND ELDERHOOD

**ADULTHOOD AND ELDERHOOD
JANDO/UZEE**

The carving is of an adult Maasai man holding a spear and shield for protecting the community. Beside him is an older Kikuyu man who has attained the status of an elder, holding a walking stick and flywhisk, symbols of his special position, authority and wisdom.

ADULTHOOD AND ELDERHOOD

Introduction

All societies worldwide celebrate stages of human development from childhood to adulthood, and from a state of adult maturity to elderhood. The change in status from childhood to adulthood is normally related to the theme of marriage, that is, a person is only seen as competent to found a family which ensures the continuation of the lineage or group, if he has attained adult status.

Adulthood and Elderhood in Africa

African societies do not take for granted the transition between childhood and young adulthood or the celebration of a mature adult as he/she enters into the world of the esteemed elders. Movement from one status to the other has profound influence on the lives of the individuals as the community singles them out and tells them in no uncertain terms how they are supposed to act from then on. Prior to becoming adults, children are often perceived as an amorphous group, neither male nor female. However, after becoming adults they are expected to put aside the things and attitudes of childhood, and begin to take adult responsibility for themselves and the wider community. In the Kuria tradition, for example, it is only after one has become an adult, that he/she is able to marry and found a family. Likewise, in the Zanaki tradition, young men who have been made adults are required to bear arms and be prepared to rush out at night to defend the community from attackers.

The movement from senior adulthood into elderhood, celebrates the fact that the person has so matured that he is no longer capable of doing evil, even having evil thoughts. He has become somewhat akin to a living saint, totally truthful, faithful and trustworthy whether with relationships, livestock or money. This signifies a new stage in life where the person puts aside the ordinary activities of adults and enters into a more contemplative stage of being. In the Kuria ritual, for example, the man pays one more bridewealth cow to his wife's family saying: "this is the last cow, there will be no more!" a ritual bringing to close the exchange of gifts instigated by the original marriage covenant.

Adulthood and Elderhood Elsewhere

In the U.S. for example, adult maturity was attained when one graduated from high school, after which, many persons married and took family and civic responsibilities. However, with the advent of college education for a large majority of youth, college graduation is now being seen as the sign that one is a mature adult and ready to take one's place in the society. Furthermore, in the U.S. elderhood is not given the place of honor it has in African societies as the elderly are often seen as unproductive members of the society and not as wise, morally upright role-models to be emulated.

QUESTION

Kindly explain in detail your understanding of the theme of ADULTHOOD AND ELDERHOOD. Does it have any meaning in your personal, social and community life? N = 68 (58 Africans, 10 non-Africans).

[Note that the meaning of the theme of adulthood and elderhood was often expressed through the domain of initiation rites.]

RESPONSES COLLATED BY NINE CATEGORIES
1. *Relevance of Adulthood and Elderhood   R = 48*
2. *Characteristics of Elders   R = 27*
3. *Definition of Adulthood and Elderhood   R = 13*
4. *Signs of Adulthood   R = 8*
5. *Responsibilities of adults   R = 7*
6. *Definition of Elderhood   R = 2*

Other Comments   R = 17

Comments relating to rites of passage
1. *Initiation into Adulthood Today   R = 19*
2. *Relevance of Rites of Passage   R = 10*
3. *Rites of Passage Today   R = 3*

AFRICAN RESPONDENTS   N = 58

Relevance of Adulthood and Elderhood   (R = 43)
It means that one is *accepted and empowered* as *an adult and a responsible member* of the community (10), it *marks the separation and entry* into a different stage of development (9), it is an *occasion for education on the community norms and values* (7), it *sanctions a person to marry and procreate* (4), it *confers on one an identity* as part of a group in the community (3), it acts as *a moral guide* (3), it *gives rise to community leaders* (2), it gives a person *the right to own property* (1), it gives a person the *right to be involved in decision making* (1), it gives a man the *right and duty of protecting* the community (1), it is an *indication of reaching an age worthy of respect* in the community (1).

Characteristics of Elders   (R = 20)
They are *custodians of wisdom* (5), are *consultants* on matters of the community as they have long experience in life and community affairs (4), are *advanced in age* (2), are *highly respected* in the community (2), are *always*

consulted to *give wise counsel* to the younger generation (1), *high moral values* (1), *high personal achievement* (1), one qualifies if *his/her children are beyond teenage years* (1), they have *authority* over other members of the community (1), they can *discern and advise* from what they have learnt in life (1), are of *high moral integrity* (1).

Definition of Adulthood and Elderhood   (R = 8)

It is the *introduction of the youth to the adult stage* of life (2), it is the *partaking or awarding of responsibilities and duties* to oneself, the family and the community (1), it is *the act of confirming that one is aged enough and has the required knowledge* to perform responsibilities of an adult and/or elder (1), it is *a process which makes an individual a full and mature member* of the community *with various duties and rights* that accompany it (1), it is the *introduction of an individual to adult life through various ceremonies* (1), it is the *process of recognizing that one has reached an age of dependability and responsibility* (1), it is *a transition into adulthood* and to *be able to transmit life through marriage* (1).

Signs of Adulthood   (R = 12)

Circumcision (3), for a *boy* this is through *building a hut* (2), a *change in one's behavior* (2), for a *girl* this is through *getting married* (1), *rituals* that accompany the rites of passage (1), for a boy to be *initiated he has to give three goats for sacrifice, eat meat from the goats with the elders who teach him the secrets of adulthood, how to behave, values and norms of the community, expectations and his responsibilities in the community* (1), *incisions* on the legs (1), one is only considered an adult if *he/she has gone through all the rites of passage* (1).

Responsibilities of Adults   (R = 7)

One is required to *have mature behavior* in the community (3), to *maintain peace and harmony* within the community (2), one's social life has to *conform* to the expectations of the community (1), *participate actively* in the *community functions as an adult* (1).

Definition of Elderhood   (R = 2)

It is *a status where you are looked upon for guidance and as a leader* (1), it is the *move from being a married normal community member with limited responsibilities and authority, to one with a broader community responsibility with more authority* (1).

Other Comments   (R = 13)

Initiation into adulthood is done through a *rigorous process*, which takes different forms *depending on one's cultural background* (1), it is *mainly relevant for the male members* of the community (1), it is important to *initiate male children* into adulthood (1), I make decisions first on the basis of my age and then the *respect accorded to me* in the community because of the *adult/ elderhood status* (1), in my community we *do not have initiation rites from childhood to adulthood* but I wish we had them, as then our *children would be educated in our cultural values* (1), *circumcision of girls* in my community *ceased after the coming of Christianity* as it was *condemned by the missionaries* (1), *as a woman I have not been initiated as an elder* despite attaining the age for this stage and I wish there was a ritual I could undergo to attain this status (1), I once witnessed my uncle being made an elder (1), there are *practices done to instill responsibility* and prepare one to be an adult or an elder (1), those who are *not yet married cannot become elders* as there is *no one they are taking care of* thus *implying that they are not yet responsible* (1), those who are *not married cannot be given positions of responsibility* in the community (1), they are stages I am hoping to pass through successfully (1), the *old today seem to have no power* as the young are referred to as great because of 'money power' (1).

Comments Relating to Rites of Passage
Initiation into Adulthood Today   (R = 19)
It *incorporates* one into the community (5), it is *a rite of passage* from *childhood to adulthood* (3), is marked by *getting a job, getting married and moving into one's own house* (1), is marked by *academic achievement or a political position* (1), a youth passes through this as one of *the rites of passage* in life (1), initiation rituals are *now defunct as they have been surpassed by time and cultural dynamics* (1), refers to when one *reaches the stage of marriage and having a family* (1), one becomes an adult when he/she gets *baptized and receives communion* (1), in the process of initiation today *there is no link with the ancestors* with the exception of the name given at birth (1), initiation into any group usually *denotes rites and passages that guide the behavior* in each particular group (1), it is a rite of passage from *childhood to adulthood either through circumcision or education* (1), it is *a ritual which is done* so as to *enable a person to take up key roles* in the community e.g., leadership (1), I see young *priests* and *politicians enthroned* as *elders* but *I think it is wrong* (1).

Relevance of Rites of Passage   (R = 10)
They *enable* one to *pass from one stage of life to the next* (3), to *incorporate* people into the life of the group in the various stages (1), they *represent the movement towards the fullness of life* (1), they are important because *certain demands had to be met for one to qualify to go through them* (1), they accord *a person certain rights* as pertains to the particular rite of passage (1), the *participants are bequeathed social roles* (1), means that one has *the vitality to*

enhance abundance of life in the community (1), one who has *passed through all rites of passage is regarded with deep respect and reverence* and is *considered wise* in the ways of life (1).

Rites of Passage Today (R = 3)
To me it means *being able to help, taking responsibility, getting married* and *bearing children or adopting them*, being *accepted and respected* in the community (1), rites of passage today *have been replaced by catechism in the Catholic Church* (1), they are *still influential though they have been watered down* (1).

NON-AFRICAN RESPONDENTS   N = 10
[The respondents answered according to their own cultures.]

Relevance of Adulthood (R = 6)
Has *no relevance in my community* (3), is *a sign* that a person can be *counted as a man in all aspects* (1), it *gives a person certain privileges as well as duties* (1), in reaching the stage of adulthood, one passes *from an active stage to a more contemplative one* (1).

Characteristics of Elders (R = 7)
They are *respected* members of the community (2), they *have more wisdom and knowledge* of life in the community (1), are *advanced in age* (1), they *must be totally trustworthy* (1), are *morally upright* (1), *have wisdom* (1).

Other Comments (R = 4)
My culture does not practice any significant ritual to *mark the rites of passage* (1), this theme *is ritualized in the African context*, but where I come from this is not the case (1), *rites and rituals* are performed in order to help people through difficult times in their lives (1), how *people relate to and communicate* with one another is very much *influenced by age* (1).

Comments Relating to Rites of Passage
Initiation into Adulthood/Elderhood Today (R = 10)
Is through *high school graduation* (2), *retirement* can be considered as *an elderhood ritual* (2), the *voting age* of *eighteen years* and the *drinking age of twenty-one years* seem to be the major marks of adulthood (1), is through *marriage and birth of children* (1), is through *a job promotion* (1), the *sacrament of confirmation* represents a celebration of becoming of age (1), in my community coming into adulthood is a long process and it seems to be getting longer as it t*akes longer to finish studies and people get married in their late twenties and early thirties* (1), is through *getting a driver's license at the age of* sixteen and one is *expected to live independently* (1).

SUMMARY
Beliefs expressed regarding Adulthood and Elderhood

<u>Definition of Adulthood and Elderhood</u>: it is *the partaking or awarding* of responsibilities and duties to an individual, family and the community, it is the recognition that one is aged enough and *has the required* knowledge to perform responsibilities of an adult or elder, *a process* which makes a person *a full and mature member of the community* with various duties and rights that accompany it, *the introduction of an individual* to adult life through various ceremonies, *the process of recognizing* that one has reached an age of *dependability and responsibility*, to be able to *transmit life through marriage*.

<u>Relevance of Adulthood</u>: means that *one is accepted and empowered* as an adult and a responsible member of the community, is an *occasion for education* on community *norms and values*, *incorporates* a person into the community, *sanctions* a person to *marry and procreate, confers* upon a person an *identity* as part of a group in the community, acts as *a moral guide*, gives rise to *community leaders, gives* a person *the right to own property*, to be *involved in decision making, to protect the community,* gives certain *privileges as well as duties,* is an *indication* of reaching an age worthy of respect in the community.

<u>Characteristics of Elders</u>: they are *custodians of wisdom, consultants* on matters of the community as they have long experience in life and community affairs, *advanced in age, highly respected, always consulted* to give *wise counsel* to the younger generation, they have *high moral values, high personal achievements, authority* over other members of the community, *wisdom and knowledge* of life in the community, *married and have children beyond the teen years*, they can *discern and advise* from what they have learnt in life, *must be totally trustworthy*.

<u>Signs of Adulthood</u>: *circumcision, building a hut, marrying, a change* in one's *behavior,* giving out of *symbolic objects, things and animals, incisions,* going through *all rites of passage*.

<u>Responsibilities of adults</u>: *mature behavior, maintain peace and harmony* in the community, *participate actively* in the community functions as an adult.

<u>Definition of Elderhood</u>: is a *status* where one is looked upon for *guidance and leadership*, the move from being a *married normal community member* with limited responsibilities and authority to one with *broader community responsibilities with more authority*.

RESPONSES FROM WORKSHEETS

[*Note that adulthood and elderhood are linked to one's level of maturity and moral rectitude. Once a person attains such a status, he is expected to act accordingly.*]

❏ Kindly explain in detail your understanding of the theme of ADULTHOOD AND ELDERHOOD. Does it have any meaning in your personal, social, and community life?

[*There were seventeen ethnic groups represented: Agikuyu (14), Luo (12), Abaluyia (9), Abagusii (4), Akamba (3), Tutsi (3), Teso (2), Aembu (2), Banyankole (1), Arusha-Meru (1), Baganda (1), Tigrinya (1), Dinka (1), Kategi (1), Bemba (1), Kipsigis (1), Akan (1). The respondents were university graduates; sixteen women and forty-two men.*]

AFRICAN RESPONDENTS   N = 58

- Initiation into adulthood is more of building a hut for a boy and getting married for a girl. Initiation into elderhood, though more ceremonial, gives rise to community leaders. Yes it does have a meaning for once I build a house I believe I will have completed my journey into adulthood. (Teso)
- Initiation into adulthood and elderhood are very important rites of passage. This is because after going through them one takes over responsibilities in the community e.g., initiation into adulthood allows people to marry, own property, be involved in decision making and protection of the community, etc. (Agikuyu)
- Initiation into adulthood in my community is especially among the males. Yes, initiation has a meaning in my personal life as it helps people to behave and become more responsible in their activities as well as their societies. (Agikuyu)
- The theme is a marking of a passage from being a child to an adult. It is the partaking or awarding of responsibilities and duties not only to oneself or family but also to one's community. This is the meaning that it has to the community and me. (Abaluyia)
- This is a rite of passage. People have to go through it. It has a lot of meaning. It marks a separation and entry into a different stage   of development. (Luo)
- Usually rituals accompany these rites of passage. Once initiated the young people begin the journey in life that would lead to elderhood. Responsible behavior is paramount in the life of an individual and usually initiation into any group denotes rites and practices that guide the behavior in each particular group. (Agikuyu)

- Initiation gives me identity to a group of friends. Lineage ideology gives me status in the society. In the community I gain recognition and respect as an adult/elder. (Dinka)
- I quite appreciate initiation into adulthood because it is an occasion for education on the community values. (Luo)
- Initiation is a rite of passage into another stage of life. In this case from childhood to adulthood/elderhood. It does have meaning in my personal, social and community life. (Luo)
- The meaning of initiation into adult/elderhood is shifting into another stage. It is a transition into a new stage. It has a lot of meaning for the community and me. Through initiation one gets a sense of belonging. (Akamba)
- Initiation into adulthood means that one is accepted as a responsible member of the society. Elderhood is a stage where you are looked upon for guidance and as a leader. (Abagusii)
- Initiation into adulthood is the act of confirming that one is aged enough and has the required knowledge to perform responsibilities of an adult or an elder. It has a meaning to myself, as it is a stage where I am authorized to carry out certain acts of an adult. The community and society looks at it as a point in one's life where he has the chance to get married and help in continuity of life. (Akamba)
- Initiation into adulthood is a process, which makes an individual a full and mature member of the community with various duties, and rights that accompany that. This influences my personal life, as I have to behave maturely in the community. My social life has also to conform to what the community expects. (Luo)
- This theme espouses the beginning of a new stage of life. You transcend childhood into maturity. To me it is a rebirth and an epoch for greater service to the society. (Abaluyia)
- Initiation into adulthood is very important. It is passing from childhood to another stage, which is very important in decision making. This implies change in status and new responsibilities. There is a change in your way of behavior. It has a practical meaning. (Teso)
- Here one gives three goats for sacrifice. He eats with the elders who reveal to him the secrets of adulthood, how to behave, the ethnic values, norms, expectations and responsibilities. (Agikuyu)
- There is no initiation into adulthood among my ethnic group. I wish we had stages of child upbringing correlating to initiation into adulthood, and then our children would be educated in our cultural values. (Banyankole)
- The initiation into adult/elderhood gives a sense of mutual linkage, relation and provides social guidance. (Luo)
- The meaning it has is that a person feels respected, and he is ready to take up responsibilities either in the family or the community at large. (Baganda)

- Initiation is a stage whereby somebody is introduced to adult life through various ceremonies. (Tutsi)
- Circumcision is the only rite of initiation I remember. This is an important period because you learn different meanings of certain behaviors, taboos, relationship, manhood and community responsibility. (Arusha-Merun)
- Circumcision to male children is done in my community to initiate t h e m to adulthood. Circumcision of girls has died with the coming of Christianity as it has been condemned but with male children it is very important to initiate them into adulthood. (Agikuyu)
- Initiation into adulthood is a kind of introduction of a youth to the next stage of life, which is adulthood. This is through a rigorous process, which takes different forms depending on one's cultural background. It has a meaning both in my personal, social, and community life. (Abaluyia)
- Initiation into adult/elderhood is a special recognition to a person by the community that he/she is of special repute. It does not however have a special meaning to me at a personal level but at the community level the initiation has a special meaning, which I recognize. (Abaluyia)
- Initiation into adulthood is the process of recognizing that one has reached an age of dependability and responsibility. We can depend on this person. I find it fairly edifying as a person. (Luo)
- In my community, initiation into adulthood was a very important stage because this marked that you were ready to settle down and be a wife and mother and be a full member of the community through procreation. (Luo)
- Initiation into adulthood is done through circumcision and the following month is for formation. It is very vital and it gives you some orientation into adulthood that you get from nowhere else. It also gives you a place in the society. (Agikuyu)
- Today getting married, getting a job and moving into one's own house mark initiation into adulthood. Today it is also marked by an academic achievement or even a political position. (Luo)
- Yes. As a Kategi child I was initiated by cuttings on my eyes and my legs and this is very important in case of death. (Kategi)
- Initiation into adulthood means being given new roles, responsibilities and status in the society. It has meaning to the personal, social and community life. (Akamba)
- Initiation into adulthood is a rite of passage from childhood to adulthood either through circumcision or education. The theme has meaning in my personal, social and community life as one has to go through initiation into adulthood at a point in life. (Agikuyu)
- Initiation signifies a transition from childhood to adulthood, young elderhood to senior elderhood. The fact that my children have now attained adulthood i.e., they are no longer teenagers, I qualify to be an elder. My own

age and position qualifies me for it even though I have not been officially initiated as an elder. I wish there was a ritual I could undergo to do this. (Abaluyia)

- It is a rite of passage, which incorporates an individual into a new social status. Initiation rituals are now defunct; they have been surpassed by time and cultural dynamics. (Aembu)

- Initiation marks the status quo towards maturity, marriage and elderhood. Elders are highly respected in our community. Personally, I do value elderhood as a custodian of wisdom. (Agikuyu)

- It is a transition into adulthood and to be able to transmit life through marriage. It is very important because it incorporates a person into the community. During initiation people are also taught about responsibilities and what the community expects of them. (Bemba)

- Initiation into adulthood marks the end of childhood and a new beginning of life as an adult so as to take the role of community activities. Initiation into elderhood is a ritual, which is done so as to make a person in the community take the key roles, for example, leadership. Through initiation young adults are initiated into adulthood and educated and empowered to assume responsibilities. (Kipsigis)

- Initiation into adult/elderhood is a stage of development. A youth passes through this as one of the rites of passage in life. It has meaning in my personal, social and community life because they are stages I am hoping to pass through successfully. (Luo)

- It is the move from being a married, normal community member with limited responsibilities and authority to a broader community responsibility with more authority. I once witnessed my uncle being given this status. (Luo)

- The rites of passage incorporate people into the life of the group in the various stages. Elderhood is a status desired and highly respected in the community. An elder, through life experiences, gains a certain level of authority over other members of the community. They can discern and advise what they have learnt from life. (Agikuyu)

- This refers to when one reaches a stage of marriage and having a family. To me it is an indication of reaching an age worthy of respect in the community. At these last stages of life one is expected to have more wisdom and knowledge of life in the community. (Luo)

- The rites of passage today have been taken over by catechism in the Catholic Church. One becomes an adult when they get baptized and receive communion. There is not much on the link to ancestors except in the name. (Abaluyia)

- These rites are about one being in the process of passing from one stage to another. In my personal and community life, they are about moving towards the fullness of life. (Tutsi)
- Rites of passage enabled one to pass from one stage of life to the next. They were important because certain demands had to be met for one to qualify. Elderhood demanded high moral and personal achievement. (Agikuyu)
- These are stages that an individual would pass through towards being at the top of society in a physical world. They are still influential though they have been watered down. (Agikuyu)
- For one to be an adult or an elder is a factor but that is not all. There are practices done to instill responsibility and prepare one to be an adult or elder. (Agikuyu)
- This is one promotion that one has to pass through. It is to be a man in the community. I make decisions by my age and the respect accorded to me in the community because of my adult status. (Abaluyia)
- Rites of passage are the ceremonies marking a transition from one stage to another in a person's growth. The rite of passage to adulthood is important in that it is only the adults who partake of community secrets. Elderhood is also important because it is connected to wisdom. (Abagusii)
- Rites of passage enable one to pass from one status to another and assign certain roles. Adulthood is a passage from youth stage and one marries and automatically becomes responsible. Hence elderhood and sometimes a leader in the community. (Agikuyu)
- Those who are not yet married cannot be seen as elders because there is nobody they are taking care of; even positions of responsibility in the community cannot be given to them. Everybody is under the obligation to undergo these rites of passage, except witches who are ostracized from the community. (Luo)
- Whether traditional or contemporary, in my community, you are considered as successful or an adult if you have gone through all the rites of passage. (Abagusii)
- This refers to rituals that are performed to make one pass from one stage to another, usually a higher status. Once one passes from adulthood to elderhood, he has earned the right to rest and be consulted. He becomes a source of wisdom. Among the Abaluyia, these are the ones who will be consulted before a funeral, marriage or any other social activity can take place. They are the clan consultants. (Abaluyia)
- The rites of passage of adulthood and elderhood are ways to instill moral nature into the young people. They are also a way to bring harmony and peace in every community. (Akan)

- Young members were prepared to take up responsibilities with time. Leaders were groomed from them. Adults were bestowed with vast respect and to guide the community, harmonize life amongst them. The old today [it seems] have no powers as the young are now referred to as great because of money power. (Abaluyia)
- These rites of passage are enveloped in rituals, which invoke the spirits. In these rituals the participants are bequeathed social roles. Their meaning is that one has the vitality to enhance abundance of life in the community. (Aembu)
- Contemporary meaning for the rites of passage for me is the same as before but as well as assuming new roles, and being responsible. It means also a change of behavior individually, socially and participating actively in the community in functions as an adult. Elderhood calls for long experience in life, community affairs and in wisdom. I see young priests and politicians enthroned as elders but I think it is wrong. One should be advanced in age and demonstrate wisdom before being declared an elder. (Abagusii)
- The rites of passage start with birth, growing up and getting involved in all the necessary stages in it i.e., naming, initiation and marriage rites, hence elderhood rites which is a culmination of all. One who has passed all these stages is regarded with deep respect and reverence and considered as wise with the ways of life. He/she always consulted to give wise counsel to the younger generation. This is the meaning, truth and reality among the Agikuyu community. (Agikuyu)
- The contemporary meaning of rites of passage in my social life is being able to help, taking responsibility, being married and have children or adopt and finally being accepted and respected [in the community.] (Tutsi)
- In my culture, the contemporary meaning of rites of passage from adulthood to elderhood is not that significant for my personal as well as for my community life. My culture does not practice any significant ritual to mark a rite of passage; however, how people relate to and communicate with one another is very much influenced by age. Mostly, elders are respected and revered for their wisdom and insight. (Tigrinya)

NON-AFRICAN RESPONDENTS   N = 10
[The respondents answered according to their own cultures.]

[There were five non-African countries represented: America (5), India (2), Paraguay (1), Spain (1), and Ireland (1). The respondents were university graduates, three women and seven men.]

- The voting age of eighteen years and the drinking age of twenty-one years seem to be the major marks of adulthood. (American)
- In my community, the theme of initiation into adult/elderhood does not have any impact. Although I don't have any knowledge about the original, traditional one. (Paraguayan)
- School graduation, marriage, birth of children, job promotion and retirement are stages of life that are celebrated as the parallels to initiation. (American)
- I think of the sacrament of confirmation as a celebration of the becoming of age. I was confirmed when I was still quite young. My cousin was my confirmation godmother and we still have a close relationship. Friends go through adolescence together and since we all were Catholic, we relied on our God and our Church. We were able to see a "bigger" church as we were stretching our comfort zones. In my society the coming into adulthood is quite a long process and it seems to be getting longer. It takes longer to finish your studies; people get married later in their late twenties or early thirties. (Spaniard)
- As I have learnt here it is a sign telling that a person can be counted as a "man" in all aspects from that day [day of initiation] onwards. Hence it draws a big importance. (Indian)
- Initiation into adulthood or elderhood gives a person certain privileges as well as duties. It has a meaning to personal, social and community life. (Indian)
- I do not see any real initiation to adulthood other than perhaps getting a driver's license at age of sixteen years when one is expected to live more independently. (American)
- This theme is not relevant in my country. (Irish)
- In order to help people in difficult times in their lives, rites and rituals are performed to initiate young people. This is done into adulthood and when one becomes an elder. High school graduation can be considered an adulthood ritual. Retirement can be considered an elderhood ritual. (American)
- In reaching the stage of elderhood, one passes from an active stage to a more contemplative one. One however does not automatically become an elder at say seventy years of age. There must be the respect and confidence of the

community in the aged person, that the elder be totally trustworthy and upright. This is ritualized in the African context, but not where I come from. (American)

EDITOR'S REFLECTIONS

Adulthood makes one a permanent member of the community, binding him/her to the ancestral world. In many African communities shedding of blood on the ground is the mark that one is bonded to the living community, the ancestors and the ancestral land upon which the blood has been shed. From that moment henceforth, the adult belongs to the community in which he/she has been incorporated and is bound by the moral code and ethics that govern that community. A person who dies as an adult is accorded complete burial rites.

In patrilineal societies, an adult is accorded respect and responsibilities, sanctioned to marry, procreate, and own land and property in his ancestral land. This status also legitimizes the male in his father's clan.

As senior adults, elderhood is a preparation towards joining the ancestral world. To become an elder one has to have met requirements such as being married, have begotten children, be seen as wise, respectable, honest and decent. In African communities, if a person has not married and has not sired children he/she is still considered an adolescent and therefore not allowed to be involved in decisions that affect the community. In many ethnic groups being polygamous is seen as a norm for entrance into elderhood.

DISCUSSION QUESTIONS

1. In your community, what are the major differences in the status of a child and a young adult?
2. In your community, what are the signs that show a person to be an adult?
3. In your community are there women elders or is it only men? Explain
4. Have you attained the status of an adult in your community? Explain.

AFRICAN ILLUSTRATION

INSTALLATION OF A LUO SENIOR ELDER

On September 24, 2004, Mzee Meshack Riaga Ogallo was installed as the most senior elder of the Luo community in East Africa. He was presented with a traditional stool, a special walking stick decorated with beads, a shield, a spear, special traditional sandals made of beads and a decorated skullcap (*Ligisa*). On his right shoulder hung a small hand woven bag decorated with beads and pieces of clothing. It is in this bag that he keeps leadership paraphernalia (*Juok Piny*), meant to unite the Luo.

For a person to be chosen to this position he has to be a respected elder of at least sixty-five years old, and knowledgeable about the community's cultural practices. He has to be a good family man, preferably a polygamist. He is anointed and identified by acclamation rather than through an election. As the overall leader of the Luo he has massive religio-judicial powers over his subjects as defender of the community's ethos, norms and values. People look to him for guidance in political, religious, judicial and educational matters. In consultation with other community elders, he is expected to advise the Luo community in East Africa on which traditions should be reviewed or discarded all together. He is meant to serve the community in this capacity for life, but can be removed in cases of abuse of office or if he is incapacitated by illness.

RECOMMENDED READINGS

Magesa, L. (1998). *African Religion: The Moral Traditions of Abundant Life.* (pp. 67-71, 92-101) Nairobi: Paulines Publications.

Pemberton, C. (2003). *Circle Thinking: African Women Theologians in Dialogue with the West.* (pp. 149-156). Leiden: Koninklijke Brill.

Van Gennep, A. (1960). *The Rites of Passage.* (pp. 65-115). Chicago: University of Chicago Press.

NON-AFRICAN ILLUSTRATION

ADULTHOOD AND ELDERHOOD
FROM A WESTERN CULTURAL PERSPECTIVE

When my father was eighteen years of age he graduated from high school. His father gave him a watch as a graduation present. He was expected from then on to be able to take care of himself and to make his own living. He eventually went through college and became an electrical engineer. He worked for the same company for thirty-five years and in 1965 at the age of sixty-five retired from the company. The company gave him a gold watch in recognition of his service to the company. In both cases it was the gift of a watch that marked the change in status to adulthood and later on to elderhood.

In 1980 at the age of eighty, my parents celebrated fifty years of marriage called the golden wedding anniversary. The ceremonies were designed to honor my parents as fully mature and responsible role models who had attained a fullness of wisdom and marital fidelity seen in the longevity of their married life. **[Verbatim report of a participant in the Maryknoll Institute of African Studies]**

CHAPTER VIII
Theme: **BRIDEWEALTH**

BRIDEWEALTH/MAHARI

The carving of a cow and goat represents livestock given as bridewealth in African patrilineal communities. Livestock is one item among many other things and services given.

BRIDEWEALTH

Introduction

Almost all societies in the world have some kind of gift-giving at the time of the marriages of its members. The reason is that marriage is the source of new life for the community, and the members feel the need to show their support, concern and solidarity with the marriage union in a tangible concrete way -- sort of buying into the relationship because of its fundamental, long term value to the society.

Bridewealth in Africa

The exchange of expensive gifts whether monetary, services, property, livestock at the time of marriage of people whose inheritance system is patrilineal, ensures that the children born of the union remain forever within the lineage of the father. This is the structural and primary reason for bridewealth -- it determines the legitimacy of children -- and is sometimes called more appropriately, "childwealth." It also has many important corollaries, namely, it is a major mechanism for the redistribution of wealth within the local communities, it relates lineages in a very strong economic union, a union that can be accessed in times of need e.g., for school fees, hospital expenses, etc. Furthermore, it creates alliances, thereby cutting down hostilities between clans as permanent in-law relationships are established. Also, it protects against divorce as the communities of both the bride and groom are intimately involved in establishing and nurturing the union. If you ask an adult from a patrilineal clan if bridewealth has any meaning in their present lives, they will most likely tell you No! However, upon reflection it becomes clear that because his/her father paid bridewealth, the person is a legitimate person within a lineage, with rights of inheritance, and attached to the ancestral world through naming. If this payment had not been made, the person would be considered illegitimate, without roots, belonging nowhere, and outside the care and protection of a lineal family -- the plight of many street children and the children of single parents.

Bridewealth Elsewhere

In the Western world where marriages are of a nuclear type, marriage gifts are given to the couple themselves with the idea that it will help them set up a new independent household. Gifts of money, blankets, toasters, dishes, linens and beddings are wrapped up and brought to wedding receptions as furnishing for the new homes. Also, the size and type of a wedding gift is a measure of a person's relationship to the couple. The closer you are to the couple, the greater is the expected gift; the gift reaffirms the social order. These days, in many urban up-scale marriages in Africa, you will find people giving wedding gifts in imitation of Western customs. However at the time of inheritance, these gifts often end up under the control of the clan elders following traditional inheritance practices e.g., the famous Kenyan case of the Luo lawyer S. M. Otieno and his Agikuyu wife.

In many Asian countries there is the custom called **dowry** in which the bride brings wealth, often in the form of jewelry, gold and silver items, into the family of the groom. The exchange, therefore, is the opposite of African bridewealth, as the wealth goes from the bride's family to that of the groom's. One of the important considerations in arranging a marriage where dowry is a factor is the wealth of the bride's family.

QUESTION
Kindly explain in detail your understanding of the theme of BRIDEWEALTH. What is its contemporary meaning in your personal, social and community life? N = 67 (57 Africans, 10 non-Africans)

RESPONSES COLLATED BY SIX CATEGORIES
1. *Relevance of Bridewealth   R = 113*
2. *Definition of Bridewealth   R = 39*
3. *Bridewealth in the Contemporary Society   R = 16*
4. *Consequences of Failure to Pay Bridewealth   R = 12*
5. *What Bridewealth Symbolizes   R = 12*
6. *People Involved in the Process of Payment of Bridewealth   R = 3*
Other Comments   R = 19

AFRICAN RESPONDENTS   N = 57

Relevance of Bridewealth   (R = 93)
It *legitimizes* the children *born in the marriage* (19), it legitimizes the *marriage* (17), it legitimizes the *children's claim to inheritance* (6), it *creates lineage identity* for the children (5), it *discourages divorce* even in circumstances where it may seem necessary such as in the case of barrenness or impotence (4), it *gives the wife/wives the right to inherit* the husband's property (4), it *facilitates the redistribution of wealth* in the community (4), it *acts as a security* for the marriage (4), the long process involved in the payment of bridewealth *gives a chance for long-lasting friendship to blossom* between the members of the two families (4) it *strengthens the relationship between the two families* (3), it *enhances the public stature of the marriage* and *confers respect* upon a married couple (3), it serves as *a token of appreciation* from the family receiving the bride (2), it *unites* the families of both the man and the woman (1), it *helps in building alliances* with other members of the community (1), it *creates a sense of responsibility* towards each other between the husband and the wife (1), it *made men work harder* since the wealthier a man was, the more wives he could marry (1), it *legitimizes the family* (1), creates *a good relationship between the family of*

the man and that of the woman (1), it creates *new friendship ties* which helps the community to expand (1), it *makes one acceptable* in the community he/ she is marrying into (1), it is *a bonding factor in marriage* (1), it makes one *always have an obligation to the in-laws* (1), it *legitimizes sex within the marriage* and makes it exclusive between the man and the woman in marriage (1), it makes a marriage to be *successful and complete* (1), it *creates families* (1), it *gives the wife the right of burial at her husband's home* (1), it *gives the husband the right to bury the wife in his land* (1), it is one *way of ensuring continuity* of the family (1), it *acts as a seal* for marriage (1), it is *a sign of goodwill* (1).

Definition of Bridewealth   (R = 34)

It is *a token of appreciation to the parents of the bride* for the good work they did in raising their daughter and preparing her for marriage (11), it is *offering compensation for the role played by the girl before being married* (4), it is *money, property or labor* given to the family of the bride to show appreciation (2),it is given *to build a new relationship between the families* of the man and the woman who come together because of the marriage (2), it is *the exchange of valuables to formalize a marriage* as a rite of passage (1), it is *a price paid by the bridegroom's family or clan to the bride's family or clan* (1), it is a *form of gift or payment* to the family of the bride *in patrilineal communities* (1), it is *the exchange of gifts* between the family of the bride and the groom (1), it is *a token of appreciation given to the in-laws* (1), these are *commodities given by a man to get a woman as his wife* (1), they are *all the things given to the bride's parents on and after marriage* (1), it is *an institution that entails the exchange of gifts* between the families of the bride and the groom with the groom's family first giving their token of appreciation to the bride's family (1), it is *a public proclamation by a man to the woman's parents that she is legally married* in his community (1), these are *products, items or things* given in marriage *to cement the relationship* between a married couple (1), this is *what is paid in exchange for getting a wife* (1), it is *an agreement for an everlasting friendship between both families* (1), it is the *legal formal identity that customary marriage has taken place* (1), it is *a reminder to the girl that she is in the family of the man permanently* (1), it is *a token from the groom's family to the bride's family as a way of legalizing the marriage and initiating a relationship* between the two families (1).

Bridewealth in the Contemporary Society   (R = 15)

It has become *a commercialized venture*, a way for the girl's parents to *enrich* themselves (3), due to economic challenges and other social dynamics, the *intention of paying bridewealth has changed* and in most areas especially *in the urban set - up the practice is slowly dying away* as *cohabitation becomes more prevalent* (3), it is *still considered relevant* but it should *not be used for business profiteering* (2), nowadays the payment of dowry *is a personal commitment rather than a family or community affair* (1), unlike the old days, today it is common to *be denied consent to marry a girl until a certain amount of money has been raised* (1), it is *seen as a payment for the bride* (1), it *has been abused due to materialism and formal education* (1), its *commercialization has overshadowed the moral dimension* that our forefathers attached to it (1), some people *still see bridewealth as an appreciation for what the family has done* in raising up the woman (1), it's *meaning has been watered down* by the money economy (1).

Consequences of Failure to Pay Bridewealth (R = 9)
The marriage is considered to be *illegitimate in the eyes of the community* (4), if a woman dies before bridewealth is paid, the husband cannot be allowed to *bury her unless he pays the required amount in full* (1), where bridewealth has not been paid, *the woman is buried at her father's homestead and the man loses claim over their children* as they are taken by the woman's relatives (1), it leads to *children losing claim of inheritance* from their father's side (1), the women for whom bridewealth has not been paid *do not feel secure* in their marriages as they can be sent away any time and there is no sense of ownership or belonging (1), a union without bridewealth *has no legal binding* (1).

What Bridewealth Symbolizes (R = 10)
It symbolizes *love and appreciation* for both the bride and the groom (3), it symbolizes that *the groom values the girl and that he will take good care of her* (3), it is *a sign of commitment* by the man marrying the woman (2), it symbolizes that *the wife has been accepted into the family she is marrying into* (1), it is *a recognition of the marriage pact* (1).

People Involved in the Process of Payment of Bridewealth (R = 3)
It involves both the *family of the man and the woman* (1), traditionally *all members of the family contributed towards the payment of bridewealth* (1), the *whole community* (1).

Other Comments (R = 12)
Bridewealth is *not buying the girl as the feminist groups and western stereotypes* portray it as it does not represent the value of the girl (3), to me *bridewealth has ceased to be meaningful and it should be phased out* because of the commercialization and unfairness to the man's parents who never get any of it (2), the payment of bridewealth is *never completed in a life time* as it is a continuous process e.g., among the Agikuyu it is said *"ruracio rutathiraga"* meaning that the payment of bridewealth never ends (1), the *amount of bridewealth given might vary* depending on the social status of

both families and other related factors (1), my community expects me *to get married and get bridewealth from my husband's family* as this is what my culture dictates (1), *I have to pay bridewealth if I am to marry* (1), I think bridewealth is *a noble institution* (1), bridewealth is *sometimes referred to as dowry* (1), bridewealth is *a tradition that has existed in many African communities for a very long time* (1).

NON-AFRICAN RESPONDENTS N = 10
[The respondents answered both according to their
own cultures and their understanding of African cultures.]

Relevance of Bridewealth   (R = 20)
It *has no relevance in my community* (4), it *legitimizes the children as lineal descendants* (2), it *facilitates the redistribution of wealth* in the community (2), it is *pivotal in African culture* (1), it *ensures the success of the wedding* (1), it gives the children the *right to inherit* (1), *how much bridewealth one is able to pay determines his quality* (1), it *protects the marriage* (1), it *protects the children* (1), it *protects the commitment of the married couple* (1), it *strengthens the bonds* amongst community members (1), the *parties involved in this form of contract are answerable to the community* (1), it is expressed with a perpetual sense of *obligations between the in-laws* (1), it *guarantees the continuity of the lineage* (1), it *legalizes the marriage* (1).

Definition of Bridewealth   (R = 5)
It is *the exchange of goods for one's child* (1), it is the *exchange of significant gifts to guarantee* that the *children remain within the family lineage of the father in patrilineal communities* (1), it is *an agreement involving subjects, objects and rights* (1), it is *a form of compensation* given after taking the daughters from their families for marriage (1), it is *a form of payment, either money, goods,* etc. given to the bride's family by the groom's family in order *to get consent to marry their daughter* (1).

Bridewealth in the Contemporary Society (R = 1)
It *has been commercialized* to the extent that until a particular amount is paid one does not get consent to marry the girl of his choice (1).

Consequences of Failure to Pay Bridewealth (R = 3)
Children suffer an identity crisis and risk being thrown into the streets upon the death of the father by members of the lineage (1), it *has led to the proliferation of street families* (1), it has led to *high rates of divorce* (1).

What Bridewealth Symbolizes (R = 2)
It is seen as *accepting the child* as now belonging to the family of the husband (1), it is a way of *showing consent and commitment* to the marriage by both families (1).

Other Comments (R = 7)
In my community *there is no bridewealth but there is bridegroom wealth* which plays a personal as well as a social function (1), society life is very much *dependent on bridewealth* (1), this institution *does not exist in my community* (1), *dowry system* is the one that is common in my culture (1), *dowry systems have a deep cultural meaning and practical application* (1), it is *an exchange that is not just formal but at times can be quite rigorous* depending on the ethnic community of the participants (1), *in some communities* it is the brides who pay wealth to the groom's family in order to get consent to marry the son (1).

SUMMARY
Beliefs expressed regarding Bridewealth

Bridewealth is: a *token of appreciation to the parents of the bride* in recognition for raising and caring for their daughter, *offering compensation* for the role played by the girl before getting married, *money, property or labor* given to the family of the bride to show appreciation, *a token* given to build a new relationship between the families of the man and the woman who come together because of marriage, *the exchange of valuables* to formalize a marriage as a rite of passage, *a price paid by the groom's family or clan* to the *bride's family or clan, the exchange of gifts* between the families of the bride and the groom with the groom's *family first giving* their token of appreciation, *a public proclamation* by a man to a woman's parents that she is *legally married* in his community, *products or items* given in a marriage to *cement* the relationship between a *married couple, an agreement* for an everlasting friendship between both families, *legal formal identity that customary marriage* has taken place, *a token* from the groom's family as a way of legalizing the marriage and *initiating a relationship between the two families*.

Relevance of Bridewealth: it legitimizes the *marriage, children born in the marriage, children's claim to inheritance, the family, sex* within marriage, *gives the wife the right* to inherit the husband's property, *the right to be* buried at her husband's home, *facilitates* the redistribution of wealth in the community, *acts as a seal as well as security* for the marriage, *strengthens* relationships between the two families, *enhances* the public stature of the marriage, *confers respect* upon the couple, serves as a *token of appreciation* to the woman's family, *unites* the man and woman's family, makes one *acceptable* to the family he/she is marrying into, is a *bonding* factor in marriage, gives the *husband the right* to bury his wife in his land, is a way of *ensuring* the continuity of the family, a *sign of goodwill, a reminder to the bride* that she is in the family of the man permanently.

Bridewealth in the Contemporary Society: has become *commercialized, an avenue for* getting rich quickly, *a personal commitment* rather than a family or community affair, it is *slowly dying off* in the urban centers as cohabiting becomes more prevalent, *seen as a form of payment* for the bride, the commercial aspect has *overshadowed* the moral dimension that our forefathers attached to it, its meaning has been *watered down* by the money economy, *still seen as an appreciation* to the bride's family and therefore relevant in a marriage, has been *abused* as a result of *materialism and formal education*.

What Bridewealth Symbolizes: *love and appreciation* for both the bride and the groom, *the groom values the bride* and will take good care of her, a *sign of commitment,* the wife has *been accepted into* the family and community that she is marrying into.

Consequences of Failure to Pay Bridewealth: the marriage is considered *illegitimate*, if a woman dies before the payment of bridewealth the husband *will not be allowed to bury her on his land,* unless he pays the required amount in full, the *woman is taken back* to her father's homestead to be buried and *the man loses claim over the children*, children lose *claim and right of inheritance* from their father's community, the woman *does not feel secure* in the marriage as well as the husband's community, the union *has no legal binding*.

People Involved in the Payment of Bridewealth: the *families* of the bride and the groom, *all members of the family* who contribute towards the payment of bridewealth, *the whole community*.

RESPONSES FROM WORKSHEETS

[Note that in Africa, bridewealth for patrilineal inheritance systems is essential for a marriage. Bridewealth negotiations and part-payment have to be fulfilled before the parents and communities of the couple give consent for a traditional union, a union which is essential prior to a church or government Western-style marriage celebration.]

❑ Kindly explain in detail your understanding of the theme of BRIDEWEALTH. What is its contemporary meaning in your personal, social and community life?

AFRICAN RESPONDENTS   N = 57

[There were sixteen ethnic groups represented: Agikuyu (16), Abaluyia (9), Luo (9), Akamba (4), Abagusii (3), Tutsi (3), Aembu (2), Kategi (2), Teso (2), Dinka (1), Bemba (1), Banyankole (1), Kipsigis (1), Tigrinya (1), Ibo (1), Akan (1). The respondents were university graduates, seventeen women and forty men.]

- Bridewealth in my community is emphasized because it legitimizes every child born in the community. It also serves to uplift the economic status of a family as well as the social status e.g., when the son of a rich man marries a girl from a poor family. (Abaluyia)
- Bridewealth secures the marriage, unites both families and gives legitimacy to the children born of the marriage. The long process involved in payment of bridewealth gives a chance for long-lasting friendship to blossom between members of the two families. Payment of bridewealth involves whole families on both sides. (Kategi)
- Bridewealth legitimizes the children, while traditionally all members of the family contributed towards it. It's more of a personal commitment nowadays. In most cases today, bridewealth has become a commercialized venture, a way for the girl's parents to enrich themselves at the man's (groom's) expense. It's common nowadays to be denied consent to marry someone's daughter until a certain amount of money has been raised. (Agikuyu)
- Bridewealth is the exchange of valuables to formalize a marriage as a rite of passage. It plays a vital role in legitimizing children, securing the relationship, discouraging divorce and building alliances, etc. Due to economic changes, and other social dynamics, the intention of paying bridewealth has changed and in most areas, especially urban, the practice is slowly dying away as cohabitation becomes more prevalent. (Agikuyu)

- Bridewealth is a price paid by the bridegroom's family or clan to the bride's family/clan. It's meaning, even in the contemporary world of today serves to legitimize children born out of the liaison. It enables the children to have roots by belonging to a particular lineage. (Luo)

- Bridewealth is a token of appreciation given to the parents of the girl because of the good work they did in bringing up their daughter. A woman feels honored if her marriage is made legitimate through the payment of bridewealth. If a woman dies before the bridewealth is paid, the husband cannot be allowed to bury her unless he pays the required amount of bridewealth in full. If bridewealth is not paid, the marriage is taken to have been illegitimate and she is buried at her father's homestead. The husband loses his claim over the children and their mother's relatives take them. Consequently, the children cannot claim inheritance from their biological father; they have no legitimate claim over his wealth. (Luo)

- Bridewealth is a form of payment or a gift to the family of the bride in patrilineal communities (communities headed by males) or to the family of the woman in matrilineal communities (communities with women as heads of household). It serves as a token of appreciation to the family receiving the bride. It gives security to the marriage, discourages divorce and makes it pretty difficult even in circumstances where it might seem necessary e.g., in case of impotence or barrenness. It legitimizes the children and gives them the right to inherit land and property in the given lineage. It also gives them identity i.e., I am son or daughter of so and so. In contemporary society, bridewealth seals the marriage, certifies the marital relationship and serves as payment for the bride. (Aembu)

- It brings legitimacy both to the children and their mother. Payment of bridewealth implies that the wife has been accepted into the family she is marrying into. (Akamba)

- Bridewealth is very important in my community. It legitimizes the marriage, creates lineage identity and legitimizes children's claim to inheritance. In my community, it's still functional. A marriage without bridewealth is not considered a marriage, it's seen more as cohabitation. (Agikuyu)

- Bridewealth is a token of appreciation given to the family of the girl. It makes the marriage legal. It also legitimizes the children. Among members of my community, we say *ruracio rutithiraga* which translates: 'payment of bridewealth is never completed.' This implies that the continued payment of the bridewealth provides a chance for both families to act together and build long-lasting friendship. It also creates a sense of responsibility towards each other. There is a saying in my community that goes like this *kaiba ka Muthoni na ka muthonwa kaguaga hamwe,* which translates: 'the corpse of one in-law, goes down together with that of the other in-law.' This implies that what endangers your in-law's life also endangers yours thus the need for mutual responsibility towards each other. (Agikuyu)

- Mahari (bridewealth) is the legal or formal identity that customary marriage has taken place. It's very important because it gives the children a sense of belonging or legitimacy. It also serves to distribute wealth among members of the community. A man with many daughters, if luck smiles on him, can change his fortunes overnight. On the other hand, it made men work very hard since the wealthier a man was the more wives he could marry. In modern times, it has been highly commercialized to a point of creating permanent ill feelings among the in-laws. (Agikuyu)

- My understanding of the bridewealth issue is that it has not changed. It still is what it was before money, property, or labor given to woman's family to show appreciation. It still serves to legitimize the children and the marriage. The amount given might vary depending on the social status of both families and other related factors. (Abagusii)

- Bridewealth takes the form of gifts given to the family of the bride by the groom's family chiefly to legitimize the children. In modern times, it has been abused due to materialism and formal education. (Agikuyu)

- *Mahari* (bridewealth) is recognition of the marriage pact but more chiefly serves to legitimize the children born of the union. (Abaluyia)

- In my own understanding, bridewealth is what is given to the parents of the bride to show appreciation for what the parents of the girl have done to bring up and prepare their daughter for marriage. When bridewealth is given, it shows that the groom values the girl and that he will take good care of her. It is not buying as feminist groups and the western stereotypes portray it. It is a sign of good will, a show of commitment, an agreement for an ever-lasting friendship between both families. (Abaluyia)

- It is the exchange of gifts between the families of bride and bridegroom. The commercialization of bridewealth has changed the moral dimension that our forefathers attached to it. (Abagusii)

- Through bridewealth, a woman is not purchased, as many people may tend to think. It's an expression of love and appreciation for both bride and groom. Secondly, it also gives children and the wife or wives a right to inherit their husband's/father's property respectively. (Agikuyu)

- Bridewealth cements family relationships and enhances the public stature of marriage. The ceremonies accompanying bridewealth provide occasions for the two families and their friends to get to know one another well and establish long-lasting bond of friendship. (Agikuyu)

- Today, *mahari* [bridewealth] is seen as an appreciation of what the other family has done in bringing up the woman. It also acts as a contract that

no one can divorce [the other partner] because of the bridewealth that
may have to be paid back in full. (Abaluyia)

- Bridewealth is a token of appreciation given to the in-laws. It stands as a
compensation for the role played by the girl before she got married.
Bridewealth is important among the Agikuyu. Marriage or family is
legitimized through bridewealth or else the children are considered not to
have a father. (Agikuyu)

- It determines the legitimacy of the children and it strengthens the
relationship of the two families. Also a woman feels proud that she was
not just picked like an object but she feels she has a right to inherit the
property of the husband. (Bemba)

- Bridewealth are commodities given by a man to get a lady as a wife.
Personally I see bridewealth as a means to legalize the marriage. It has the
same meaning socially and at the community level. (Tutsi)

- Bridewealth are all things given to the bride's parents on and after
marriage. It comprises all responsibilities that go with it. It legitimizes the
marriage and all responsibilities that go with it e.g., children. (Abagusii)

- It is seen as an appreciation of the groom's family for the girl they have
incorporated in the family. It is also seen as a compensation for the girl. It
is also a way of legitimizing the marriage and the children and
incorporating the children into the father's lineage. (Akamba)

- It is given to the family of the wife in appreciation for their daughter. It is
also given to build up a new relationship between the two families that is
the husband and wife's families who come together because of the
marriage. Bridewealth has meaning in my personal, social as well as
community life. (Agikuyu)

- Bridewealth is very important in my community and in my personal life.
My community and parents expect me to get married and get bridewealth
from my husband's family. My husband's family must give bridewealth
and cannot get away with it, as this is what my culture dictates. (Agikuyu)

- Bridewealth is an appreciation of one's spouse. (Luo)

- To me bridewealth has ceased to be meaningful and it should be phased
out. This is because of commercialization and unfairness to the man's
parents who never get any of it. My community still practices it though
most people nowadays opt for "come-we-stay" marriages when the man
cannot afford to pay the bridewealth. (Agikuyu)

- Bridewealth is of social importance because it legitimizes me in a
particular family, of which I have a right of inheritance. (Dinka)

- Bridewealth is very important within all African marriages up to date. A
marriage is not considered complete unless bridewealth has been given. It
legitimizes the marriage institution, inheritance of wealth, and creates

good relationships. Unfortunately today its meaning has been watered down by the money economy. (Agikuyu)

- Bridewealth is a token of appreciating the bringing up of a lady (the bride) to the family. It has meaning in my life because I have to pay bridewealth if I am to marry. (Teso)

- It is an appreciation to the parents of the girl for their care and concern for the bride who is to live with the husband's family for life. It has a lot of meaning. If it is not paid then the union won't be legitimate. (Luo)

- Bridewealth entails offering compensation for a girl when you marry her. In modern day society bridewealth has assumed a commercial dimension and personally I think it should be done away with. (Abaluyia)

- It is an institution that entails exchange of gifts between two families of the bride and the groom with the latter giving first their token of appreciation to the former's family. All this is meant to cement the relationship between the two families/clans. It has a meaning in my personal, social and community life. (Abaluyia)

- Bridewealth was given to the parents of the bride as a token of appreciation and compensation for the services lost. This is in the sense that there would be no one to replace the girl in the responsibilities she used to do at home. (Luo)

- It has a meaning to the community and me. My understanding of bridewealth is that it is a means of appreciation. (Luo)

- Bridewealth is the token of appreciation by a man to a woman's parents, for their daughter who is to be taken up for marriage to go and help the man, get his children, and take care of his homestead. (Abaluyia)

- It is a public proclamation and witnessing that one is married legitimately in the community. It is significant in the sense that before you honor it you are not married in the eyes of your community. It is a noble institution in my personal, social and community life. (Abaluyia)

- Bridewealth legitimizes the children born out of the marriage, legalizes the marriage, shows appreciation from the side of the groom [to the bride's family] and it is a bonding factor in a marriage. It acts as a reminder to the girl that she is there permanently. It does not represent the value of the wife. (Luo)

- For some bridewealth is a gift of appreciation to the girl's parents while for others it is an exchange for an increase of wealth and still others think it should be abolished because its meaning and significance has changed over the years. It is practiced in my community. I have my reservations about it. (Banyankole)

- This is a creation of new friendship ties, which help the community to expand. It has a personal, social as well as community meaning because it makes one acceptable in the community he/she is marrying from or to. (Akamba)

- It makes one belong; it legitimizes my being in a family. It is a community affair and makes one always have an obligation to his in-laws. It makes a woman to be recognized and have a right to be buried in her husband's land. It must be paid as a token of appreciation to the parents of the woman for a good upbringing. It legitimizes sex within marriage and makes sex exclusive between the man and woman in marriage. Its payment is never completed in a lifetime. It is a continuous process. (Teso)

- These are products, items or things given in marriage to cement the relationship between a married couple. Bridewealth is still meaningful today and so it has a social or community life meaning. (Aembu)

- Bridewealth is what is given to a girl's parents by the family into which she is marrying as a token of appreciation. It is also a sign of commitment on the part of the man marrying her. She feels she belongs and is valued if some bridewealth is paid for her. Her children also have a sense of belonging and she feels secure in her new home. Women for whom bridewealth has not been given do not feel secure in their marriage. They can be sent away any time and there is no serious sense of ownership or belonging. The union without bridewealth has no legal binding. (Abaluyia)

- Bridewealth makes marriage legitimate. It makes the children belong. It is also an appreciation and a way of sharing wealth. In a situation where there was no bridewealth, the man and his wife were mocked and looked upon with disrespect. (Ibo)

- Bridewealth is what is paid in exchange for getting a wife. It is sometimes called dowry. It has a major meaning in my personal, social and community life because it makes a marriage become successful and complete. (Luo)

- Payment of bridewealth gives legitimacy to the children born out of marriage. It is also a token of appreciation given to the parents of the bride. It is also a tradition. In my community (Agikuyu) bridewealth is a tradition that has been there for a very long time and is therefore very important. (Agikuyu)

- Bridewealth simply means a token from the groom's family to the bride's family as a way of legalizing the marriage and initiating a relationship between the two families. It has a great meaning in my personal, social and community life. (Kipsigis)

- It was meant for creating a relationship. It was not to make one party pay the other. (Akamba)
- Money, animals and labor that you give to a girl's family to legitimize the marriage and to show appreciation to the family. I carry my father's family name because he paid bridewealth for my mother. Bridewealth creates families. (Agikuyu)
- Bridewealth is the gift taken to a girl's family. It is a sign of appreciation for the girl's family. It legitimizes the marriage and sanctions the sons as heirs of their father's estate. It gives the wife the right of burial at the husband's home. For me bridewealth is relevant and should be propagated but not used as a commercial business for profiteering. (Agikuyu)
- Bridewealth helps in legitimizing the marriage and burying one's wife. It has a great significance to me. (Luo)
- This is one way of ensuring the family will continue because it legitimizes the marriage. (Kategi)
- Dowry system is common in my culture. Nonetheless, I tend to believe that because it has survived the test of time, dowry systems have deep cultural meaning and practical application for African societies. Because I am a religious person, I cannot say that dowry system has any significant meaning in my personal life. However, dowry has meaning to the social life of the ethnic community that I belong to. (Tigrinya)
- Bridewealth is a form of compensation given after taking daughters [from their families]. It also legalizes the marriage and legitimizes the children. (Tutsi)
- Paying of the bridewealth is a way of showing consent and commitment to the marriage by both families. In the present time, it has been commercialized. Until a particular amount has been paid, many unfortunate fellows will not get consent to marry someone's daughter. (Akan)
- Bridewealth is a form of payment. Can be money, goods, etc. given to the bride's family by the groom's family in order to get consent to marry their daughter. In some communities, it is the other way around. (Tutsi)

NON-AFRICAN RESPONDENTS   N = 10
[The respondents answered both according to their
own cultures and their understanding of African culture.]

[*There were five non-African countries represented: America (5), India (2), Spain (1), Italy (1) and Ireland (1). The respondents were university graduates, four women and six men.*]

Mixed African and non-African Perspective

- My understanding is that it is pivotal in African culture. It ensures the success of the wedding, legitimizes the children as lineal descendants and qualified for inheritance and it redistributes the wealth. It has no relevance in my life. (American)

- I am beginning to get a deeper understanding of the meaning that the payment of bridewealth has for the African cultures and for any culture. Beyond the materialistic interpretation it is a payment that protects the marriage institution and children, the commitment, and strengthens the bonds amongst the community at large and it facilitates the redistribution of wealth. (Spaniard)

- Bridewealth is the exchange of goods for one's child. It is seen as accepting the child as now belonging to the family of the husband. This does not exist in any form in my society. (American)

- Bridewealth is the exchange of significant gifts to guarantee that the children remain within the family lineage (of the father in patrilineal communities). Among those who have not exchanged bridewealth, children suffer an identity crisis and risk being thrown into the streets upon the death of the father, by the members of the lineage. Among the consequences of not paying bridewealth is the proliferation of street families and high divorce rate (failed marriages). (American)

- Bridewealth is a clever way to guarantee the continuity of a certain lineage It's an agreement involving subjects and objects with obligations and rights. It's not very different from a formal contract only that in this form of arrangement, the parties involved are answerable to the community. It is an exchange that is just formal, sometimes, but can be quite rigorous in other cases depending on the ethnic community of the participants. It is expressed with a perpetual sense of obligations between in-laws. (Italian)

Non-African Perspective

- In my community there is no bridewealth but 'bridegroom' wealth, and it plays a personal and social function. (Indian)

- Society life is very much dependent on bridewealth. How much one is able to pay decides his status in the society. Also how much one is getting as bridewealth measures his "quality." So there is no "free" marriage, even if one is in love with a girl. (Indian)

- I do not see bridewealth as having any relevance in my community. (American)
- This does not apply in Ireland. (Irish)
- There is no such thing in my culture. (American)

EDITOR'S REFLECTIONS

In Africa, marriage is the major rite of passage into adulthood. A marriage is considered to be in process in a patrilineal community only after a portion of the bridewealth has been paid. The bridewealth is not paid all at once as it is considered to be an ongoing process since the relationship between the couple, their families and communities continues to grow. In most communities it is said that one can never finish paying bridewealth as gifts continue to be exchanged between the two families. Failure to pay the agreed upon bridewealth could lead to children being repossessed by the family of the wife. This is a shameful thing as in patrilineal societies the children belong to the father's family.

In most communities, the number and type of livestock to be paid are already set and are standard. Gifts such as money and other items vary from clan to clan. Male elders from both communities decide the amount and mode of payment of the bridewealth. In bridewealth discussions the elders from both sides display their oratory skills and the discussion is mainly conducted using metaphors, rituals and proverbs. Women are not directly involved in the bridewealth negotiations but are only informed of the outcome by the men. A woman for whom bridewealth has been fully paid has more authority and confidence in her marital home than one for whom it is still being paid.

In cases of a married woman dying before the promised bridewealth has been paid, the husband's family would pay the bridewealth lest her family repossess her body for burial and the children. In such an event the children would not be legitimate heirs of the father but would belong to the woman's family. This would be a great loss to the building of the father's lineal family.

It should be noted that bridewealth in Africa is different from the Asian custom called **dowry** in which the bride brings wealth, often in the form of jewelry, into the family of the groom. In Africa, bridewealth can be any goods or services that are exchangeable including livestock, money, accommodation, land, labor, etc.

DISCUSSION QUESTIONS

1. Why does the payment of bridewealth legitimize the children into the lineage of the father?
2. Against popular wisdom, a recent research project in Nairobi showed that all economic classes whether wealthy, middle or poor, continue to pay and follow bridewealth customs. Why is this so?
3. Can a church and/or government wedding substitute for a traditional bridewealth wedding and be accepted by the couple's families as a legitimate marriage?
4. Are you married with bridewealth payments or hope to be married in this manner in the future?

AFRICAN ILLUSTRATION

BRIDEWEALTH AND LEGITIMACY OF CHILDREN

A couple had been living together in a come-we-stay relationship for about fifteen years and had borne five children. Unfortunately the wife fell sick and died before they were married according to traditional patrilineal rites, which always involve bridewealth payments. The parents of the woman came to collect the body for burial at their home since, according to Maragoli traditions, she could not be buried at her husband's home. His family had not formally consented to the union through payment of bridewealth. They were also to take the five children as the father could only claim them if bridewealth had been paid.

Elders from the man's clan had to hurriedly convene a meeting to solve the problem as it would be a big shame and loss for the man's family and clan -- they knew they had no legal claim to the children. All the man's age mates and clan members quickly contributed towards the bridewealth as it was necessary that it be paid before burial arrangements were finalized. Once the bridewealth was paid, the woman was buried in her husband's homestead and the children were forever legitimized in the family of the father. This incident confirms the saying, "whoever pays the cows owns the children." **[Verbatim of a field assistant.]**

RECOMMENDED READINGS

Magesa, L. (1998). *African Religion: The Moral Traditions of Abundant Life.* (pp. 122-127). Nairobi: Paulines Publications.

Ngubane, H. (1987). The Consequences for women of marriage payments in a society with patrilineal descent. In Nyamwaya, D. & Parkin, D. (Eds.). *Transformations of African Marriage.* (pp. 173-182). Manchester: International African Institute.

Nagashima, N. (1987). Aspects of change in Bridewealth among the Iteso of Kenya. In In Nyamwaya, D. & Parkin, D. (Eds.). *Transformations of African Marriage.* (pp. 183-198). Manchester: International African Institute.

NON-AFRICAN ILLUSTRATION

MARRIAGE GIFTS IN A WESTERN CONTEXT

At a recent Church wedding in the US, an elaborate reception was held in a local country club where the invited guests numbered close to a hundred. All came with gifts wrapped with special paper and cards. There were gifts of appliances, blankets, and many things that the young couple could use when setting up their household.

After the wedding, the couple sat down and began to go through the list of gifts in order to thank the people involved. In the process, it became clear that a particular gift was an expression of the gift-giver's closeness or distance to the couple. Those that were closely related gave larger gifts, and those that were less closely related gave smaller gifts.

In one case there was concern that a person whom they thought was close to them only gave a small gift. It indicated that there might be something negative about the person's attitude towards them. In another case, the gift was much larger than they expected and it invoked the comment that perhaps the person was more interested in them than they had thought. In other words, gifts given at weddings are an expression of the closeness of one's relationship to the couple.

CHAPTER IX

Theme: **MARRIAGE**

The carving is an image representing an African family. It shows a man carrying a bundle on his shoulder, surrounded by children who are doing different activities. The woman on the left is pounding food using a pestle and mortar. To marry and procreate is a continuation of one's life -- a gift given by ancestors to be shared and passed on to the new generation.

MARRIAGE

Introduction

In order to ensure the continuation of the community, and to be able to determine the legitimacy of its offspring, all societies worldwide, have special rites, rituals and permanent structures surrounding the sexual unions of its male members to females from other lineages and clans, called marriage. These marital unions between a husband and a wife are rooted in the fertility of the couple for the sake of responsible parenthood. The so called same-sex unions that are currently under consideration are in no sense marriages as there is no possibility of fertility -- the root and focus of marriage relationships worldwide.

Marriage in Africa

The passing on of life, which is seen as a gift of the ancestral community, happens through procreation. One lives forever through one's offspring. Not to marry and procreate is seen to be a negative and selfish stand, a stopping of one's life that was given as a gift to be shared and passed on. Marriages in African societies continue beyond the grave, there is no "till death do us part." Marriages are community affairs in which the elders must agree upon the prospective bride or groom. If the society is patrilineal it determines the bride price to be paid, arrange and pay for the marriage celebration, put the newlyweds under the guidance and protection of an older couple, and ensure the continuation of the union even in the face of an untimely death of the husband through the custom of widow inheritance. There is a pledge given to the couple at the time of the marriage by the community that the family will survive and prosper no matter what happens in their lives. Divorce, especially among patrilineal peoples, is rare as there has been careful preparation to ensure that the bride and groom are compatible and come from well respected families.

The payment of bridewealth in patrilineal societies determines the legitimacy of the children in the lineage of the father. It also results in a substantial amount of wealth being redistributed around the community reinforcing the equalitarian nature of property and goods. Furthermore, due to the fact that the marriages are exogamous, the relationship cuts down potential hostility between the clans of the bride and the groom (the old Romeo and Juliet story -- you marry your enemies -- played out for centuries in Africa).

Marriage Elsewhere

As far back as recorded history, all societies have had marriage institutions involving a man and a woman. In Africa and many parts of Asia there are also polygynous marital unions involving a man with two or more legally accepted wives, and in some parts of Asia, a woman can be married to two men, usually brothers, called polyandry. Worldwide, expensive gifts are usually given at the time of marriage celebrations.. In Asia for example, there is a custom called dowry in which the bride brings wealth into the household of her husband. This custom is the opposite of African bride price where wealth goes to the bride's homestead.

Presently in many cultures worldwide there are common law marriages (called in Kenya "come we stay") in which a couple merely move in together and share a common table and bed. Some of these unions are recognized as legal by local governments after a period of time e.g., in the U.S. but not in Kenya. These unions tend to be unstable and result in the women and children fending for themselves when the unions break up.

In the West, marriages are of a nuclear style as the couple starts their own household independent of their parents. Consequently, gifts are given to the newlyweds to help them start their new household. In all cultures, marriages are a major rite of passage into responsible and full adulthood.

QUESTION

Kindly explain in detail your understanding of the theme of MARRIAGE. What is its contemporary meaning in your personal, social and community life? N = 64, (53 Africans, 11 non-Africans).

RESPONSES COLLATED BY SIX CATEGORIES
1. *Relevance of Marriage   R = 46*
2. *Definition of Marriage   R = 28*
3. *Significance of Marriage   R = 27*
4. *Elements of Marriage   R = 18*
5. *Marriage Today   R = 14*
6. *Why People get Married   R = 12*

Other Comments   R = 9

AFRICAN RESPONDENTS   N = 53

Relevance of Marriage   (R = 38)
It *sustains the lineage* through procreation (11), brings *order* in the community (4), helps to *sustain the community* (3), brings *together* two families (3), creates *friendships* within the community (2) *unites individuals, clans and whole communities* (2), is the *basis of a person's social and community life* (2), *incorporates* one in a family and the community (2), provides *a legal base for the legitimacy* of children (1), *creates families* which eventually make communities (1), families of the husband and wife become *related* (1), *legitimizes the family* (1), helps in *propagating a family name* and the *reincarnation* of its members (1), is a condition for *elderhood* (1), socially *a married couple form a source of support* for one another (1), to an

individual, it helped *solve the problem of loneliness, placed him in a family unit* and made him *a leader as the head of a household* (1), the couple acquires *new social responsibilities* (1).

Definition of Marriage (R = 26)

Is the *union of two people of the opposite sex* for the purpose of *procreation* and for *companionship* (6), is an *institution* in which *a mature couple* comes to unite with the *aim of propagating their lineage* (4), is a union of man and woman who through *love decide to live together* as husband and wife (2), is a *formal agreement* between a man and a woman *in front of a witness/ witnesses* making them husband and wife (2), is *a bond of union* between two people with *mutual obligations as established traditionally* (1), is a *socially accepted union* between *a man and woman/women* (1), is *a rite* that unites members of *two lineages to cement kinship ties* through uniting two individuals in *a marital covenant* (1), is a union of two people of the opposite sex who *take vows to legally stay together* (1), is a union between *two separate clans* where the family of the man and that of the woman play an important role *of creating another family from their own* (1), is *an intimate relationship* between a man and a woman (1), is *the willingness* of two individuals to live together (1), is the *unification* of two persons to become one to help each other (1), is *a social relationship that is founded on the need to perpetuate human life* through procreation (1), is a relationship of two opposite sexes of adults who *love each other and want companionship* (1), is the relationship of two adults of the opposite sex who make *an emotional and legal commitment underscored by group sanctions* to live together as husband and wife with *a primary aim of raising a family* (1), is the union between two members of the opposite sex and of *different lineages* with the aim of raising children (1).

Significance of Marriage (R = 19)

It is *God's way to ensure the continuity of life* (2), marks the *rite of passage* from youth to adulthood (1), is a *binding institution* for different clans in any community (1), it is *God's way of uniting humanity* (1), is *a bond* that brings two people together so that they may *serve God and a family* through their relationship (1), is a *personal, social and communal* matter for the couple (1), it is the *foundation* of a family (1), *binds two clans and two individuals socially and emotionally* (1), is a *ritual* that confirms you as an adult and *tests one's capability in leadership* (1), it *defines* the socially accepted way *for procreation and sexual gratification* amongst *two spouses* (1), I am *my ancestor* and in marriage I get children who are *my future* (1), is the *rite of passage* which *incorporates* a person in the society *as an adult* (1), it is the *institution* through which *the human race is preserved* (1), once a person is married *it is permanent* until death parts him/her with the spouse (1), it *enables members to procreate* within *a limited and orderly institution* (1), is the only way *life is continued legally* (1), is the *continuation of life* through bearing children (1), it is the only way the *life of a community can continue and be transmitted* through the ancestors (1).

Elements of Marriage (R = 14)

It is usually *cemented by various ceremonies* such as payment of *bridewealth* (2), children are *important* and are normally expected in a marriage (2), is *a union blessed by God* (1), is *deeply rooted* in the *traditional setting* (1), it must be *legitimized* (1), is a *communal rather than an individual* affair (1), each person in the society is expected *to marry after attaining the right age* (1), *traditional ceremonies* are done *to bless* the marriage (1), is *a sacred institution* (1), children are *gifts from God* and the *fruits of a marriage* (1), is *a continuation of love* (1), lack of children should *not destroy the harmony* in a marriage (1).

Marriage Today (R = 11)

There is *an increase* in the number of *single parents, divorces and neglected children,* which is *an indication* that marriage is an *endangered institution* (2), on a *personal level* marriage is very *challenging from the socio-economic* point of view (1), *marriage bonds are taken temporarily* and take *the form that suits the concerned parties* (1), the institution of marriage is *on the decline* (1), it means *a mature couple coming together for convenience* and for *procreation if they wish* (1), is *losing meaning* as many couples do not bother to *legitimize* their union (1), has taken the form of *'come-we-stay'* (1), seems to be a union between a man and woman *with or without the consent of their families* (1), *documentation of the relationship* is considered sufficient to legitimize it (1), marriage is *still relevant* despite the setbacks it is facing (1).

Why People get Married (R = 12)

For *procreation* (4), *unmarried people in Africa are sometimes looked upon with contempt and even considered social outcasts or seen to be cursed* (3), because *marriage is a must for all members* of the community (2), for *social recognition* in African cultures (1), for *companionship* (1), for *continuation of the family name* (1).

Other Comments (R = 3)

There is a *strong connection* between *God, ancestors and procreation* (1), [I] would encourage people to marry as it *is the only way to sustain our existence* (1), being from *a matrilineal tribe*, I have all rights on *my mother's side* and my children will be *named as my maternal uncle's children* (1).

NON-AFRICAN RESPONDENTS   N = 11
[The respondents answered both according to their
own culture and their understanding of African culture.]

Relevance of Marriage   (R = 8)
The couple *support each other* towards achieving *a holistic personal growth*
as well as contributing towards development (1), involves *sharing of one's
talents, skills and material possessions* with the larger community (1),
expectation is that the *lineage* will be continued (1), *joins two families* (1), it is
through the institution of marriage that *I came into being* (1), through it *a
family is legalized* (1), through it the *offspring get identity* (1), it *gives
structure* to the community (1).

Definition of Marriage   (R = 2)
Is *the coming together of a man and woman who love each other* (1), is *the
uniting of two people who have come to a mutual decision to unite and spend
their lives together* (1).

Significance of Marriage   (R = 8)
Signifies *the creation of a lasting union* between *two opposite sexes* (1), for a
couple it is *a choice to change life* and *keep some responsibilities* (1), it is
facing challenges together to create happiness (1), for the community it is a
sort of *a guarantee* to survival through procreation (1), *socially* it is one way
of *organizing* people's life, while *communally it is a rite* (1), it is the *highest
social contract* (1), it is *a union that should not be entered into lightly* and
should last for one's life (1), is *a sacramental bond* that is life long (1).

Elements of Marriage   (R = 4)
There is the aspect of *procreation* in marriage (1), in the African context it is *a
community event* (1), marriage is between *two individuals* (1), people *get
married in church* (1).

Marriage Today   (R = 3)
In the *Western culture*, marriage *remains the hope and ideal* for all people
(1), the view that *marriage should be taken seriously and last forever is dying
out* in the West (1), is *not respected* and considered so worthy nowadays (1).

Other Comments   (R = 6)
Marriage is *an essential element of the Spanish culture* (1), in Spanish
culture, *divorce* was *only legalized twenty years ago* (1), in the *Western
culture there is no stigma attached to unmarried persons* (1), in *USA divorce
is prevalent* and there are *many second marriages* that are successful (1),

social life revolves around married people (1), in *some developed societies, marriage and children are considered a liability* [or only] *for personal happiness* (1).

SUMMARY
Beliefs expressed regarding Marriage

<u>Marriage is</u>: the *union* of *two people of opposite sex* for the *purpose of procreation and companionship*, an institution in which *a mature couple unites* with the aim of *propagating their lineage*, union of a man and a woman who *through love* decide to live together as husband and wife, a *formal agreement* between *a man and a woman* in front of witnesses making them husband and wife, a *socially accepted union* between a man and a woman/women, a *rite* that unites members of two lineages to *cement kinship ties*, a *social relationship of two adults of opposite sex* who make an *emotional and legal commitment* underscored by *group sanctions* to live together as husband and wife with the *aim of raising children.*

<u>Relevance of Marriage</u>: *sustains* the lineage, brings *order* in the community, *unites* families, clans and communities, is *the basis* of a person's social and community life, *a condition* for *elderhood, legitimizes* children born of the union, helps in *propagating the family name and reincarnation* of its members, *the couple acquires new social responsibilities*, gives the *offspring an identity*.

<u>Significance of Marriage</u>: is *God's way of uniting humanity* and ensuring the *continuity of life*, an *institution* through which the *human race is preserved, permanent* until one of the spouses dies, the only way *life is passed on legally, continuation of life* through bearing children, a *sacramental bond* that is life long, a *binding institution* for different families, clans and communities, a *bond* that brings two people together so that they may serve *God and a family* through their relationship, the *foundation* of a family, a *ritual* that confirms one as an *adult* and *tests one's capability in leadership*; marks the *rite of passage* from youth to adulthood, *defines* the *socially accepted way for procreation and sexual gratification* amongst spouses.

<u>Elements of Marriage</u>: is a *community* event, between two people of *opposite sex*, usually *cemented* by payment of *bridewealth, deeply rooted* in *traditional* setting, a *sacred* institution, a continuation of a *couple's love,* an *expectation* of the society that each person must marry after attaining the *right age*, it must be *legitimized, children* are important and normally expected, *traditional ceremonies* are done to bless the marriage.

<u>Why People get Married</u>: for *procreation, social recognition, companionship, propagation of the family name*, to *avoid social stigma, fulfill* a community *obligation.*

Marriage Today: is on the *decline* as indicated by the prevalence of *single parent families, divorces, neglected children, challenges from the socio-economic* point of view, is *not respected* nor considered so *worthy*, is still *relevant despite the setbacks* facing it, is for *convenience,* in the form of *'come-we stay,'* takes place *with or without the consent of the wider families*, may or may not be *legalized.*

RESPONSES FROM WORKSHEETS

[Note that in African heritage, marriage is a sacred institution involving two people of the opposite sex for the purpose of responsible parenthood through procreation, while under the supervision and protection of the lineal community.]

❑ Kindly explain in detail your understanding of the theme of MARRIAGE. What is its contemporary meaning in your personal, social and community life?

AFRICAN RESPONDENTS N =53

[There were sixteen ethnic groups represented: Agikuyu (11), Luo (11), Abaluyia (7), Akamba (5), Abagusii (4), Aembu (3), Teso (2), Tutsi (2), Kipsigis (1), Kategi (1), Akan (1), Arusha-Meru (1), Ibo (1), Bemba (1), Banyankole (1), and Tigrinya (1). The respondents were university graduates; fourteen women and thirty-nine men.]

- Marriage is a rite of passage from being youthful to adulthood. Marriage on a personal level is very challenging i.e., from a social and economic point of view. The community always welcomes the new couple in terms of social responsibilities. (Agikuyu)
- Marriage is a bond of union between two [people], with mutual obligations as established traditionally. This institution has undergone many changes. Bonds are today temporary and take the form that suits the concerned parties. Some bonding cannot stand hard times together. (Abaluyia)
- Marriage is a union or partnership of man and woman who through love decide to live together as husband and wife. Socially, the two form a source of support for one another. I do not know its contemporary meaning since I am not married. (Abagusii)
- Marriage is a union of two people of the opposite sex for the purpose of procreation and for companionship. Personally, marriage is a binding institution for the different clans in any community. It also contributes in building allies in any community. (Agikuyu)
- Marriage is meant for procreation. Through marriage, the lineage system is sustained. There exists a strong connection between God, the ancestors and procreation. (Abagusii)
- The anthropological meaning of marriage in our community is a socially accepted union between a man and a woman or women. (Tutsi)
- Marriage is an institution in which a mature couple comes to unite with the aim of propagating their lineage. In contemporary times, the term

marriage means a mature couple coming together for convenience and for procreation if they so wish. (Luo)

- Marriage is as old as mankind. It is God's creation to ensure continuity of life. It was deep-rooted in the traditional setting. Today, it is a dying institution. Personally, I would still encourage people to marry for it is the only way to sustain our existence. (Luo)
- Marriage is a very important institution that sustains the survival of the lineage. (Akamba)
- Marriage is meant to perpetuate the lineage system. (Luo)
- Marriage unites individuals, clans and the whole community. It is God's way of uniting humanity. Marriage is thus a union blessed by the creator God. (Abaluyia)
- Marriage is a rite that unites members of two lineages to cement kinship ties. This is done through uniting two individuals into a marital covenant. Marriage is the foundation of a family. (Aembu)
- Marriage is a union of two people of opposite sex who take vows to stay legally together. In contemporary times, it is losing its meaning in that many cases exist where couples do not bother to legitimize their marriage and instead just stay together (i.e., come-we-stay). The increase of single parents is proof that marriage is an endangered institution. (Agikuyu)
- Marriage involves the union of two partners, families and clans. It must be legitimized and its main purpose is procreation. Today, marriage is taking a different shape. We can now witness many divorces, single parents, and neglected children, which were facets that were absent in traditional settings. Personally, it is still meaningful despite the setbacks it is facing. (Abaluyia)
- Marriage is necessary in African cultures for one to be socially recognized. Marriage is a community issue and not just a confidential issue between two individuals. (Kategi)
- Marriage is an institution meant to sustain the lineage through procreation. It binds two clans and the two individuals socially and emotionally. Marriage also provides a legal base for the legitimacy of the children. (Akamba)
- Marriage is important in society for it provides lineage continuation through procreation. Marriage is still important today for it still brings order and continuity of the family tree in the community as a whole. (Agikuyu)
- Marriage is a commitment between two individuals of the opposite sex to come together, to live and procreate, to protect and nurture the offspring. Marriages create families. These families eventually make up the community. (Agikuyu)

- Marriage is a union between two separate clans where the family of the man and that of the woman play an important role of creating another family from one of their own. Marriage in the contemporary sense seems to be a union between a man and woman with or without much consent of the two families. (Akan)

- Marriage is an intimate union between a man and woman that is consummated with mutual love and commitment and nourished by sexual intercourse. Personally, marriage has solved the problem of loneliness, placed me in a family unit and made me a leader i.e., head of a household. (Luo)

- Marriage is the union between two persons of different sexes who mutually consent and decide to live together and fulfill the family's obligations e.g., procreation. (Tutsi)

- Marriage is an intimate relationship between a man and a woman. This relationship is usually cemented by various marriage ceremonies. The ceremonies include paying of bridewealth. Children are normally expected from these relationships. In the modern times, legal documentation of the relationship is considered sufficient to legitimize the relationship. (Abaluyia)

- Yes, it is a simple unit, which leads to a person's social and community life. (Abagusii)

- My tribe is matrilineal (follow the side of the mother). My child will be named as my uncles' children. I have all the rights on the side of my mother's family. (Arusha-Meru)

- Marriage is the coming together of people (man and woman) for the sake of companionship and procreation. Without it the society would be chaotic. (Luo)

- Marriage involves the union of two people of the opposite sex with an intention of continuity of life. It also brings together two families. It has some meaning to my personal, social and community life. (Abaluyia)

- Marriage is a bond that brings two people together so that they may serve God through their relationship and also as a family. (Luo)

- Marriage is a ritual that confirms you as an adult and tests one's capability in leadership. A well managed family clears someone for outside marriage [societal] leadership. It is also a go-ahead to continue the lineage to the next generation. (Agikuyu)

- The theme of marriage defines the socially accepted way or leeway for procreation and sexual gratification amongst two spouses. This is the African context. To me marriage is a unification of two persons to become one to help each other. (Abaluyia)

- Marriage means the union of different sexes with the aim of [the] continuation of life in the lineage/community. (Agikuyu)
- Marriage is the coming together of two people (male and female) to bear children. In this way, the name of the family is continued. The families of the husband and the wife then get related. (Agikuyu)
- Marriage is where a man and a woman agree to live together as husband and wife for the purpose of raising children. It has a lot of meaning in my personal life. (Akamba)
- Marriage is the peak of one's life and means a lot in social circles. (Luo)
- It is the only way the life of the community can continue and be communicated from the ancestors. I am my ancestor made present and in marriage I get children who are my future. (Luo)
- Marriage is the rite of passage which incorporates a person in society as an adult and marriage is made for procreation and each person in the society is expected to marry after getting to the right age. (Akamba)
- Marriage is a very big theme in the social and community life of Africa. I share the same idea of importance of marriage. As it was stated in the scripture, not all are called to be eunuchs for the kingdom of God. I think there is need for people to marry and procreate. In the social and community life of Africa, unmarried people are sometimes looked upon with contempt. (Ibo)
- Marriage is the center of human life through procreation. It is important because it prolongs the lineage of the clan. (Bemba)
- Marriage is the institution through which human race is preserved. Children are therefore important. If this is to happen, marriage is permanent in that once married you stay together until death separates you. (Abaluyia)
- Marriage is what legitimizes a family, which consists of a father, mother and children. I have found it [marriage] meaningful when with my larger clan members. Marriage makes one belong to the larger group or community. (Agikuyu)
- Marriage is a formal agreement between a man and a woman in front of a witness or witnesses making them husband and wife. Marriage is a ritual that is passed on from generation to generation. Marriage is a personal aspect for the marrying couple and also a social and community aspect. (Agikuyu)
- Marriage is a very sacred part of culture for it is the base of lineage continuity and the carrying on of a family name and reincarnation of its members. (Teso)
- Marriage enhances continuity of life in the lineage and kinship. (Abagusii)
- Marriage institution brings together two families. It involves paying of bridewealth. Traditional ceremonies are done such as blessings by elders and feasting. It has a great meaning in my life/community because for one to pass [graduate] to be an elder, he must be married. (Kipsigis)

- Marriage is the unity between a husband and a wife through love. It incorporates one in a family. (Luo)
- It is a social relationship that is founded on the need to perpetuate human life through procreation. (Aembu)
- Marriage in my community is a must and one who fails to marry or be married is considered a social outcast and this may be seen as a curse. (Luo)
- Marriage is a social institution that brings order to the otherwise chaotic situation. It enables the members to procreate within a limited and orderly institution. Marriage is a must for all members of the community. (Agikuyu)
- This is the union of/between two people of the opposite sex who accept to live together as husband and wife and accept certain conditions in the presence of witnesses. Marriage is the only way life is continued legally. (Luo)
- Marriage is a relationship of two opposite sex adults who love each other and want companionship. The children who are gifts from God are the fruits of marriage but the lack of this should not destroy the harmony in marriage. (Teso)
- Marriage is a relationship of two adults of the opposite sex who make an emotional and legal commitment underscored by group sanctions to live together as husband and wife with a primary aim of raising a family. Thus marriage is a continuity of love, and increase of social friends through in-laws, which gives a community a sense of belonging and stability as well as solving conflicts. (Akamba)
- Marriage has a meaning because it is the continuation of life through the bearing of children. (Banyankole)
- Marriage is a union between two members of the opposite sex and of different lineages, with the aim of raising children. (Aembu)
- Marriage signifies the creation of a lasting union between two opposite sexes. The two individuals support each other towards achieving a holistic personal growth as well as contributing towards community development. At the center of this holistic growth is procreation and sharing of one's talents, skills and material possessions with the larger community. (Tigrinya)

NON-AFRICAN RESPONDENTS   N= 11
*[The respondents answered according to both their
own culture and their understanding of African culture.]*

*[There were four non-African countries represented: America (6), India (3),
Spain (1), and Italy (1). The respondents were University graduates; four
women and seven men.]*

Mixed African and Non-African Perspective
- In the African context, marriage is a community event, where the whole community is part of the preparations and celebrations with the expectation that the lineage will be continued. In my culture, marriage remains the hope and ideal for all people. However, unmarried people and childless couples do not suffer the plight of similar people in the African setting. (American)

Non-African Perspective
- Meaning of marriage varies depending on the subject. For a couple, this is a choice to change life and keep some responsibilities. It is facing challenges together to create happiness. For the community, it is a sort of guarantee, a control through which the community is guaranteed to survive through procreation. Personally, I see marriage as a big responsibility and a vocation that not every one has. Socially, it is one way of organizing people's life. Communally, it is a rite, an expectation that at times becomes the source of pride or problems. (Italian)
- Marriage to me is the highest social contract. It is a union, which should not be entered into lightly and should last for all of one's life. However, this view is dying out in my society. (American)
- Marriage is between two individuals although it does join two families. It's a sacramental bond that is life long. (American)
- Marriage is an essential element of the Spanish culture. Until twenty years ago we did not have legalized divorce. It has a lot of meaning to me as a daughter of a married couple and a lot of meaning to all in the society. The worth and respect of marriage is a bit sweetened nowadays. (Spaniard)
- Marriage is basic to social and community life. Through marriage, a family is legalized and the offspring get the identity from marriage. Marriage also gives a structure to the community. (Indian)
- Marriage is very important but there is no stigma attached to unmarried persons. Divorce is prevalent in the USA but many second marriages are very successful, including mine. Social life revolves around married persons. (American)

- Marriage is strictly coming together of a man and a woman who love each other. It has great meaning for my personal, social and community life. (American)
- Marriage with its implication of the continuation of life is challenging the values of certain developed societies where marriage and children are considered as a liability for personal happiness. (Indian)
- Marriage is the uniting of two people who have come to a mutual decision to unite and spend their lives together. In my community, people are married in the church. (American)
- Marriage is the willingness of two individuals to live together. The society has existence only as long as the marital relationship is strong. Well-defined marriage customs keep and bring the community together. (Indian)

EDITOR'S REFLECTIONS

In Africa, marriage continues to be a sacred and essential institution. It is solely the union of two adults of the opposite sex; Africans are appalled at the idea of same sex marriages. The purpose of marriage is procreation. Traditional requirements for patrilineal people, such as the payment of bridewealth, still persist as they are the African seal of the marriage and legitimize the children born of the union. Today, common law marriages (come-we-stay) are common even though they are not recognized by the families of the couples as marriages. The couples are only considered to be cohabiting friends, no matter how long they stay together. Furthermore, children born of such a union are considered to be illegitimate until traditional requirements of marriage are fulfilled. Usually Western-style marriage celebrations are conducted only after traditional marriage requirements have been fulfilled. Otherwise, the couple is considered by their lineal families to be cohabiting friends and not married, even though they might have a government marriage license.

DISCUSSION QUESTIONS

1. In Africa why do marriages continue beyond the grave-- there is no "till death do us part?"
2. Is the traditional custom of polygamy for the sake of power and prestige or for the sake of a large homestead with many children?
3. In African patrilineal communities, why are marriages not considered fully completed unless children have been born? Explain.
4. What is your present personal marital situation, or your plans for the future?

AFRICAN ILLUSTRATION

NECESSITY OF MARRIAGE AND PROCREATION
FOR ALL ADULTS

A Dinka Catholic Priest from the Sudan related to a missionary while on a flight from Khartoum to Juba, that his family was unwilling to accept the fact that as a Catholic priest he would never marry and beget children. Consequently his life, given to him as a gift, would not be passed on and his name would be lost forever. To overcome his lifelong celibate situation, he reported that his family would marry a wife in his name after his death, and any children born of the woman would be seen as his offspring, continuing his life and name. In effect, he would have his family posthumously.

The objections of his family to his celibate state would be an ordinary reaction of most African families when dealing with a son or daughter who contemplated entering a Catholic religious community in which celibacy was mandatory.

RECOMMENDED READINGS

Magesa, L. (1997). *African Religion: The Moral Traditions of Abundant Life.* (pp. 110-143). Nairobi: Paulines Publications.

Hastings, A. (1973). *Christian Marriage in Africa.* (pp. 27-44). London: SPCK.

Ayisi, E.O. (1972). *An Introduction to the Study of African Culture.* (pp. 6-12). Nairobi: East African Educational Publishers.

NON-AFRICAN ILLUSTRATION

MARRIAGE FROM A WESTERN PERSPECTIVE

In Western societies marriage for many people has become an option. Life is seen as linear and is given to one as a gift, which one can do with what one likes. Therefore, if the person procreates or does not procreate, the quality of their life is not at risk as it is in African societies. This reality has created a large group of people in western societies that will marry and purposely not procreate, as well as a significant group that remains single, some of whom purposely procreate as single parents. This marital reality is a direct effect of Western cultural knowledge that sees life as linear and infinite and not recyclable.

On the other hand, a number of people in Western countries are appalled that the lack of interest in procreation will redound to childless couples to their own detriment. For them, an integral and critical dimension of being a fully mature and responsible human being entails nurturing new life and accompanying that life to maturity. Furthermore, the aging societies of the Western world are in danger of stagnating as there are not enough children being born to renew and reinvigorate the societies.

CHAPTER X
Theme: POLYGYNY

POLYGYNY/WAKE WENGI

The carving is a representation of polygynous marital relationships common in African communities.

POLYGYNY

Introduction

The English word "polygamy" means many wives or many husbands. The technical term for many wives is "polygyny" as used in this document. Interestingly only a few African countries after independence legalized polygyny through national laws, one of which is Tanzania. Polygynous marriages in most African countries continue to follow traditional laws.

Polygyny in Africa

In a number of African ethnic groups (some would argue all), polygyny, that is having more than one wife simultaneously, is not only culturally acceptable, but seen as the ideal way to found and nurture a family. It is the men with many wives who are seen as the leaders and pillars of the local community. Their ability to manage a large homestead is testimony to their personal social skills and maturity. Monogamy, having only one wife, is merely a stepping-stone to adding other wives and reflects the situation of the youth or those who do not have the resources to marry another. However, when resources to marry become available, usually a monogamous man will marry a second wife. Following on this, it is said that all marital relationships in Africa are potentially polygynous. **The basic reason for many wives is to have many children to support, develop and continue the homestead and the life of the lineage.** It also gives status to the man, and furnishes helpmates for the wives. The latter is a reality that is often overlooked, namely, that women play an important role in promoting and supporting polygynous relationships. For many women, a second wife represents a helper for the housework, cooking, caring for children, and cultivating the fields. At times, a first and only wife will encourage, even harangue her husband until he marries another woman who might even be her sister or her best friend. The end result is that the first wife gains power and dominance over another woman to the point that some scholars argue that one of the basic reasons polygyny continues in Africa on a wide scale is precisely because it enables women to dominate their fellow women socially and economically.

Polygyny Elsewhere

Polygyny, having multiple wives, is in no way peculiar to Africa. It is currently practiced in one form or another in cultures all over the world, and has been part of human history from the earliest time. Witness the polygynous relationships of most of the Old Testament leaders and heroes, beginning with Abraham and continuing with his descendents. In fact, many of the Luo speaking people of North Mara Tanzania when told by the Christian missionaries that polygyny was wrong and against God's laws, responded that this was a fabrication of the missionaries as God obviously had no problem with the polygynous marital situations of the OT leaders and prophets.

In the Western world where almost all countries have outlawed polygyny, many men get around the law by taking mistresses, women with whom they are sexually involved, and whom they maintain and support in some discrete fashion on a long-term basis. Unlike Africans, the second woman is not desired for the sake of procreation, rather for companionship, variety of experiences and sexual release. The problem with such relationships is that there is no legal protection for the woman in the case of children or inheritance. Often the mistress is known to the man's wife who will turn a blind eye to the relationship to keep her marriage together.

Another way of having a new marital partner is to divorce one's husband or wife in order to marry another, a custom called **serial polygyny**. Again, as in the African polygynous relationships, women are major actors and intimately involved in either serial polygyny or in mistress relationships -- they are not passive bystanders. For every unfaithful husband there is another woman responding to his attention and affection, and for every unfaithful wife there is another man open to receiving her attention and affection.

In Asia and Latin America, especially among the wealthy, there are both mistress-type relationships, and (in some countries) legally binding marriages with more than one woman e.g., Japan...The underlying issue here is why, since the beginning of recorded history, have men actively sought to have multiple domestic, marital partners, whether socially acceptable as wives, or as mistresses?

QUESTION
Kindly explain in detail your understanding of the theme of POLYGYNY. What is its contemporary meaning in your personal, social and community life?   N = 57 (53 Africans, 4 non-Africans)

RESPONSES COLLATED BY FIVE CATEGORIES
1. *Relevance of Polygyny   R = 57*
2. *Definition of Polygyny   R = 34*
3. *Polygyny in the Contemporary Society   R = 24*
4. *Challenges to Polygyny today   R = 23*
5. *Who Sanctions Polygyny   R = 3*

Other Comments   R = 29

AFRICAN RESPONDENTS   N = 53

Relevance of Polygyny   (R = 45)
It was a *symbol of wealth* (8), it was for *perpetuation of the lineage* (6), one *enlarged the progeny* (4), a man was *accorded more respect* depending on the number of wives and children he had (4), it is seen as *a symbol for higher social status* (3), it is seen as an *indication of good leadership and*

management of the family (2), it was considered *an economic achievement* (2), through it *work is shared easily* (2), when one has *many wives they each learn to be independent* unlike in a situation where there is only one wife who becomes dependent on him (1), it is *vital in widening the kinship network* (1), many wives served to *strengthen and develop the lineage* (1), it served as *a relief to the many women who would have remained unmarried* due to fewer males compared to the female population (1), it was necessitated by the *high mortality rate of the males* (both young and old) as a result of incidences such as accidents during hunting expeditions and inter-tribal wars casualties (1), it *brought family security* in terms of labor and security in old age (1), it *ensured a wider range of families/clans coming together* and hence the unity of the community (1), the *co-wives supplemented each other* in their many responsibilities of taking care of their offspring (1), the many children born of polygynous unions would *act as a source of labor* (1), it helped in the *spacing of children* (1), it helped in *reducing infidelity* (1), it was *desirable in cases where one was the only son* in the family among the Abagusii (1), helped in *redistribution of wealth* in the community (1), gives *rise to interactions* of many clans (1).

Definition of Polygyny   (R = 31)
It is the *practice of one man having more than one wife* (22), it is the *marriage of many women by one man simultaneously* (3), it is the *practice of having more than one wife in a legally binding arrangement* and especially with the approval of the community (2), it is either *one man marrying many wives or vice versa* (2), it is *marrying as many wives as one can be able to feed and take good care of* (1), it is marrying more than one wife in *a legally organized and recognized ceremony* (1).

Polygyny in the Contemporary Society   (R = 17)
It is *still relevant* in the present society as it *gives reprieve* to those women who would otherwise have missed an opportunity to get married (1), the *social and economic changes have gone against polygyny* although many African men would not mind having an extra wife if conditions would allow it (1), today it is *seen as a threat to a stable and responsible parenthood* among the Agikuyu community (1), the practice *has virtually died out* in some communities (1), currently polygyny *has turned out to be a hide and seek game* where people *keep concubines without the knowledge of their wives* (1), the *ideals have changed over time*, but polygyny still persists in my community (1), *Christian families are discarding polygyny* but men or women can have five to six spouses secretly (1), polygyny is *no longer being practiced* in my community today *because of Christianity and socio-economic conditions* (1), in the contemporary world, polygyny *would mean marrying one wife and keeping other concubines or mistresses* outside your

marriage (1), it *should be discouraged* because it *has lost meaning and may encourage promiscuity* by unsatisfied wives (1), the *modern version of polygyny is "free floating" marriages*, which is going on in many communities (1), in my rural home today, *a polygamous man is still respected* as the practice is welcome and still encouraged (1), it *gives every woman a chance to marry* and *for the rich man to share his wealth* (1) polygyny now *should be looked at anew and understood in the context of the present day* and not the past (1), it is *not very present and prevalent* in the society today (1), it *was valued in the past* but nowadays it is *seen as risky in terms of contracting HIV/AIDS* and also the economic aspect cannot allow its practice anymore (1), in the contemporary society polygyny *is not acceptable as it is uneconomical and exploitative* (1).

Challenges to Polygyny Today   (R = 23)

Harsh economic conditions (6), *Christianity* (5), the *AIDS scourge* (4), *gender sensitization programs and feminist movements* who portray it as negative and discriminating to women (1), *erosion of cultural beliefs* (1), *scarcity of land* (1), *globalization* (1), impact of *education* (1), it is now *a burden and expensive* to afford bridewealth (1), *population control campaigns* (1), *Western culture and capitalism* (1).

Who Sanctions Polygyny   (R = 3)

It is *legally sanctioned by the customs of the community* in which it takes place (2), it is sanctioned by *the society* (1).

Other Comments   (R = 22)

To me polygyny *is untenable* as I cannot think of a situation where several women share one man (2), there is a belief that *Africans are polygamous at heart*, thus even when a man is in a monogamous set-up, he desires to have a second or even a third wife (2), *some women enjoy being a second or even fifth wife* (1), polygyny *was a preferred form of marriage in the Agikuyu community* (1), polygyny *involves some kinds of ceremonies and exchange of gifts* (1), polygyny is an *age-old tradition within the Nubian community* (1) I was brought up in such a system but I do not see myself getting involved in it (1), among the Agikuyu *the women insisted on the man taking a second wife,* and would work hard to get enough sheep and goats to enable the husband to pay bridewealth for the second wife (1), in some communities, *the woman was given the freedom to decide whom she wanted to become her co-wife* (1), if a woman insisted on a monogamous set-up she was seen as *very selfish and shunned by other women in the lineage* (1), some men who opt for polygamy are neither leaders nor wealthy, they *just desire to have more than one wife* (1), in the Agikuyu community it was the *responsibility of the father to get his son the first wife* through paying bridewealth for him (1), polygyny *has no place in a marriage based on mutual love* (1), as *a Christian I believe in monogamy* and also because I have been socialized in this way (1), these days *there are men who do not want to officially have a second wife* but they have girlfriends (1), as a Christian I feel *polygyny is no longer practical* as it was in the traditional society as a man does not need many children to provide labor as he can easily hire workers (1), today both men and women *encounter similar hazards* and although women generally survive, *good medical care has seen the male to female ratio stabilize* to a point where it is possible for men to be monogamous without exposing women to the risk of being single (1), reasons for marriage have *undergone drastic changes* e.g., people *now marry because they love each other and want to be together not necessarily to beget children* (1), not many people are interested in many wives as *that means more mouths to feed and cater for* (1), it *has been abused by concubinage and other illegal practices* but it is good when properly practiced (1).

NON-AFRICAN RESPONDENTS N = 4
[The respondents answered according to
their understanding of African cultures.]

Relevance of Polygyny   (R = 12)
To *allow for many children* and in turn *ensure the continuity of the lineage* (2), it was *a way of ensuring continuity of life* especially where *the first marriage was childless* i.e., the woman was barren (1), it *ensured faithfulness on the part of the husband* (1), it ensured there was somebody to take care of the man *when the woman was expecting* and little work was expected of her (1), it has *no significant meaning in my cultural group* (1), it is *a strategic plan to guarantee good management of a man's wealth* (1), the many children from a polygynous family *guarantees the continuity of the activities started by the father* (1), it is *a way of ensuring every woman gets to have a mate/partner* (1), it is *a sign of wealth* (1), it *provides for plenty of children* to take care of the *shamba* and protect the community (1), provided *a helpmate to the wife* (1).

Definition of Polygyny   (R = 3)
It is a situation where *one husband marries many wives* (1), it is the *state of having more than one wife according to the dictates of the culture and sanctioned by the community* (1), it is *a man having multiple wives* in order to have many children (1).

Polygyny in the Contemporary Society   (R = 7)
The *gender movement sees it as an abuse of women's rights* (2), the *church has branded polygyny a sin* (1), *due to social, economic and cultural*

changes, polygyny has been *rendered less popular among many communities* in Kenya but it is *still far from extinct* (1), nowadays among the well-off and educated men, there is the *merging of a people's cultural heritage with the pleasure they receive from the new economy by marrying many wives* and *placing them as managers of the business enterprises* (1), in my community it *has been abolished but people still practice it secretly* (1), as circumstances of life in Africa have changed, *polygyny is less prevalent* (1).

<u>Other Comments</u>   (R = 7)
Polygyny is *not practiced in my culture* (2), any form of polygyny is *neither legally sanctioned nor culturally acceptable action in my culture* (1), it is true that *some males do keep mistresses* but such unions are never officially recognized (1), traditionally the *strength and stability of the community relied on numbers* and the more land frontiers a community conquered the stronger it was (1), polygyny *should be reintroduced to clear up messes caused by clandestine affairs* (1), we *do not have this institution in my community* as it is against the law (1).

SUMMARY
Beliefs expressed regarding Polygyny

<u>Polygyny is:</u> the *practice of having more than one wife*, *the marriage* of many women by *one man simultaneously*, having more than one wife in *a legally binding* arrangement especially with the *approval of the community*, *marrying as many wives* as one can be able to feed and take good care of, marrying more than one wife in a *legally organized and recognized* ceremony, having more than one wife *according to the dictates of the culture and sanctioned* by the community.

<u>Relevance of Polygyny:</u> was a *symbol of wealth*, considered an *economic achievement*, vital in *widening* the kinship network, necessitated by the *high mortality* rate of the males, a way of *ensuring the continuity* of the lineage especially in cases where the first marriage was childless, to *perpetuate* the lineage, *enlarge* the progeny, *increase the number* of male offspring in the lineage, an *indicator of* a higher social status, *good leadership and management* of the family, for *labor* through the children, *security in old age,* helped in *spacing* the children, *redistribution of wealth* in the community, *reducing infidelity*, gives rise to *interaction* of many clans and communities, *unity* between families, clans and communities, provided a *help mate and companion* to the wife.

<u>Challenges to Polygyny Today:</u> *harsh* economic conditions, *Christianity, HIV/AIDS, gender sensitization* programs, *feminist* movements that portray it as negative and discriminative towards women, erosion of

cultural beliefs, scarcity of land, globalization, formal education, population control campaigns, *Western culture, capitalism,* the *inflation* of bridewealth costs.

<u>Polygyny in the Contemporary Society</u>: it is *still relevant,* has *reduced* due to social and economic challenges, should be discouraged as it *promotes promiscuity* by unsatisfied spouses, should be looked at anew and *understood in the present day context,* seen as *risky* because of the HIV/AIDS scourge, not accepted as it is *uneconomical and exploitative,* many men *keep concubines* without the consent of their wives, in the rural set-up *polygynous men are still respected* as the practice is welcome and encouraged.

<u>Who Sanctions Polygyny</u>: it is legally sanctioned by the *culture of the community in which it takes place, the society*.

RESPONSES FROM WORKSHEETS

[Note that in many African societies a man with only one wife would not be allowed to drink beer from the same pot with polygynous men. This is because he is considered to still be a junior adult and has nothing of importance to tell those with more than one wife. In Luo and Abaluyia communities, such a man is referred to as "a man with one eye." It is only a fully mature man that can manage a polygynous household. As a result, local community leaders are usually polygynous.]

❑ Kindly explain in detail your understanding of the theme of POLYGYNY. What is its contemporary meaning in your personal, social and community life?

AFRICAN RESPONDENTS   N = 53

[There were sixteen ethnic groups of Africa represented: Agikuyu (15), Luo (10), Abaluyia (9), Tutsi (3), Akamba (2), Abagusii (2), Aembu (2), Teso (2), Nubian (1), Kipsigis (1), Ibo (1), Kategi (1), Banyankole (1), Bemba (1), Tigrinya(1), Akan (1). The respondents were university graduates, fourteen women and thirty nine men.]

- Polygyny is the practice of having many wives by one man. Such a marriage is legally sanctioned by the customs of the community it takes place in. It's still relevant in the modern society as it gives those women who would otherwise have missed an opportunity to get married. (Luo)
- Polygyny is a practice of marrying more than one wife. It's different from concubine relationships in that it is legally sanctioned by the customs of the community and involves some kind of ceremonies and exchange of gifts. The social and economic changes have gone against polygyny although many African men would not mind an extra wife if only the conditions would allow it. (Agikuyu)
- It's the practice of having more than one wife. The practice is still very much in the life of my community. It is seen as a symbol for higher social status and those who have only one wife find it very difficult to cater for their dependent wives, but when wives are many, every one of them learns to be independent. Some women enjoy being a second or even the fifth wife. (Luo)
- Polygyny was a preferred form of marriage in the traditional Agikuyu communities. More wives meant more hands and therefore more work would be done. This led to increased operation of wealth capability. It was also vital in widening the kinship network. Today, it's seen as a threat to a stable and responsible parenthood among the Agikuyu community and the

practice has virtually died out. Economic pressure has also contributed to the death of the practice. (Agikuyu)

- Polygyny is an age-old tradition within the Nubian community. I was brought up in the system, but I don't see myself getting involved in it. (Nubian)
- Practice of having more than one wife in a legally binding arrangement and especially with the approval of the community. Polygyny has currently turned out to be a hide-and-seek game where people keep concubines without the knowledge of their wives. (Abaluyia)
- It implies many wives married to one man in a community-sanctioned way. Many wives served to strengthen and develop the lineage. One begot many children, enlarged the progeny and perpetuated the lineage through polygyny. Polygyny is nowadays uneconomical mostly due to decreasing land frontiers and increased access to educational facilities for women. (Agikuyu)
- It served as a relief to the many women who would have remained unmarried due to fewer males compared to female's population. Also of note was the high mortality for males both young and old compared to women and girls. Men faced hazards during inter-tribal wars and hunting expeditions. This caused high mortality among them hence the necessity of those who remained to take more than one wife. Nowadays, men and women face similar hazards and although women generally survive, good medical care has seen the male-female ratio stabilize to a point where it's possible for men to be monogamous without exposing women to the risk of singlehood. In addition, gender sensitization programs and feminist movements have served to destroy the practice by portraying it as negative and discriminating to women. Erosion of cultural beliefs and effects of Christianity caused the greatest havoc to the practice. (Luo)
- Polygamy is the marrying of more than one wife. It was a symbol of wealth and brought family security in terms of labor and security in old age. (Agikuyu)
- Polygyny is a form of marriage where one man has many wives. Its meaning in my personal, social and community life can only be seen if I belong to a polygamous family set-up. (Luo)
- It is the marrying of many wives. It ensured a wider range of families/ clans coming together and hence the unity of the community. The co-wives supplemented each other in their many responsibilities of taking care of their offspring. Among the Agikuyu, contrary to what many foreigners to our culture believe, the women insisted a lot on the man taking a second wife. Actually, the woman worked very hard to raise enough sheep and goats to enable the husband to pay dowry for the second wife. Women were given the freedom to decide the girl they would like as

a co-wife. Today, harsh economic conditions, lack of land and the AIDS scourge has served to destroy this age-old custom. (Agikuyu)

- It's said that we Africans are polygamous at heart implying that even when a man is in a monogamous set-up, his heart desires to have a second or even a third wife. Traditionally, marrying many wives was an indication of wealth. Children born of these liaisons would be many and would act as a source of labor. (Aembu)

- Polygyny helped child spacing and reduced infidelity. If a woman insisted on monogamous set-up, she was seen as very selfish and would be shunned by the other women in the lineage. Globalization and Christianity have contributed to the demise or near demise of this form of marriage. In addition, reasons for getting married have also undergone great changes. People now marry because they love each other and want to be together, not necessarily to beget children. (Agikuyu)

- Among the Abagusii community, those with many wives had a reason. They either were the only children in their family or came from a lineage endowed with wealth and leadership. Thus, polygamy gave high social status. (Abagusii)

- It's a form of marriage involving one man and many women (more than one). It has disappeared and I think it's because of the economic challenges of supporting more than one wife and their dependents. (Agikuyu)

- It was a form of marriage that met the cultural demands made on the individual by the community e.g., marriage was necessary, and many children were preferred. It was expected that sons would contribute to the continuation of the lineage. These ideals have changed overtime, but the practice persists in my community. (Abaluyia)

- This is when a man marries more than one woman. I have heard it said that men are polygamous by nature. It doesn't surprise me when I hear that a man wants to take another wife. Some men who opt to be polygamous are neither leaders nor wealthy. They just desire to have more than one wife. (Abaluyia)

- Polygyny is the practice of marrying more than one wife. It's burdensome economically and especially if one had to provide for the livelihood of the wives and the children single-handedly. It's not acceptable to many Christian churches. (Abagusii)

- Polygyny was mainly encouraged because of the need to have many children, which was seen as a sign of wealth. A man with many children was greatly honored in the kinship. Having many wives was also a source of dignity and wealth for a poor person could not afford to pay bridewealth for a second wife. It's of note that in the Agikuyu community, it was the responsibility of the father to get the son the first wife i.e., to pay bridewealth in full. (Agikuyu)

- In my opinion, polygyny is untenable. I cannot think of a situation where several women share one man. It has no place in a marriage based on mutual love. (Agikuyu)
- Christian families are discarding polygyny today but men or women can have five to six spouses secretly. (Abaluyia)
- The theme of polygyny in African tradition is a term used in cases where a man has more than one wife. It was a source of pride and respect in the traditional African society. It may still hold for some communities today but not in my own community because of Christianity and the socio-economic situation today. Not many people are interested in many wives as that means more mouths to feed and cater for. (Ibo)
- Polygyny was accepted and respected in my community. (Kategi)
- It is the marrying of more than one wife. It is part of my culture and therefore its value is connected to leadership and good management of a family. (Luo)
- Polygyny is marrying more than one wife. This could be to the extent that one can feed and take good care of them. In the contemporary world, polygyny would mean marrying one wife and keeping other concubines or mistresses outside your marriage. (Abaluyia)
- Personally I do not advocate for it, because I cannot imagine sharing a man with another woman. It is selfishness of one party. (Akamba)
- Polygyny is a type of marriage where one man marries more than one wife. Traditionally polygyny was the norm, but today it is slowly losing meaning and popularity because of influence of Christianity, western culture and capitalism. (Agikuyu)
- Polygyny had much significance traditionally but it is now outdated and should be discouraged. This is because it has lost meaning and may encourage promiscuity to the unsatisfied wives. In my community, it used to be highly practiced but the practice is dying out. (Agikuyu)
- Polygyny is men having many wives and not vice-versa. As a Christian I believe in monogamy and also because I have been socialized this way. (Teso)
- Polygyny is whereby a man marries more than one wife. I have no interest in polygyny as such. (Tutsi)
- Modern version is "free floating" marriages going on in many communities. (Banyankole)
- Polygyny is whereby one man has more than one wife. This was practiced in all African communities. It has a meaning in my personal, social and community life in the contemporary situation because it helps many

African men to get another wife if the other one is dead. He remains with someone to assist him in one way or another. (Luo)

- Polygyny is having many wives simultaneously. In the contemporary society, with the influence of Westernization, and Christianity, many people disregard it. (Luo)

- Polygyny played an important role in the society because those who considered themselves wealthy married more women thus more children. They would divide their property among these family members thus not too much was taken by few people. Today polygyny should be highly discouraged mainly because of AIDS. (Agikuyu)

- Polygyny means either a man marrying several wives or vice versa. I personally value polygyny as far as social roles are concerned. Polygyny was considered as an economic achievement. (Agikuyu)

- Today in my rural home, a polygamous man is still respected. The practice is welcome and is still encouraged. (Luo)

- Marrying more than one wife under legally organized and recognized ceremony. Resources not withstanding, polygyny is a good thing. My grandfather was a polygamist, which enabled our family to grow big. (Agikuyu)

- It is the marriage of many wives or husbands. This practice is not commonly carried out due to the advent of HIV/AIDS pandemic, impact of education and social economic hardships. (Abaluyia)

- It has been abused by concubinage and other illegal practices. It is good when properly practiced. (Luo)

- Polygyny is a man marrying many wives, which extends the lineage, brings more economic/agricultural production into a family. Work is shared easily. It brings many children. Now this is threatened by HIV/AIDS. It is now a burden and expensive to afford bridewealth. The idea of a wider community is now diminishing because of economic crisis. Polygyny now should be looked at anew and understood in the context of the present day and not the past. (Teso)

- Polygyny is the state of marriage where a man marries several wives. This practice is sanctioned by the society. In the contemporary meaning it gives every woman a chance to marry and for the rich man to share his wealth. (Agikuyu)

- Polygyny is the marrying of many wives by one man simultaneously, which gives interactions of many clans. (Akamba)

- Polygyny refers to a man marrying many wives. To me, the concept has limited significance because of the influence of Christian teachings and economic circumstances. (Abaluyia)

- Polygyny is the simultaneous possession of two wives or more. It exhibits a man's wealth and ability to manage a large number of people i.e., wives and children. It is not very prevalent in the contemporary society. It has no meaning in my personal life. (Abaluyia)

- Polygyny is having many wives commanded by one husband. (Luo)
- It is to have more than one wife. It was valued in the past but nowadays it is seen as risky in terms of contracting HIV/AIDS and also the economic aspect cannot allow it. (Bemba)
- [I t is] the practice of marrying many wives. In the contemporary society, polygyny is not acceptable as it is uneconomical and exploitative. (Aembu)
- Polygamy refers to that act of having more than one wife. This is due to the fact that some people want many children and others marry more than one wife as a sign of prestige. (Kipsigis)
- This is one man having many wives. These days there are men who do not want to officially have a second wife but they have girl friends. As a Christian I feel that polygyny is no longer as practical as it was in traditional days. A man does not need many children to provide labor as he can easily hire workers. These are also days of population control and there is really no need to have many wives for the sake of many children. The children need to be cared for. It is not just for numbers sake. (Abaluyia)
- Polygyny is a situation where one husband marries many wives. Polygyny is not practiced in my culture. It's true that some males do keep mistresses but such unions are never officially recognized. Any form of polygyny is neither legally sanctioned nor culturally acceptable action in my culture. I can safely say that polygyny has no significant meaning in my personal as well as the social and community life of my ethnic group. (Tigrinya)
- In my community, it has been abolished but people still secretly practice it. It should be re-introduced to clear up messes caused by these clandestine affairs. (Tutsi)
- Polygyny was a way of ensuring continuity of life especially where the first marriage was childless i.e., the woman was barren. It also ensured faithfulness on the part of the husband, it ensured there was somebody to take care of the man when the woman was expectant and little work was expected of her. The church has branded polygyny as a sin and the gender movement sees it as an abuse of women's rights. (Akan)
- In my personal opinion, polygyny is a way of ensuring every woman gets to have a mate/partner, though looked down upon by many women as an abuse of their rights. (Tutsi)

NON-AFRICAN RESPONDENTS   N = 4
*[The respondents answered according to
their understanding of African cultures.]*

*[There were three non-African countries represented; America (2), Italy (1),
and Spain (1). The respondents were university graduates, three women and
one man.]*

- Polygyny is the state of having more than one wife married according to
  the dictates of the culture and sanctioned by the community. The primary
  reason is to allow for many children that in turn ensure the continuity of
  the lineage. It's important to note that traditionally, strength and stability
  of the community relied on numbers and the more land frontiers a
  community conquered the stronger it was. Due to social, economic and
  cultural changes, polygyny has been rendered less popular among many
  communities in Kenya but it's still far from extinct. (American)
- In my own opinion, polygyny is a strategic plan to guarantee good
  management of a man's wealth. Even nowadays, among the well-off and
  educated men, we have the merging of a people's cultural heritage with
  the pleasure they receive from the new economy by marrying many wives
  and placing them as managers of their business enterprises. The many
  children from such families guarantees the continuity of the activities
  started by the father. Polygyny is not practiced in my culture. It's strange
  but a married man once explained to me the possibility and the advantage
  of being a second wife. At the beginning, it was something out of my
  reality (I thought never!) but now through long discussions I have found
  polygyny not such a strange idea and possible but I am still trying to
  understand. (Italian)
- Polygyny is a man having multiple wives in order to have many children.
  It is a sign of wealth as to how many wives one has. We do not have this
  in my community. It is against the law. (American)
- Polygyny is the existence of more than one wife in a family unit. It
  provides for plenty of children to continue the lineage, take care of the
  shamba, protect the community and also provide a helpmate to the wife.
  As the circumstances of life in Africa have changed, polygyny is less
  prevalent. (Spaniard)

EDITOR'S REFLECTIONS

For centuries polygyny as a form of marriage has been practiced in Africa. Efforts have been made by some national governments and most mainline Christian churches to eliminate it and yet it persists. Indeed, Moslem religion openly accepts it. Furthermore, the missionary churches still consider polygyny to be incompatible with biblical teachings, despite the polygynous Old Testament heroes and prophets such as king David and Abraham. Moreover, the colonial administration in most African countries opposed it saying that the tradition was not in keeping with modern civilization.

Most African countries after independence maintained a stance similar to that of the colonial governments in which traditional polygyny was allowed alongside official government monogamous marriages.

In contemporary Africa it is common to find wealthy business men, local leaders and politicians in polygynous relationships. In polygynous relationships the man can either marry into the clan of his wife or from different clans depending on circumstances. What is not understood is that women are often fully involved in polygynous unions to the point of encouraging and initiating the process that lead a husband into a polygynous relationship. The reason, as mentioned earlier, is that a woman/wife gains a companion and helpmate, but more importantly gains social control over another woman. Some proponents of polygyny have argued that polygyny should be legalized in order to curb prostitution, the spread of HIV/AIDS and the street children menace.

DISCUSSION QUESTIONS

1. Is it correct to speculate that polygyny in Africa will only end because of economic reasons rather than as a result of the influence of Christianity or Western culture/education? Explain .
2. It is argued that women encourage and perpetuate polygynous relationships. Do you agree? Explain.
3. Would the legalization and encouragement of polygyny minimize prostitution, the number of street children and the spread of HIV/AIDS in Africa?
4. Would you personally enter into a polygynous marital relationship? Explain.

AFRICAN ILLUSTRATION

RESPONSIBLE POLYGYNY: A MARK OF LEADERSHIP

A politician in western Kenya had been staying with his younger wife in a town away from his traditional homestead. He went home to seek an elective office. The people in his home constituency told him that they could only vote for him if he came back and began taking care of his first wife. He had to build a stone house for her just as he had done for the younger wife, furnish it, and live with her throughout the campaign period. In the end he failed to get elected as the constituents felt that he had failed in his duties of taking care of his first wife and their children as she was the one officially recognized in his home constituency. For them, abandoning the first wife and their children was an indication of his lack of leadership skills and abilities. **[Verbatim of a field assistant.]**

RECOMMENDED READINGS

Mailu, D.G. (1988). *Our Kind of Polygamy.* Nairobi: Heinemann Kenya.
Pemberton, C. (2003). *Circle Thinking: African Women Theologians in Dialogue with the West.* (pp. 144-149). Leiden: Koninklijke Brill.
Hillman, E. (1975). *Polygamy Reconsidered: African Plural Marriage and the Christian Churches.* New York: Orbis Books.

NON-AFRICAN ILLUSTRTION

POLYGYNY FROM A WESTERN PERSPECTIVE

Polygyny in the Western world, due to national laws, is not recognized as a legitimate type of marriage. However, the Western world has circumvented this by a phenomenon called **serial polygyny** in which a person will divorce a spouse, and then marry a second person in a legally accepted union. However, if there are children from the first marriage, the couple continues to interact in a marital manner in terms of the needs and development of the children, and often share the children back and forth. In a structured way therefore, the first marriage continues to have a major influence on the lives of the separated parents. It is even said that in the second marriage, until the couple have their own children, the new spouse is a step-husband or step-wife. Polygyny therefore, although it is not legal within most Western nation states, does have its **serial-polygyny** form.

CHAPTER XI
Theme: HERBALIST

HERBALIST
BWANA MITI SHAMBA

The carving is an image of an elderly herbalist seated on a traditional stool holding a staff. Around his neck is a gourd used for carrying medication made from natural sources e.g., roots, leaves, etc.

HERBALIST

Introduction

All biological life is subject to unending threats to its existence through sickness, disease as well as physical and social violence. The law of the talon that "living things eat living things to live" expresses the violent and anti-life principal underpinning biological existence. All societies, therefore, have performers/actors who specialize in treating, warding off, and curing diseases.

African Herbalist

In all African communities you will find men and women who have been trained, either through apprenticeship or by deep mystical experiences, to diagnose, treat, cure and ward off anything that might harm one's life. Their instruments of healing are various types of medicines made with roots, leaves, minerals and dried parts of animals together with special rituals for healing and warding off evils. It is said, for example, that every home in the squatters' camps surrounding Nairobi has an object/charm hidden in its roof for protection. The same, they say, is also true for the houses of the middle and upper class Kenyans.

The herbalists in the minds of the people are seen as doctors of African medicine in contrast to the doctors who were trained in Western medicine. Presently, both kinds of doctors have their roles to play; if one type of doctor does not bring relief, then the other is consulted. For example, at Bugando hospital in Mwanza, Tanzania, a major district referral hospital, a survey a number of years ago showed that 90% of the three hundred out-patients seen on a daily basis had already used local African medicines, or were going to use them if the hospital medicines were not effective.

In point of fact, some of the local African medicines have powerful medicinal value and are being studied by Western medical facilities to ascertain their efficacy. Some have even been accepted and are in use by Western medical personnel. The late Kofi Appiah-Kubi, a Ghanaian theologian, at the time of his death was working on a Ghanaian government program to evaluate the medicinal value of the various compounds and herbs being used for remedies.

The reality is that the rituals and medicines of the herbalists usually bring about a certain amount of relief and healing, consequently for many they continue to function as the first source of help when stricken with sickness and disease.

Herbalists Elsewhere

Most third world countries would have practitioners like African herbalists. For example, a former Maryknoll missionary studied all the herbal remedies used by the Aymara shamans in the Alti Plano, Peru and published his findings in a book that was cited for excellence by the American

Anthropological Society. At the same time, there is a similar mixing of local and Western medical rituals, medicines and techniques by indigenous people throughout the world.

In the so called first world, the pharmacists play the role of herbalists as they recommend and sell to a willing public millions of shillings worth of compounds, salves, powders, and lotions, many of which are clearly marked as having no medicinal value. One needs only to stop at one of the local pharmacies in Nairobi to observe this reality, yet ordinary people still buy and consume these products with some feeling that they are helpful, at least psychologically.

QUESTION
Kindly explain in detail your understanding of the theme of HERBALIST. What is the contemporary meaning in your personal, social and community life? N = 74 (61 Africans, 13 non-Africans)
[Note that the question asked about this theme evoked some responses that included diviners as well as rainmakers under the category of herbalists.]

RESPONSES COLLATED BY EIGHT CATEGORIES
1. *Characteristics of Herbalists   R = 29*
2. *Herbalists today   R = 27*
3. *Role of Herbalists in the Community   R = 24*
4. *Relevance of the Theme of Herbalists   R = 20*
5. *Definition of Herbalists   R = 25*
6. *How One Becomes a Herbalist   R = 15*
7. *Unique Qualities of a Herbalist   R = 6*
8. *Types of Herbalists   R = 5*
Other Comments   R = 28

AFRICAN RESPONDENTS   N = 61

Characteristics of Herbalists (R = 25)
They use *locally available and natural herbs* to heal the sick (4), can *diagnose and cure diseases and misfortunes* (3), they do not promote *division or misunderstanding* in the community as they do not look for the cause and source of the disease *nor do they harm others* (2), are *highly respected* in the community (2), have *exceptional skills* in healing (1), have *good diagnostic skills* to tell which medicines to give for what (1), have *medicines of mysterious origin* (1), they keep the *combination of their herbs secret* so as to keep up the *sacredness* of the medicine (1), *train their children* who later inherit their practice (1), their *role strictly touches* on *healing* rather than *divination* (1), they claim to have been *called to the profession by God* (1), they exercise their trade and pass on their knowledge to *others freely* (1), they

have *supernatural powers* (1), are *ritual experts* (1), are *spiritual leaders* as they *discern God's guidance* on diagnosis and treatment (1), are *specialists* in treating different ailments (1), some *do not charge* for the services they offer (1), at times herbalists *invoke mystic power* as part of the treatment method (1).

Herbalists Today   (R = 21)
They are still *relevant and effective* (3), their *medicine has no side effects* making them earn respect as any doctor of *modern medicine* (2), I believe a herbalist is a *nurse, doctor and counselor*, all in one (1), socially traditional healers are becoming quite *influential* in the society (1), they are somewhat *overlooked* today despite the fact that they played a very *big role before the advent of modern medicine* (1), many are *commercially minded* (1), traditional healers need to be *studied and institutionalized* for the betterment of modern society (1) they are like *chemists* for they deal with *diagnosis and administering of medicine* (1), the society at large needs to *recognize their importance* and they should be allowed to continue their work (1), today herbalists are the *medical doctors* in hospitals (1), there are traditional herbalists who *still treat* people in *rural areas* (1), the *church ought to* understand traditional healers fully before condemning them (1), contemporary understanding of herbalists is that *they are not scientific* (1), herbalists are *assumed to be witches* (1), *science has failed to acknowledge* their knowledge of medicine (1), there are people who are well educated in *botany* and *use herbal extracts* to *treat chronic ailments* especially where *Western medicine* has failed (1), role of the herbalist *is beginning to be recognized* once again and people now have *more confidence in herbal medicine* (1), they are like any doctor today who is charged with the *well - being* of the community (1).

Role of Herbalists in the Community   (R = 20)
To treat both *physical and psychological* sicknesses (4), to *sustain life* through curing diseases (3), to keep the society *healthy* (3), are *African pharmacists* (1), to *give medicines* for sicknesses (1), have *special knowledge* which helps people to acquire local medicine (1), help the community to *deal with* certain forms of sicknesses (1), they *cooperate with God* in the well-being and good health of human beings (1), to *treat and guide* people (1), to *relieve pain and suffering inflicted by evil spirits* (1), to *keep in check* any disease that may afflict the health of the community (1), they *play a great role socially* in the community (1), they can *tell the cause* of an illness and avert it in future (1).

Relevance of the Theme of Herbalists   (R = 14)
Have a *great meaning* in the life of an individual and that of the community (4), *not relevant* to me or my community (3), many people in my community *still practice traditional healing* (1), are important because they are *life givers*

(1), the theme explains the *ability of bio-diversity in medicine* (1), my community believes so much in them and they *influence their lives* (1), *three of my family members were completely cured* by a *traditional healer* after *hospital treatments had failed* to cure them (1), they have an *exceptional role* as they heal taking into account that the *individual belongs to a family* and *a community* (1), the theme provides for both *vertical (in relation to ancestors and spirits) and horizontal (in relation to the community)* healing (1).

Definition of Herbalists (R = 23)
Are *special people* in the community who *understand diseases and can treat them using herbs* (11), are *herbalists, medicine men, diviners, rainmakers* and *all who positively contribute* to the community's life in a special way of healing (2), are those who are *consulted and heal sickness using traditional methods of healing* (1), are people who have *skills in identifying medicine* and treating certain specific traditional medicine (1), are persons *who treat* people in the village (1), are *African* diseases (2), they are persons who can *read people's illnesses and treat them* using *doctors* (1), are *ritual experts* who normally restored life to normalcy and *promoted abundance* of life (1), are *wise men* who know the *interconnection of elements in the universe* and understand how the *vital force works* (1), are *experts in the community* who have a *thorough knowledge* in understanding a number of diseases and providing the right treatment using *traditional medicine* (1), are people with *special gifts to treat illness* (1).

How One Becomes a Herbalist (R = 14)
Through *inheritance* (6), through *apprenticeship* (5), *given the power* of the trade *by God,* as He is the only one who knows the past, present and future (3).

Unique Qualities of Herbalists (R = 6)
There are *certain diseases that can only be treated by them* (1), *have cheaper rates in comparison with hospitals* (1), many of them are *credible* (1), have *spiritual power* to *understand and discern* what ordinary people may not discern (1), are *powerful and perhaps the greatest benefactors* of the community (1), their *medicines are effective* (1).

Types of Herbalists (R = 5)
Fake and genuine healers (2), *medicine men* (1), *rainmakers* (1), *diviners* (1).

Other Comments (R = 19)
Human life is *sacred, of paramount importance* and must be *safeguarded* (2), to my understanding traditional healers are *unprofessional as they lack a*

standard unit of measure in their prescriptions (1), *traditional healing is outdated* (1), I know of many people -who have been *helped by going to traditional healers* (1), I encourage anyone I know who wants to visit a traditional healer to seek the *services of a genuine one* (1), I *cannot disassociate myself* from relatives and friends who go to traditional healers (1), I *do not take herbal medicine* and therefore would not frequent a traditional healer's home (1), I believe that they *are not exposed* to many diseases and *can only cure a few*, thus they are *not well versed* with many diseases (1), I *do not believe* in what the traditional healers do and the way they practice their healing (1) there are *some herbs such as (mwarubaini) Neem tree* that *cure diseases more effectively than modern medicine* (1), traditional healers *should be encouraged and supported* in their fields to *compliment a government's efforts* to have better care for its citizens (1), *condemnation* of traditional healers *by missionaries* was not only unessential but unfair too (1), my father *knew many herbs* that were very helpful when we had attacks of malaria and bad stomachs (1), *at times traditional healers are misused* to harm others with their knowledge of herbal medicines (1) problems including *barrenness are believed to be caused by* the *curse of a witch* (1), *herbalists are just like any other doctors* so long as they are trained (1), through the *discouragement of missionaries*, African Christians were compelled to go to hospital for treatment (1), the *secret of the combination of medicines used by traditional healers* is only acquired by those closely related to them (1).

NON-AFRICAN RESPONDENTS N = 13
[The respondents answered both according to their
own culture and their understanding of African culture.]

Characteristics of Herbalists   (R = 4)
Use natural resources like plants, seeds and barks of trees (1), they *know well the properties of their medicines* through knowledge accumulated from generation after generation (1), *possess some kind of cultural knowledge* regarding sickness (1), most of them *do not possess written knowledge* of their profession (1).

Herbalists Today   (R = 6)
Herbalists are present in my culture and even my uncle was a well known herbalist (1), they *are physicians and nurses* who hold positions of respect in the society (1), the theme of traditional healers *is almost non-existent* in my community (1), there is *more of an emphasis on alternative medicine* and *healthy living through good diet and exercises* (1), it would be of great help if traditional healers *received support especially from the missionaries* (1), they are *represented by social workers and psychologists* (1).

Role of Herbalists in the Community (R = 4)

Are *mediators* between human beings and ancestors who are the link to creator God (1), he/she is *a specialist in herbal medicine* (1), involved in *treating* common ailments within the community (1) with the help of *roots and rituals, he/she recommends treatment* based on the diagnosis of the sickness (1).

Relevance of the Theme of Herbalists (R = 6)

They *embody knowledge* that is handed over *from one generation to the next* (1), they *make use of healing methods* that form part of the accumulated wisdom of a people (1), have no relevance to me or my community (1), play *a significant role* in societies where they are accepted (1), in my life, the theme *has a meaning and my appreciation* too (1), the theme is *important in African culture* (1).

Definition of Herbalists (R = 2)

Are *people trained in the art of healing*, usually by family mentors preceding them with years of experience (1), are *people who are knowledgeable on particular herbs* that can be used to cure certain physical or psychological ailments (1).

How One Becomes a Herbalist (R = 1)

The response: through *training* (1).

Other Comments (R = 9)

Unlike in African culture where herbalists are believed to have some kind of supernatural powers, *in my culture they are recognized* only as *people who know that certain herbs are effective for certain illnesses* (1), at times the *valuable knowledge that traditional healers embody* is *often distorted* by superstitious practices that creep in (1), in African culture a healer is different from my culture where *healers are medical doctors* (1), African healers use more *natural means of medication* such as herbs (1), *Jesus is a Christian's only mediator* and *advocate* with God (1), I do *not have an understanding* of traditional healers from my culture except that it *might be mostly based on myths and superstitions* (1), many *condemn* the theme of the traditional healer *without knowing or even understanding* it (1), I think of *a herbalist as a pharmacist* who prescribes herbal concoctions after a *diagnosis of the disease that has been made by a witchdoctor* (1), *herbalists exist in my community* back at home *but they remain suspect* in the view of the overall society (1).

SUMMARY
Beliefs expressed regarding Herbalists

<u>Herbalists are</u>: *special people* in the community who *understand diseases* and can treat them using *herbs, have good knowledge of using herbs for treatment and in performing cultural ceremonies, medicine men, diviners, rainmakers, African doctors, ritual experts,* those *consulted* and heal sickness using *traditional methods* of healing, who have *skills in identifying medicine* and treating some *specific diseases,* who can *read* people's illnesses and treat them using *traditional medicine, experts* in the community who have a thorough knowledge in understanding a number of diseases and providing *the right treatment* using traditional medicine, those with *special gifts* to treat illnesses.

<u>Characteristics of Herbalists</u>: they *use locally available and natural* herbs, *diagnose and cure* illnesses and misfortunes, are *highly respected, ritual experts, spiritual directors,* have *exceptional skills* in healing, *good diagnostic* skills, *supernatural powers, cultural knowledge* regarding sickness, keep the *combination of their medicines a secret* so as to maintain its sacredness, *pass down the knowledge* of their practice to their children through *training,* offer their services *freely* to all, they may *invoke mystic* powers as part of the treatment, *know well the properties* of their medicines through knowledge *accumulated* through generations, most of them *do not possess written* knowledge of their profession.

<u>Role of Herbalists in the Community</u>: *treat* physical as well as psychological diseases, *sustain life* through curing, keep the society *healthy, treat and guide* people in the community, *relieve* pain and suffering caused by *evil spirits, recommend* treatment based on the diagnosis, are *African pharmacists, mediators* between human beings, the spiritual world and creator God.

<u>Relevance of the Theme of Herbalists</u>: to *explain* the ability of bio-diversity in medicine, *influence* people's lives, *cure* people. They *heal* taking into account that the individual belongs to a family and a community, *provide* for vertical healing in relation to the ancestors and horizontal healing in relation to the community, *embody knowledge* that is passed on from one generation to the next, *make use* of healing methods that form part of the accumulated wisdom of a people.

<u>How One Becomes a Herbalist</u>: through *inheritance, apprenticeship, training, power from God.*

<u>Unique Qualities of Herbalists</u>: they *treat* some diseases that modern medicine is not able to, have *cheaper rates* in comparison to modern medical establishments, most of them are *credible, combine spiritual powers as well as knowledge* of herbs to treat the sick, their *medicines are effective with few side effects.*

<u>**Types of Herbalists**</u>: *medicine men, rainmakers, diviners.*

<u>**Herbalists Today**</u>: are *physicians and nurses, practitioners* of alternative medicine, *social workers and psychologists, counselors, influential* in the society today, somewhat *overlooked* despite the fact that they played a big role in the society before the advent of modern medicine, like *chemists* for they deal with diagnosis and administering medicine to the sick, *people who are well-educated* in botany the use of herbal extracts to treat chronic ailments especially where Western medicine has failed, some are *commercially oriented*.

RESPONSES FROM WORKSHEETS

[Note that the power of the herbalist is derived from the belief that all evil is personalized i.e., caused by someone. Hence the herbalist can ward off evil by a combination of medicines and rituals that are not only scientific and psychosomatic but also effective against evil doers. The end result is that persons are healed and restored to health.]

❑ **Kindly explain in detail your understanding of the theme of HERBALIST. What is its contemporary meaning in your personal, social and community life?**

AFRICAN RESPONDENTS   N = 61

[There were eighteen ethnic groups represented; Luo (14), Agikuyu (12), Abaluyia (9), Akamba (6), Abagusii (3), Tutsi (3), Kategi (2), Teso (2), Bemba (1), Banyankole (1), Arusha-Meru (1), Baganda (1), Ibo (1), Aembu (1), Dinka (1), Kipsigis (1), Akan (1), Tigrinya (1). The respondents were university graduates; eighteen women and forty-three men.]

- The traditional healers in my own understanding include herbalists, medicine men, diviners, rainmakers and all those who positively contribute to the community's life in a special way of healing. They have a great meaning in an individual's life and the life of the community. (Akamba)
- To my understanding, traditional healers are unprofessional. They lack a standard unit of measure in their prescriptions. The act of traditional healing is also outdated. Traditional healing does not have much meaning in my personal life. However many people in the society and my community (Agikuyu) still practice traditional healing. (Agikuyu)
- Traditional healers are those who are consulted and heal sickness using traditional methods of healing. They have a meaning in my life because they are important in my personal, social and community life. (Luo)
- These are people who use natural medicines to heal the sick. I see them as important because they are life givers. They do not promote division or misunderstanding in the community because they do not look at the causes of the sickness and where it comes from. (Bemba)
- I know many people who have been helped by going to traditional healers. I have no doubt that their medicines are effective. I also know there are some who are not genuine. If anyone I know feels that he will
  get better by going to see a traditional healer I encourage him or her but tell them to look for a good one. (Abaluyia)

- Traditional healers have a lot of meaning. There are certain diseases that only traditional healers can treat. (Luo)
- Traditional healers have no influence on my personal life. Socially they are becoming quite influential in the society, though many are commercially minded these days. In community life, they have not been influential. (Agikuyu)
- Traditional healers are African pharmacists, known as herbalists. These are the people charged with the curative role of the people in the community. This theme holds a lot of meaning to my community, for it provides for the sustenance of life through the curing of diseases. To me this theme explains the ability of bio-diversity in medicine. (Abaluyia)
- Traditional healers are special people in the community who understand diseases and can treat using herbs. They can also be able to tell the cause of an illness and how to avert it in future. Usually the knowledge can be inherited or learned through training. (Agikuyu)
- Traditional healers are people who have special skills in identifying medicine and treating certain specific diseases. It does not really affect my life so much as I have never consulted them. My community believes so much in them and they influence their lives. (Luo)
- Traditional healers or herbalists are medicine men who use herbs to cure or heal certain sicknesses. They train their children who later inherit their work. They were highly respected in the community. (Luo)
- Traditional healers are people who give medicine for illness and sicknesses. It has meaning to community and social life because I cannot disassociate myself from my relatives and friends who go to traditional healers. I personally do not take herbal medicine and would therefore not frequent a traditional healer's home. (Abaluyia)
- Currently it does not have a meaning in my life because I believe that they are not exposed to many diseases and can only cure few. So they are not well versed with many diseases. (Luo)
- Traditional healers are extremely important in the society because some people have the ability to harm others through magic. My family members (three of them) were completely cured of their illnesses by traditional healers after hospital treatments had failed. (Arusha-Meru)
- Traditional healers are persons who can read people's illnesses and treat them using traditional medicine. They are important people to the community because they treat some illnesses, which occasionally herbalists cannot. (Abaluyia)
- A traditional healer is someone who treats people in the village and is always identified that when people are sick they must go to him. He is the African doctor. (Kategi)

- Traditional healing is a method in which special people use herbs and cultural practices to try to cure even the most chronic diseases. (Akamba)
- For me there is not much meaning because my belief in what they do and the way they practice their healing is that it is never true. I always doubt what they say and do. (Baganda)
- They are an important group of any African society who ensure the vital force of life is maintained. Their role strictly touches on healing and not divination and their power is God-given (Luo)
- They have a special knowledge, which helps people to acquire local medicine. They have cheaper rates and help the community to deal with certain forms of sicknesses. (Akamba)
- The traditional healers were and still are respected in my community. I respect and appreciate them. They cooperate with God in the well-being and good health of human beings. (Ibo)
- Traditional healers have an exceptional role because they heal taking into account that the individual belongs to a family and community. It provides for both vertical (in relation to ancestors and spirits) and horizontal (in relation to the community) healing. (Luo)
- These are ritual experts who normally restored life to normalcy and they promoted the abundance of life. (Aembu)
- Traditional healers played a very big role in healing people before [the advent of] modern medicine even if they are somehow overlooked today. (Tutsi)
- Traditional healers are very important in my community and they have a lot of meaning. People go to them for treatment and guidance. (Akamba)
- We as Luo community believe in vital forces. Because of that, I personally believe that the traditional healers play a great role socially in the community. (Luo)
- A traditional healer is one with the knowledge of herbal medicine. It has a meaning to me because there are some herbs that cure diseases more effectively than modern medicine. For example, the **Neem** tree can cure more than forty diseases. (Teso)
- Traditional healers are of importance to the society. They need to be studied and institutionalized for the betterment of the modern society. (Dinka)
- Traditional healers are relevant and effective today. (Agikuyu)
- There is a great regard for traditional healers in my personal, social and community life because healing relieves us of pain and suffering inflicted upon us by evil spirits. (Abaluyia)
- Traditional healers are people with skills. They claim to have been called into this profession by God and they inherit this knowledge from their fathers and grandparents which they exercise in the community and pass to others freely. Besides sickness, they can cure misfortunes. They claim to

know and can cure misfortune because they have supernatural powers from God. They should be encouraged and supported in their fields to compliment the government offer to have better health care for its citizens. Many are credible and the church should understand them fully. (Teso)

- Traditional healers are people with special powers in the use of herbs for treatment. In most cases they inherit the power from the older generation but one can also learn through apprenticeship. They are like chemists for they deal with diagnosis and administering of medicine. (Agikuyu)

- Traditional healers are as important today as they were long ago. The condemnation by the missionaries was not only unessential but also unfair. The society at large needs to recognize their importance, hence be allowed to continue with their work. (Agikuyu)

- Traditional healers are wise men that know the interconnection of the elements in the universe and understand how the vital force works. They are powerful people and perhaps the greatest benefactors of the community. They keep the society healthy. (Luo)

- They are important as they treat both physical and psychological sicknesses. (Luo)

- I am sixty-seven years old but I have no idea of who these are and how they cure, although I am aware of the herbalists. My father knew many herbs that were helpful when we had attacks of malaria and bad stomach [ache]. Thus I am not sure whether traditional healers and herbalists are the same. (Banyankole)

- Traditional healers are those experts in the community who have a thorough knowledge in understanding a number of diseases and providing the right treatment using traditional medicine. They have a great meaning in the Kipsigis community. (Kipsigis)

- These are ritual experts, vested with the role of restoring and promoting abundant life in the community. (Abagusii)

- Traditional healers are people with special gifts to treat illnesses. They are also spiritual leaders as they discern God's guidance on diagnosis and treatment. (Abagusii)

- Herbalists contribute to healing through the provision of herbs to the sick. Today, herbalists are the medical doctors in hospitals. There are also traditional herbalists who still treat people in the rural areas. (Abaluyia)

- Contemporary understanding of herbalists is that they are not scientific. However, they have the art of diagnosing ailments and administering herbs. Science has failed to acknowledge their knowledge of medicine. (Abaluyia)

- A herbalist is that person in the community who has good knowledge of herbs to be used to ease various discomforts community members have. From my experience of interviewing herbalists, I learned that they also have extra powers (call them spiritual powers) to understand and discern what ordinary people might not discern. They must have good diagnostic assessment skills to tell which medicines to give for what. They also must know how to do a good and accurate diagnosis. (Abaluyia)

- Herbalists are traditional healers. At times, they are misused and harm others with their knowledge of herbal medicines. (Abagusii)
- The contemporary society seems to value the role of a herbalist. There are some sicknesses that herbal medicine has proved to be very effective in curing without any side effects. The problem however is telling a genuine herbalist from a fake one. (Agikuyu)
- Herbalists take care of psychosomatic problems. Life, regardless of whether it is personal, social or communal, is sacred. Today, we have courts to prosecute all murderers. However, life is at stake these days. (Agikuyu)
- I have never been to a herbalist personally, but in my community, people believe that the herbalist or the diviner is given the power of his trade by God. He is the only one who knows the future, the present and the past. (Tutsi)
- Herbalists are traditional healers in our community who treat people using herbs. They have some important skills and are specialists in treating different ailments. In my personal, social and community life, I would say herbalists differ from one another. They use locally available herbs to treat various diseases. If a herbalist does not harm, he/she is regarded as important in the community. (Luo)
- Herbalists are people who are knowledgeable in administering herbal treatment to the sick, weak and women who are barren. (Kategi)
- A herbalist is a person who has a distinct knowledge of using herbs for treatment and performing cultural ceremonies. Some of the herbalists do not charge for the services they offer. (Akamba)
- A herbalist is somebody who cures diseases using herbs. Herbalists are still active today and are still treating various ailments using herbs. (Tutsi)
- The herbalist helps keep in check any disease that may afflict a community's health. In contemporary society, herbalists are assumed to be witches. (Agikuyu)
- Herbalists give treatment to the sick or those suffering from various problems. These problems can either be physical, mental or psychological. These problems, including barrenness, are seen to be caused by the curse of a witch. Herbalists are just like the other doctors as long as they are trained in their work. (Akamba)
- A herbalist is a traditional doctor who treats common ailments using herbs. This meaning remains the same in the contemporary situation

although through discouragement by missionaries, the African of Christian faith is compelled to visit a hospital rather than a herbalist. (Luo)

- A herbalist is someone who has the gift of power to heal. They use herbs to cure/treat various forms of illness. (Akan)
- A herbalist deals with psychosomatic problems in the society. Human life is of paramount importance and must be safeguarded. I believe a herbalist is a doctor, a nurse and a counselor all in one. (Agikuyu)
- In the contemporary society, there are people who are well educated in botany and use herbal extracts to treat chronic ailments especially where western medicine has failed. (Agikuyu)
- Herbalists are healers in traditional African societies. They use herbs for treatment of various diseases. At times, herbalists invoke mystic powers as part of the treatment method. (Luo)
- These are people who have acquired healing skills through either inheritance or apprenticeship. They use local herbs to heal different illnesses. Today, the role of the herbalist is beginning to be recognized once again and people are now more confident in herbal medicine. (Agikuyu)
- A herbalist is that person who has acquired the art of using herbs to cure diseases. (Luo)
- Herbalists are like any doctor today who has a role in the well-being and health of the community. Today, we have these people as part of us. Their medicine has no side effects making them really respected as any doctor of medicine from Harvard University. (Abaluyia)
- These are people who are knowledgeable on particular herbs that can be used to cure certain physical or psychological human ailments. Herbalists are present in my culture. My late uncle was a well-known herbalist. However, unlike in [other] African cultures where herbalists are believed to have some kind of supernatural powers, in my culture, they are recognized only as people who know that certain herbs are effective for certain illnesses. (Tigrinya)

NON-AFRICAN RESPONDENTS   N = 13
*[The respondents answered both according to their
own culture and their understanding of African culture.]*

*[There were five non-African countries represented: America (7), India (3),
Spain (1), Italy (1), and Paraguay (1). The respondents were university
graduates, five women and eight men.]*

African Perspective
- In African culture, a healer is different from my culture where healers are medical doctors. African healers use more natural means of medication such as herbs. (American)
- I understand them to be essential in traditional Kenyan culture and religion. I understand them to be mediators between human beings and ancestors who are the link to creator God, and thus are most important to traditional culture. Jesus is a Christian's only mediator and advocate with God. (American)
- The theme of herbalist is important in African culture. This person, who may also be a diviner, is involved in treating common ailments within the community. With knowledge of roots and rituals, he/she recommends treatment, based on the diagnosis of the sickness. Herbalists do exist in my cultural community back at home, but they remain suspect in view of the overall society. (American)
- A herbalist is a key person in the community. He is a specialist in herbal medicine. Most of them possess no written knowledge of their profession. They are social workers and psychologists. Personally, I think of a herbalist as a pharmacist who prescribes herbal concoctions after diagnosis of the disease has been made by a witch doctor. (Italian)

Non-African Perspective
- Traditional healers are people trained in the art of healing, usually by family mentors preceding them with years of experience. They use the nature resources like plants, seeds and the barks of trees, and they know their properties well through knowledge accumulated from generation after generation. (Spaniard)
- Traditional healers embody knowledge that is handed over from one generation to the next. But this valuable knowledge often is distorted by superstitious practices that creep in. (Indian)
- Traditional healers make use of healing methods that form part of the accumulated wisdom of a people. They generally have no impact on my personal, social and community life. (American)

- My understanding of traditional healers [is that they] are physicians and nurses who hold positions of respect in the society. (American)
- I think traditional healers possess some kind of cultural knowledge regarding sickness and they play a significant role in the society where they are accepted. (Indian)
- It is nearly non-existent. However, there is more of an emphasis on alternative medicine and healthy living through good diet and exercise. This helps my personal, social and community life. (American)
- I do not have an understanding of them from my culture except to say that it might be mostly based on myth and superstition. (American)
- The traditional healer is a very positive one. It would be a great help to the community if they received support, especially from the missionaries. It happens that many people condemn it without knowing or understanding it. In my life, it has meaning and also my appreciation. (Paraguayan)
- The medicines given [by the traditional healers] for the sickness are known to be of mysterious origin. The combination of herbs is not revealed to all. Often it is kept as a trade secret. This also believed to keep up the sacredness of the medicine. This is only acquired by those closely related to the herbalist. (Indian)

EDITOR'S REFLECTIONS

All African communities have their herbalists who specialize in African traditional medicine in order to restore health to the community. They provide the community members with an effective and affordable alternative to Western medicine. Their medicines are from natural sources known to the users and often have little or no side effects. Some African herbalists are said to cure diseases that Western medicine has been unable to cure effectively e.g., breast cancer. There is strong evidence that for ordinary African people, African medicine and Western medicine co-exist as valid means of health and healing; if one is ineffective the other is sought.

DISCUSSION QUESTIONS

1. Why are the mainline Christian churches negative towards African herbalists, even though many of their members secretly go to them for health and healing?
2. Are the African herbalists similar or different from the alternative medicine practitioners of the Western world?
3. Is the healing by herbal medicine mostly psychosomatic or do the herbs have scientific medicinal potency?
4. Do you personally visit herbalists and take the medicine they prescribe?

AFRICAN ILLUSTRATION

AFRICAN AND WESTERN MEDICAL PRACTICES PERCEIVED AS ALTERNATIVE THERAPIES

An African student and her field assistant made an appointment with a herbalist in Ongata Rongai area of Nairobi to research his work and medicine. As they were waiting for the herbalist, the field assistant struck a conversation with one of the clients, a young woman who had brought in her child for check up. She said that the child had been having a cough that had persisted for over two weeks. She had taken the child to several government hospitals where Western medicines were prescribed. The child would stop coughing for a day or two and then the cough would reappear. So she was advised by a friend to bring the child to this herbalist. She did that and after the herbalist examined the child, he cut off the epiglottis and prescribed some herbs for the child to take. The child stopped coughing and was said to have recovered.

RECOMMENDED READINGS

Mbiti, J.S. (1991). *Introduction to African Religion.* (pp. 153-157). Nairobi: East African Educational Publishers.

Kokwaro, J.O. (1993). *Medicinal Plants of East Africa.* Nairobi: Kenya Literature Bureau.

Swantz, L. (1990). *The Medicine man Among the Zaramo of Dar Es Salaam.* Dar Es Salaam: Dar Es Salaam University Press.

NON-AFRICAN ILLUSTRATION

HERBAL MEDICINE FROM A WESTERN PERSPECTIVE

One of the common cancers for older men in the Western world is prostrate cancer. At this point there is no one therapy that is fully recommended. It can be treated either with radiation, drugs, surgery or, if the person is elderly, to leave it untreated. At the time of a general physical, a PSA test is done to see whether or not there is an elevated level of a chemical in the blood indicating a problem with the prostrate.

In a recent case, an older man found that his PSA was elevated, and instead of following his doctor's advice for treatment he took the advice of a friend, and went to a store selling herbal medicines. They sold him a specific herbal medicine that was made for lowering the PSA count. He took the medicine as recommended and two months later when he had his PSA tested by his regular doctor, it was found that the PSA level had dropped dramatically. The doctor was surprised. . . Herbal medicines are becoming more and more common in the Western world as well as alternative therapies such as acupuncture.

CHAPTER XII
Theme: DIVINER

DIVINER/MWAGUZI

The carving shows a diviner at work. He is using a horn as a means of calling up ancestral spirits in order to consult them on issues under consideration, and make their responses known to the living.

DIVINER

Introduction

All cultures worldwide have religious leaders, some of whom are charismatic and others functionary, who interpret for people life and death issues. These leaders come in a variety of styles such as pastors, priests, prophets, spiritual directors, sheikhs, etc.

African Diviners

The diviners of African cultures whether functional e.g., the priests of the royal shrines of Uganda, or the more familiar charismatic diviners of most of the ethnic groups of East Africa, are the priests, spiritual directors, counselors of African spirituality. This spirituality, expressed publicly in rituals and songs, is so profound and extensive that it touches all facets of a person's life. The men and women diviners are the mediums through which societies and individuals are able to ward off evils that threaten human life, so that it remains lively and vigorous according to the wisdom and lore of the ethnic group. They are the persons who walk with the living along the razor edge of life and give answers and consolation as one falls in and out of chaos.

Religious Leaders Elsewhere

All cultures have religious leaders who function, in fact, like the African diviners -- they are the counselors and teachers dealing with the ordinary and extraordinary issues of human life. There are the functional religious leaders and evangelizers of the Christian churches, the royal priests of the tribal societies, the divine-like figures such as the Dalai Lama of Tibet, the Moslem Sheikhs, the Hindu holy men, the prophets and seers of Chinese temples. All claim the ability to be able to listen to and/or enter into the spiritual world and make present the will of the spiritual powers to protect and enhance the life of their petitioners, and to answer the ultimate questions regarding the meaning of life and death.

QUESTION

Kindly explain in detail your understanding of the theme of DIVINER. Does it have any meaning in your personal, social and community life? Who functions in your life as a diviner? N = 78 (55 Africans, 23 non-Africans)

RESPONSES COLLATED BY SEVEN CATEGORIES

1. *Role of Diviner in Society R = 81*
2. *Definition of Diviner R = 32*
3. *Characteristics of a Diviner R = 31*
4. *Diviner in Modern Society R = 28*

5. *Relevance of the Theme of Diviner R = 26*
6. *When People Seek the Services of a Diviner R = 13*
7. *How One Becomes a Diviner R = 3*
Other Comments R = 16

AFRICAN RESPONDENTS N = 55

Role of Diviner in Society (R = 58)
Mediates between the *people and the spirit world* (9), *mediates between God and the people* (7), *predicts* future events (5), is the *moral guardian* of the society (5), offers *solutions to problems* (4), *restores harmony* in the society (3), *reverses the harm caused by witches* (3), is *a religious leader* (3), is *a healer* (3), ensures the *safety of the community* (2), *mediates* between the *living and the living dead* (2), acts as a *counselor* (2), is the *community's wise man* (2), *harmonizes* the happening of *events in the society* (1), *exorcizes evil spirits* (1), *performs rituals and rites* (1), would be *positively identified as prophets* as they hold people together (1), give *information and assurances in cases of misfortune* (1), *reveal secrets, possible dangers and their solutions* (1), offers *advice* (1), is *involved in the life of the community* (1).

Definition of a Diviner (R = 19)
Is able to *counteract the forces of evil* (2), the person to whom people turn when they want *to understand a mystery in life* (1), a *reconciler of the living with the living dead* (1), who *links the living with the ancestral/spirit world* (1), the *personification of good, abundant life and benevolence* (1), one who *foretells* events (1), who can *assist someone to understand life* (1), *finds out* what is going on in people's lives (1), who *tells things happening in one's life* and *gives reasons for these happenings* especially if they are *bad ones* (1), *gifted by God* to *find out and discover secrets* and *unknown things or activities* (1), *communicates* directly with the *spirit world* (1), has *special powers to comprehend the mysteries* that ordinary people do not understand, and *prescribes* how to deal with the puzzling situations in life (1), has *traditional powers* that he/she uses for the *betterment of the community* (1), *exercises the values and traditions* of African *religion* (1), is *able to help people identify the root cause of their problems* so as to overcome or cope with them (1), a *priest of African religion* and a *spiritual director* of his community (1), to whom *God gave the knowledge to act like a mediator* (1), is the person I find in my *relationship with an elderly* Luo man at home (1).

Characteristics of a Diviner (R = 24)
Is a *friend of the community* and *involved in all aspects of the community* (3), a *leader* (2), *knowledgeable in many fields* (2), can *provoke spirits and*

communicate with them (2), *respected* (2), can be *a herbalist* (2), an *elder* (2), *considered holy* since he/she is *used as an instrument* by *creator God or the living dead* (1), is *a ritual expert* (1), *promotes life* (1), relates to the *ancestors in spirit form and to the people in physical form* (1), has *powers that enable him/her to manipulate forces* and *penetrate the spirit world* (1), some are *genuine* others *fake* (1), is *gifted* (1), a *rainmaker* (1), can be *very young* (1).

Relevance of the Theme of Diviner   (R = 18)
Has *no relevance*/influence (8), I do *not believe* in diviners (2), *relevant [only]* in an individual's life (1), the theme shows the *mediatory role* between *God and the people* (1), he/she *occupies a central position in African culture today* (1), the *theme offers a way of knowing the hidden truth* (1), are *important* because through them *healing is accomplished* (1), *used to be more functional* in the old days than they are today (1), people *tended to believe* in them especially in *solving their problems* (1), today the *diviner is remotely important* as many *social problems* have found solutions in other contexts (1).

Diviner in the Modern Society   (R = 15)
Jesus has taken the place of the diviner in modern society (6), the *priest* has taken the role of the *diviner* as a *religious leader* in modern society (5), the *pastor* is the diviner in the present society (2), are becoming *non-existent* in present society (1), *no longer has a meaning* because of the introduction of *Christianity* (1).

When People Seek the Services of a Diviner   (R = 9)
In *times of problems* (3), times of *crisis* (1), when in need of *healing* (1), for *intervention* (1), in *extreme and unexplainable* circumstances (1), when *feeling disturbed* (1), [when] a person has *lost something* (1).

How One Becomes a Diviner   (R = 3)
Through *training* (1), one is *born with the skill* (1), through *inheriting* the powers of divination (1).

Other Comments   (R = 13)
[I] believe in the *creator God* rather than *diviners* (2), have *seen and know* the work of diviners (1), his/her work is *useful when it is applied in the correct way* (1), a diviner *positively contributes to development* (1), divination is *a positive force* (1), is a *mysterious field* and unless one is a diviner, the actual understanding of the works of divination will not be to the fullest (1), is *a gift from above* that was *not to be abused* as the *ancestors* could *rescind it in case of mischief* (1), if something goes wrong one has to visit someone *who can pray to*

correct the situation (1), *God* is the only *source of life and protection* (1), there are moments in life when the *intervention of a diviner is necessary* (1), would *not* go to a diviner (1), the community has *faith in them because they do not harm people* (1).

NON-AFRICAN RESPONDENTS N = 23
[The respondents answered both according to their
own cultures and their understanding of African culture.]

Role of Diviner in the Society (R = 23)
Mediates between *people* and the *spirit world* (5), helps *those in need* to find *solutions to difficult situations* (3), acts as *an intercessor* in times of *natural calamities/war* (3), *explains* the *causes of* problems/situations (2), is the *moral guide of the community* (2), *protector* (2), is the *spiritual guide* of the community (2), *social guide* (1), *counselor* (1), *advisor* (1), helps in the *continuity of life* (1).

Definition of a Diviner (R = 13)
Is *a person who has special contact* with the *spiritual world* and he *is able* to keep people *informed about their problems* (2), someone who can *explain* to you the *meaning of a situation* or things that would be *puzzling to the common individual* (2), one who *knows the right thing* for one to do (2), has *talents* that you *cannot get from book knowledge* (1), has *contact with the ancestors* (1), can *identify a problem, find its solution and solve it* (1), an *African functional* equivalent of a *counselor or spiritual director* (1), a *priest of African religion* who has already agreed to be *a medium for ancestral spirits* (1), can *communicate* with the *spirits because of a near death experience* (1), one who *plays tricks and tells lies* (1).

Characteristics of a Diviner (R = 7)
Resembles a *magician* (1), can be *either man or woman* (1), has the *interests of his people at heart* (1), will only *charge a minimal fee* for his *healing services* (1), can be a *herbalist* (1), *respected* (1), is an *expert in human relationships* (1).

Diviner in the Modern Society (R = 13)
The *priest* has taken over the services of the diviner in the modern society (2), can be compared with the *western counselors* (2), *church minister* functions as a diviner today (1), is the *pastor* (1), *modern doctor* (1), *spiritual director* in the community (1), *mother* (1), *friends* (1), [like] *literature in religious traditions* (1), is *someone who you trust* for various reasons such as his *age, experience*

and demonstration of great capability in particular situations (1), *fake diviners* nowadays have *a lot of power* within the community because *people are too busy making money* that they prefer to *pay someone* to give them *fast solutions to their problems* (1).

Relevance of the Theme of Diviner   (R = 8)
Has *no relevance* (5), makes the *ancestral will present* (1), helps *solve life's problems* (1), because they are *powerful in the community* (1).

When People Seek the Services of a Diviner (R = 4)
Consulted when *serious problems* arise (2), called when *things go wrong* to give *advice* to an individual or the community (1), when in need of *guidance* (1).

Other Comments   (R = 3)
Sometimes *selfish interests* affects the *positive role* of the diviner (1), though he does not have an influence on my personal life, he *was very important in the traditional community* of my forefathers (1), his *influence depends on different people* and the *power ascribed* to him by an individual (1).

SUMMARY
Beliefs expressed regarding the Diviner

A Diviner is: a *person,* who is *gifted* by God to *counteract the forces of evil, unravel* the *mysteries* of people's lives, is a *link* between the *living,* the *spirit world* and *God.* He/she uses his/her *powers* for the *betterment* of the *community,* is a *priest, leader, and spiritual director* of African religion, and can *identify* a *problem* and provide a *solution* for it. A person regarded as a diviner is a *friend* of the *community* as he/she is *involved* in *all aspects* of the *community, knowledgeable* in many fields, *promotes life,* and is a *ritual expert.*

Role of a Diviner in the Society Includes: *mediates* between *people, the spirit world and God.* He/she *restores harmony* in the society, *predicts* the future, *reverses* the harm caused by witches, *harmonizes* the happening of events in the society, *exorcizes* evil spirits, performs *rituals and rites, reverses* the harm caused by the witch, and offers *advice.* He/she is the *moral guardian, a religious leader,* and a *healer.*

Characteristics of a Diviner Include: he/she is a *leader, an elder, a ritual expert,* at times he/she is *a rainmaker, a herbalist* and is considered a *holy person.* The diviner *promotes life,* relates to the *living* in physical form and to the *ancestors* in *spirit form.*

Relevance of the Theme of Diviner: it shows the *mediatory role* played by the diviner between the people, ancestors and God, he/she occupies a central position in Africa today, it offers a way of knowing the *hidden truth,* and through them *healing* is accomplished.

Diviner in the Modern Society is: *Jesus, a priest, a pastor, and any religious leader.*

People Seek the Services of a Diviner: when *in need of healing, times of problems, seeking intervention,* and in *extreme and unexplainable circumstances.*

A Person Becomes a Diviner: through *inheritance, training or is born with the skills.*

RESPONSES FROM WORKSHEETS

[Note that in every society, there are mediums who are able to communicate with the spiritual world in order to foretell the future, unravel the mysteries of life, identify problems and provide solutions. In most African communities there are charismatic diviners who are able to communicate the will of the ancestors to the community. The diviners use instruments such as gourds, old coins, horns and cowry shells to interpret messages from the spiritual world.]

❑   Kindly explain in detail your understanding of the theme of DIVINER. Does it have any meaning in your personal, social and community life? Who functions in your life as a diviner?

AFRICAN RESPONDENTS   N = 55

[There were twelve ethnic groups represented: Agikuyu (14), Luo (13), Abaluyia (8), Akamba (5), Abagusii (4), Aembu (2), Kategi (2), Teso (2), Tutsi (2), Ibo (1), Kipsigis (1), and Akan (1). The respondents were university graduates, twenty-two women and thirty-three men.]

• A diviner is the person to whom people turn when they want to understand a mystery in life. As a Christian, I turn to God through Jesus Christ when there are things I do not understand. (Abaluyia)

• A diviner is a reconciler of the living dead. They restore harmony in society by removing evil caused by the witch. A diviner has no meaning in my personal or social life. God or Jesus functions in my life in place of a diviner. (Abaluyia)

• A diviner is a person who links the living with the ancestral spirit world. They are consulted in times of crisis either to heal or to help alleviate the problem being experienced. They reverse the harm caused by witches. (Agikuyu)

• The diviner is the personification of good, abundant life and benevolence. The theme of the diviner is quite meaningful to my life. Jesus functions as a diviner to me. (Aembu)

• A diviner is regarded as a mediator between God and the people. He influences the life of people by communicating God's message to the people and he also communicates people's petitions to God. (Luo)

• The diviner is an intermediary between spirits and human beings. He/she is a medium who gets in touch with the spirit world. A person who has disturbances or has lost something may consult a diviner. I have seen and I know diviners. (Teso)

- A diviner is a person who foretells events and is trained or born with the skill. They can act as herbalists as well. (Agikuyu)
- A diviner is a person who can assist me to understand life. (Luo)
- According to my own understanding, a diviner is one who helps people to understand the spirit that helps people in day-to-day living and gets rid of evil spirits. (Luo)
- My understanding of a diviner is that he/she connects the human world with that of the living dead. In recent times, diviners are becoming non-existent. The priest is the one who has taken this task. (Teso)
- The diviner was a religious leader. They were the mediums of ancestral spirits. They guided the moral aspects of life. Currently, I am a Catholic by denomination hence a priest now acts as an advisor in today's life. (Luo)
- I think a diviner's work is useful especially when it is applied in the correct way and positively contributes to development. (Akamba)
- A diviner is for predicting future events in the society. (Akamba)
- A diviner is a helper in time of need. He mediates between the ancestral spirits, God and the living people. The diviner is a positive force. He is consulted in times of problems. (Agikuyu)
- A diviner is a person who finds out what is going on in people's lives. Most Abagusii's believe that if something goes wrong, then you have to visit someone who can pray to correct the situation. In my life, if I suspect that something is wrong, then I pray to God. (Abagusii)
- A diviner tells you about things happening in your life and gives you reasons for these happenings especially if they are bad ones. Personally, I do not believe in them, and thus believe in God my creator. (Agikuyu)
- The diviner is a respected person in the society who intervenes between the living dead and the living. He/she is thus considered holy since he/she is used as an instrument by creator God or the living dead. A priest in the church acts as a diviner in my life. (Agikuyu)
- A diviner is a person gifted by God to find out and discover secrets and unknown things or activities. (Akamba)
- Diviner is a person whom people would run to in times of difficulties and is able to tell people the cause of the problem. Diviner has no meaning in my life because I see God as the only source of life and protector. (Ibo)
- Diviner is the person who communicates directly with the spirits e.g., interacting with the ancestors, seeking refuge from the ancestors, [and is a] facilitator between people and the ancestors. The diviner no longer has meaning because I have been introduced to Christianity, where Jesus is the mediator. (Kipsigis)

- The diviner is someone who intervenes in times of trouble. He/she tries to make things right and is knowledgeable in many fields. In my life the diviner is Jesus Christ who affects my life in various ways. When I seem not to be able to make decisions, I ask for His guidance and find solutions to whatever is troubling me. (Luo)

- The diviner makes the will of the ancestors and creator God known and done by the community. Christian priests remind us every now and then the will of God the creator, the moral values and keep the society in unity and helping each other. (Agikuyu)

- The theme of the diviner has some meaning, as the concept cannot exist without some truth in it. People must have experienced something like this and as such came up with the term. (Luo)

- A diviner has some meaning in my life although the concept is known better by my sister. (Tutsi)

- The theme shows [a] mediatory role between God and the people. The diviner helps the people to acknowledge their ignorance towards responsibility. Personally, I believe the diviner occupies a central place in African culture even today. (Agikuyu)

- The priest, the very social and stoic leader, the magician - - all describe my understanding of the diviner. In my life, my diviner is the very special and unique person I find in a relationship with an elderly Luo man back home. (Luo)

- Personally today, I do not believe in diviners. Since, when I started doing research in MIASMU, I have discovered several skills that they use. (Luo)

- A true diviner is equivalent to a modern, religious, spiritual priest. The priest and his bible is a diviner. He uses the bible as his tool for divination. (Abagusii)

- Divination is a mysterious field and unless one is a diviner, the actual understanding of the works of divination will not be to the fullest. (Agikuyu)

- According to 1 Samuel 28:8-16, the diviners are practicing evil things. Samuel could only consult her after God had departed from him. But if here the diviner means a priest, then a diviner has a meaning in my life. (Luo)

- Diviner is a wise man in the village who has wisdom. He can also provoke the spirits and communicate with them. (Kategi)

- Diviners would be positively understood as prophets as they hold people together and become the society's conscience. (Abaluyia)

- This is someone who has special powers to comprehend the mysteries that ordinary people do not understand and prescribes how to deal with puzzling situations in life. Personally, I would not go to a diviner but faced with a challenge in my life, I would go to my pastor, a counselor or someone with some understanding of what I am going through so that I can be helped. (Abaluyia)

- My understanding of the diviner is that unlike the witch, he is a friend of the community. He supplies information and assurance in case of misfortune, reveals secrets and possible dangers and solutions. He advises and counsels people in need. Up to now, I have not had a need for a diviner, so I do not know how far they would influence my own life. (Abagusii)

- The diviner is the community's wise man. He can predict what may happen to the family - good or bad. (Kategi)

- A diviner is a ritual expert, promoter of life, guardian of morality and an enemy of the witches. Currently it has no meaning in my life. (Aembu)

- Diviners are important because through them healing is accomplished and people get to know what is expected of them. The role of the diviner is important to the community life but personally I don't find them relevant. I [often] talk to a pastor who performs religious tasks for the sake of believers. (Agikuyu)

- The diviner determines the good of the community. He/she is a well wisher. He/she brings peace to my life when conditions are restored. (Agikuyu)

- A diviner is one who is able to counteract the powers of evil. I believe they played an active and significant role in the society. The community that I come from has faith in them since they do not harm people but are protectors of the society. (Luo)

- The diviner is the correction tool of the community. He/she relates to the ancestors in spirit form and to fellow human beings in physical terms, hence the term "mediator." (Agikuyu)

- The diviner is the medium between the physical and spiritual world. He is the high priest to be consulted during extreme and not easily explained difficulties. At a social level, he/she suggested/provided solutions to complex issues and made the community feel safe. (Agikuyu)

- A diviner in my view is someone who has "traditional" powers, which he/she uses for the betterment of the community. They are powers that enable them to manipulate forces and penetrate the ancestral/spirit world. Genuine diviners have meaning in my personal life because they are able to foretell what will happen to me in the future. (Luo)

- The diviner is a religious priest. He/she can give spiritual guidance on my personal, social and community life. (Abagusii)

- The theme of the diviner has a lot of meaning in my life as it offers a way of knowing the hidden truth. (Akamba)

- A diviner is one who exercises the values and traditions of African religion. They are religious leaders who act as priests. They perform rituals and rites that meet African needs. The diviner however, has no meaning in my personal, social or community life. (Luo)

- The diviner is one who is able to help people to identify the root cause of their problems so as to overcome them or cope with them. There are moments in my life when the intervention of a diviner is necessary. (Agikuyu)

- The diviner played a crucial role of doing away with uncertainties and solving problems in the society. The diviner today is remotely important given that many social problems have found solutions in other contexts. (Abaluyia)

- Diviners possess special powers to foretell the future and predict whether one will have good or bad luck. People respect such a gifted person. They are held [in] high esteem in the community. (Abaluyia)

- A diviner is a mediator between God and a community or God and a family. Traditionally, diviners used to be more functional than today and people tended to believe in them more, especially in solving problems. (Akamba)

- A diviner is not a witch but an instrumental person who harmonized the happenings of events in a society. It was a gift from above that was not to be abused as the ancestors could rescind it in case of mischief. (Abaluyia)

- A diviner is a person with skills and abilities to neutralize the harm caused by the witch. (Tutsi)

- A diviner is a priest of African religion and a spiritual director of his community. He can be an elder, a leader, a rainmaker, etc. He is involved in all the aspects of the community, social and personal life of the people. The theme thus has lots of meaning in my personal life. (Luo)

- A diviner is the healer of his people. By the use of herbs and performance of rituals, he administers healing among his people. He is the intermediary between the people and the spirit world - the ancestors, the living dead and God the creator. He is deeply involved in the personal, social and community life of the people. He is deeply respected and loved in the community. He can be young or very old. Usually, a diviner's powers are inherited. A grandfather would pass the powers to the grandchildren. The theme has no relevance in my life whatsoever. (Abaluyia)

- A diviner was a person to whom God gave the knowledge to act like a mediator between man and his creator, heal people from sickness and solve their problems, etc. The diviner has no influence on my personal life. (Agikuyu)

- A diviner helps control the moral life of the people. I have learned to believe that a diviner helps in the continuity of life, but sometimes selfish interests affects his positive roles. (Akan)

NON-AFRICAN RESPONDENTS N = 23
*[The respondents answered both according to their
own cultures and their understanding of African culture.]*

*[There were seven non-African countries represented: America (14), Norway
(4), Poland (1), Ireland (1), Indonesia (1), Italy (1), and Spain (1). The
respondents were university graduates, fifteen women and eight men.]*

African Perspective
- A diviner is the person who has special contact with the spiritual world and who is able to keep people informed about their problems. A diviner is an African functional equivalent to a counselor or spiritual director. This role has a great meaning for me since I am a psychologist. (American)
- The diviner is a priest of African religion who has already agreed to be a medium for ancestral spirits. They make the ancestral will present. They are usually consulted when serious problems arise. You can compare them with western counselors. (Norwegian)
- The diviners acted as mediators between the ancestors and the living in African cultures. They were highly regarded and were sought out in many circumstances. (American)
- A diviner is the one who has contacts with the ancestors. In this way he passes information from the ancestors to us. He can explain the causes of our troubles and give advices of what to do. In my culture, we do not have diviners as such, but for me my diviner was my mother. (Polish)
- A diviner is a person who can identify a problem, find out its solution and solve it. He protects people from witchcraft and evil spirits. He can assist people in times of personal crisis e.g., barrenness in the case of a woman. In community life, he can intercede in times of famine, disease outbreak and during war. He has the interest of his people at heart and will only charge a minimum fee for his healing services. He could be a herbalist. Though he doesn't have any influence on my personal life, he was very important in the traditional community of my forefathers. (American)

Non-African Perspective
- A diviner is someone who plays tricks and tells lies. It has no meaning for me. (Norwegian)
- A diviner is somebody who has talents that you cannot get from book knowledge. (Norwegian)
- The diviner is in touch with the spirits and interprets the will of the ancestors for the community. In my culture, I use the priest as the diviner. (American)

- A diviner normally works like a magician. They can be men or women. They deal with the question of finding out why something has gone wrong. The diviner has no meaning for my personal, social and community life. (Norwegian)
- If the diviner is a priest or a spiritual director, then his role is essential for good spiritual health. (American)
- The diviner is the one who is called when things go wrong to give advice to an individual or community. He/she is taken as a good counselor, spiritual or a wise mentor. (American)
- In my present life, a spiritual director would be the closest [person] known as a diviner. I can share my experiences of life with the spiritual director and notice where God is in that experience and where God is calling me. (American)
- A diviner is a spiritual and social guide of the community. Everyone has some spiritual guide. My friends are all diviners and so is literature in religious traditions. (American)
- A diviner is one who knows what is the right thing to do for me. He gives the best advice for my spiritual life. (Irish)
- My pastor, friends and myself; we all serve as diviners by offering spiritual advice. (American)
- The diviner is somebody who knows. He/she is in contact with the ancestors, so they orientate, counsel and help. They are experts in human relationships. (Spaniard)
- A diviner is someone who can communicate with the spirits because of a near death experience. People visit the diviner for guidance. This is the function of a counselor or doctor in my society. My diviner is a minister. (American)
- The diviner is the medium between the present world and the life hereafter. The diviner helps a person sort out life issues. The diviner in my life is a pastor at a church who offers spiritual guidance. (American)
- A diviner does not have any meaning in my life and in the community because I don't see the values that bring meaning. (Indonesian)
- The diviner is the one who is "connected" to the spirit world as well as keenly observant in this world. These connections give wise counsel in solving life problems. In my personal life, I have at times been in the role of divining and I have therefore been used as a diviner. (American)
- Diviners are powerful people in the community who can direct people in times of trouble or confusion. They are respected for their role in communication with the spirit world and then informing our world of what is happening. (American)
- The diviner is someone who can explain to you the meaning of a situation or things that would be puzzling to the common individual. Someone that

you trust for different reasons e.g., because he is older than you, has more experience and has demonstrated great capability in particular situations etc. It depends on the people's beliefs and the power given to a diviner to influence your life. The diviners (or the fake wizard) nowadays has a lot of power within my community because people are too busy working and making money and have failed to give attention to themselves and the environment. Consequently, they prefer to pay someone else to give them fast solutions to their problems. (Italian)

- The diviner is someone who is able to explain to you the meaning of something that you cannot explain. (American)

EDITOR'S REFLECTIONS

Diviner, a religious, spiritual and charismatic leader, still plays an important role in African cultures. The diviner is a powerful figure in Africa whose services are recognized and understood by African people. They are like the very astute spiritual directors of the Christian religion, and claim the ability to enter into the ancestral world -- they have a presence in both worlds. There is no doubt in people's minds of their powers or the cosmic vision underlying them. Whenever people are faced with spiritual or medical problems, especially those that cannot be resolved by Christianity or Western medicine, they engage diviners to unravel the mystery. Diviners are so influential that even those who are known to be staunch Christians will turn to them for help in secrecy, mostly under the cover of darkness. Some African politicians are said to rely on the mystical powers of the diviners to win elections. In 2003 in Sirisia constituency in Western Kenya, an election was nullified due to accusations of using rituals of divination to win.

DISCUSSION QUESTIONS

1. Despite the large number of Christians who openly preach against divination as diabolic, why are diviners still alive and active on all levels of African societies ? Explain.
2. Are diviners the priests of African religion? Explain your answer.
3. What do you think of a Christian who regularly consults a diviner when Western medicine fails to solve a particular medical problem?
4. Do you have a personal relationship with someone who functions as your diviner/spiritual director? Explain.

AFRICAN ILLUSTRATION

TABOOS CONCERNING DIVINERS

A Kenyan member of parliament died in 2003 on his way to his constituency. He was accompanied by a diviner who was to perform rituals at his home before he hosted a party for his constituents. Items normally used for divination among the Akamba were found in a traveler's bag at the accident scene. Apparently, according to Akamba traditions, some diviners are not supposed to step in water when going to perform a divination. If he/she steps in water, then misfortune will befall him/her. This is because it is believed that if he/she stepped in water, his/her powers would be drawn into the river leaving him/her powerless. Thus it I believed that the death of the member of parliament was as a result of the diviner not being able to come out of vehicle because of the restrictions placed on her by the person who initiated her into divination.

RECOMMENDED READINGS

Zahan, D. (1979). *The Religion, Spirituality and Thought of Traditional Africa.* (pp. 81-91). Chicago: University of Chicago Press.

Turner, V.W. 91985). Religious Specialists. In Lehman A.C. & Myers, J. E. *Magic, Witchcraft and Religion.* (pp. 85-92). Mountain View, California: Mayfield Publishing Company.

Ray, B.C. (1976). *African Religions: Symbol, Ritual and Community.* (pp. 102-130). Englewood Cliffs, New Jersey: Prentice-Hall Inc.

NON-AFRICAN ILLUSTRATION

CHRISTIAN ILLUSTRATION OF THE TRANSMISSION OF GOD'S DIVINE POWERS THROUGH A HUMAN MEDIUM

In the Catholic church a person is only declared a Saint if there are several authenticated miracles, usually medical recoveries, that are unexplained by human and scientific knowledge. The power of God therefore is manifested in the direct intercession of the sanctified person e.g., Saint Padre Pio.

CHAPTER XIII
Theme: WITCH

WITCH/MCHAWI

The distorted human-like figure pictured above with a horn growing out of the head and the eyes becoming ears is called a witch. This is the effect of his/her total and complete perversion. Such a person is no longer seen as human.

WITCH

Introduction

From the beginning of time, religious traditions worldwide have been attempting to understand the nature of evil both moral and cosmic. No tradition has been able to produce a totally satisfying answer. Some traditions go to the extent of perceiving two gods, one evil and one good, and others, such as Buddhism, say that evil is an illusion and beyond human comprehension. However, all cultures have to deal with the problem of evil, and most have a personal symbol of evil as a representation of total perversion, such as the African witch. The Christian and Islamic personal symbol of evil is a totally corrupt spirit commonly called the devil or Satan.

Witch in Africa

According to African thought, the world should be ordered and harmonious as it is the work of the creator God. However, this is not the reality. There is disharmony and evil that constantly threatens the lives of the lineal families, socially and personally, physically and spiritually. The answer to this problem is found in an African theology which states that evil comes from within the human heart (or liver if a Luo) whether living or ancestral. Furthermore, the image of the totally evil person is that of the witch, the one running naked at night with fire coming from the mouth. Such a person is considered so perverted that he/she is no longer a human being and if caught, is killed (a not uncommon story in the daily newspapers of Kenya). Moreover, since everybody is capable of evil, everybody is potentially a witch. The witch therefore, is "you who are immoral"- - a very powerful and sophisticated moral theology. This theology extends to everything that threatens to destroy or interrupt life, including storms and famines together with all evil actions. In fact, when evil strikes a lineal family, it triggers in the minds of the adults that there is some immorality, whether personal or social, that is causing it. Consequently, diviners are engaged to find the source of the evil in order to counteract it.

Witch Elsewhere

Again, all living cultures are faced with the problem of evil and offer various and sundry answers trying to explain it. Some anthropologists call the problem of evil the nightmare of all religious traditions. No religious tradition, including Christianity and Islam, has a simple and a totally satisfying answer to this problem. Some cultures make distinctions between "natural" evils caused by storms and lightening, and moral evils caused by human actions, that are seen as sinful. Others deny the existence of "natural" evils and focus on those attributed to human actions. In real time, everybody is personally challenged to make some sense out of the evils that impinge on their daily lives, and ultimately culminate in physical death.

QUESTION
In terms of African cultural knowledge, what is your understanding of the theme of WITCH? N = 76 (58 Africans, 18 non-Africans)

RESPONSES COLLATED BY SEVEN CATEGORIES
1. *Characteristics of a Witch* R = 55
2. *Definition of a Witch* R = 39
3. *Social Control of a Witch* R = 28
4. *Impact of a Witch on Society* R = 27
5. *Where a Witch is Found* R = 26
6. *How one Becomes a Witch* R = 9
7. *Other Effects of a Witch* R = 4

AFRICAN RESPONDENTS N = 58

Characteristics of a Witch (R = 49)
Is *fearful* (6), *kills people* (5), *runs naked at night* (5), has *superhuman/ mystical powers* (4), *anti-life* (4), *jealous* (4), *destroyer* (3), has *bad/evil eye* (3), always *a woman* (2), has a *grotesque appearance* (2), causes *harm to others* (2), *inhuman* (2), *evil hearted* (2), always *a man* (1), *hated by all* (1), uses *bones, seeds* and other items *to harm others* (1), *anti-social* (1), *becomes an evil spirit at death* (1).

Definition of a Witch (R = 25)
Is *an evil person* (11), one who *propagates evil* (4), *does not live in accordance with societal rules* (3), a *representation of evil/immorality* (3), a person *harboring ill feelings/thoughts* towards others (2), uses *different methods to harm others intentionally* (1), an *evil spirit that exists in the community* (1).

Social Control of a Witch (R = 23)
Killing them in a painful manner such as *lynching, or rolling them, tied to a beehive, down a waterfall and left to be eaten by crocodiles* (6), *ostracizing* them from the community (6), by *leading a moral life* (3), is *counterbalanced by the witchdoctor* (2), through *cleansing rituals and ceremonies* (2), *denouncing* the practice in the society (2), *by punishment* (1), *not naming the newborn after a witch* (1).

Impact of a Witch on Society (R = 23)
Is an *agent of social control* (5), causes *misfortunes and calamities* such as *death, insanity and sickness* to an individual and the society as a whole (5), causes *disharmony* (5), is *an indicator of the immorality of people in the society* (2), *threatens life* (2), *spreads evil spirits to people* (1), is *associated*

with animals such as a black cat and the owl (1), the *family* of the witch is *feared and ostracized as one cannot marry or be married to a member* of such a family (1), it is *a bad omen to meet a witch in the morning* (1).

Where a Witch is Found   (R = 11)
In each one of us (11).

How one Becomes a Witch   (R = 7)
By *doing evil to others* (1), *failure to control evil* that *emanates from one's heart* (1), through *marriage to a member of a family of witches* (1), being *born by a parent/family of witches* (1), having *bad blood* (1), being *used by the devil to adversely affect people's lives* (1), as a result of a *curse* (1).

Other Effects of a Witch   (R = 4)
Controls the morals of individuals as well as the community (1), sometimes helps to *solve problems that are considered to be difficult* (1), *can be engaged to counteract the power of other witches* (1), helps some members of the society to *climb up the ladder of economic success* (1).

NON-AFRICAN RESPONDENTS   N = 18
[The respondents answered according to their understanding of African culture.]

Characteristics of a Witch   (R = 6)
Runs naked at night (2), living *immorally* (1), has *evil intentions* (1), *fearful* (1), *not trustworthy* as they are *intrinsically evil* (1).

Definition of a Witch   (R = 14)
Anyone who harms or does evil to others (5), one *who acts in a perverted manner* (3), *symbol of evil and immorality* (3), is the *African answer to the problem of evil* in our lives (1), the *explanation* for some of the evil that has happened among us (1), are *people who are lacking in love* (1).

Social Control of a Witch   (R = 5)
By *killing* (1), *ostracizing* them (1), *getting rid of the desire to do evil* (1), *Christianity* (1), they are *held in check by creative and life-giving forces in the human heart* (1).

Impact of a Witch on Society   (R = 4)
Can *cause bad things to happen to the family* (1), *warn us of what we are capable of doing or being* (1), *harms* other people (1), *destroys relationships* (1).

Where a Witch is Found   (R = 15)
Within human beings (15).

How One Becomes a Witch   (R = 2)
Having *ill intentions/thoughts towards others* (1), doing *evil repeatedly* (1).

SUMMARY
Beliefs expressed regarding the Witch

A Witch is: a *human being* who is *totally evil, immoral, untrustworthy, who runs naked at night, has superhuman and mystical powers* and *does not live in accordance with societal rules.*

A Witch's Activities Include: to *harm* people, *bring misfortunes, calamities, disharmony, to threaten life,* and is often associated with a *black cat.*

A Witch is Controlled through: *painful killing, ostracizing him/her* from the society, by the witch being encouraged to *lead a moral life,* by the *witchdoctor (diviner)* through *cleansing ceremonies* and by *punishment.* The practices of witches are discouraged by *denunciation,* and by *not naming a newborn after a witch.*

A Person can Become a Witch through: *doing evil to others, failing to control the evil that emanates from the heart, marrying into a family of witches, being born in a family of witches, having bad blood, a result of a curse,* and by *being used by the devil* to adversely affect other people's lives.

Other Effects of a Witch Include: at times *controls* the morals of individuals and the community, sometimes *helps to solve difficult problems, helps* some members of the society to *climb up the ladder of success,* and *can be engaged to counteract the power of other witches.*

RESPONSES FROM WORKSHEETS

[Note that the understanding and resolution of the problem of evil is the central task for all religious traditions worldwide. The question posed: Why is humanity involved with and confronted by evil of all types and manner both cosmic and moral? In African cultures, the witch, the personification of evil, is considered so corrupt as to no longer be a human being and therefore is killed if caught. The witch is African religion's equivalent to the Christian and Islamic cosmic, non-human principle of evil called the devil/Satan/Beelzebub -- an unknown actor in African religion.]

❑   In terms of African cultural knowledge, what is your understanding of the theme of WITCH?

AFRICAN RESPONDENTS   N = 58

[There were twelve ethnic groups of Africa represented: Agikuyu (16), Luo (12), Abaluyia (9), Akamba (5), Abagusii (4), Tutsi (3), Aembu (2), Teso (2), Akan (2), Kipsigis (1), Bemba (1), Tigrinya (1). The respondents were university graduates, twenty-six women and thirty-two men.]

- The witch is within each one of us, simply dormant and any bad feelings towards the neighbor, friend or family can/could trigger it to reality. Africans never die without a cause, so they say. People do harm to others when they cease to love their fellow beings and especially close related kin. (Abaluyia)
- A witch is someone who uses different methods to harm in different ways other human beings even without having any differences. (Akamba)
- The witch is a common person in the African context. Witchcraft as practiced is indispensable in the notion of religion, spirits, etc. It is part and parcel of the Africans but as a negative aspect. (Akamba)
- Where I come from, a witch is the source of evil. Animals like black cats are always associated to that [a witch] so are birds like an owl. The punishment or the best way of bringing harmony in our society is by getting rid of these sources of evil by killing them and letting them die a painful death. (Bemba)
- The witch is the evil that exists within us. Because of our human weaknesses, a certain part of us is evil e.g., we desire things that do not belong to us and sometimes these desires push us into situations that make us create harm to others and ourselves. Therefore this wickedness or evil is referred to as being a witch. (Luo)
- In terms of African cultural knowledge, a witch is a person who does evil to other people intentionally. If you met a witch in the morning it was a bad

omen. He/she practices witchcraft and makes people die. It is believed that normal people could not visit a witch without a "bad motive." (Agikuyu)

- The witch is evil and associated with bad things in the society. For example, causing misfortunes like death of a person, being insane, and sickness. This was highly discouraged because it does not bring progress in any way. This was and still is a source of fear because if a witch is identified in a certain family, then that family is feared and isolated. This will make them uncomfortable in relating with other members of the society, and if there are daughters in that family they will not be married. This is the same case with sons from the family as they will not find ladies to marry. (Kipsigis)
- The witch among the Agikuyu is the propagator of evil. The witch is always a woman never a man. She is considered to be the source of evil in the community. In the local language she was known as *Murogi*. She personifies "dark forces." The witch is counter balanced by the witch doctor *Muganga* who works to undo the evil of the witch. (Agikuyu)
- The witch is an evil person who spreads terror and leaves death in his wake. He/she can be killed if caught and the society ostracizes the family of such a person. Cleansing rituals are done to cleanse the society of such evil. Witchcraft is an abhorred practice but it can never end, as there are evil people in our culture. (Abagusii)
- In my culture, the witch is out to spread evil spirits to people. It is said it is always a woman who is the witch. She causes evil to the people and the community at large. A *Muganga* has to be called upon to remove the evil caused by the witch. The *Muganga* is the witch doctor. (Agikuyu)
- A witch is hated and feared. A witch is considered an outcast and once it is known that a particular homestead has a witch, people in the village fear that home especially at night when they are said to carry out their activities. For the Iteso community, once a witch has been identified, he/she is burnt for they are causing disharmony in the community. (Teso)
- A witch is that person who is evil. The anatomy of a witch is a perversion of a human being. Evil in the society is personalized in a witch. (Aembu)
- In my understanding in terms of African cultural knowledge, the theme of the witch is the one of evil, wrongdoing and manipulation, which is denounced and feared by an African person. (Teso)
- A witch is someone who is anti-life. Witches can either be men or women. In most cases they are treated as outcasts in the society because everything evil that happens in the society is attributed to them. There are different kinds of witches e.g., the evil eye, those who use items such as bones, seeds and other such items. (Agikuyu)
- The witch is anybody who does evil to others. (Abaluyia)
- The witch is seen as an evil spirit, which exists in the community and is out to cause harm not [just] to bad people but [anyone] out of jealousy. Most of

the negative things that happen to anyone in the African setting are initially linked to some evil spirit working against them, in most cases witchcraft. Witchcraft is also used to solve problems believed to be difficult to handle. In such cases a witch is consulted. (Luo)

- A witch is an evil person. He is the person with the bad eye, malicious and can bring harm to others. He does anti-social things. No one wants to be associated with a witch unless of course he is seeking the witch's help to destroy another person. It is the personification of all that is evil. In African thought, evil comes from the heart of a witch. Since all have potential to do evil, there is the potential of being a witch. To avoid becoming a witch, one must seek to do that which is the opposite of evil -- good. (Abaluyia)

- The theme of the witch is related to the human heart. In Africa it is evil and indicates the immorality of the persons living in the society. (Luo)

- Witches are living people who do ill to others. They are ostracized from the community and when they die they form "evil spirits" who disturb the peace of the living. Ceremonies are conducted to cleanse the evil. (Agikuyu)

- A witch is anything that is evil and immoral. Every one of us is a potential witch as long as one involves himself/herself in an evil deed. A witch is condemned in the African cultural society, and if one is caught practicing witchcraft, he/she is killed. Witchcraft is very strong and feared and seen as the main cause of every evil, calamity or downfall in life. Witchcraft in my community (Akamba) is seen as the cause of every death. (Akamba)

- A witch is a person who does not live well according to a society. A witch does not wish other people well. (Luo)

- He is the evil one who with impunity causes harm to fellow folk. Every one of us has the potential to be like him if we fail to control the evil that emanates from within our hearts. Misfortune is caused by the evil witch who daily affects the community and individual lives. (Luo)

- The witch is everyone who harms, does bad things, or who behaves badly. Each person sometimes has in himself something which causes him to cause disappointment to another person. It is in every person. The witch is myself. (Tutsi)

- The witch is someone who performs perverted things, things that are not allowed in the community. A witch may have been someone cursed or may be someone that runs naked at night. A witch is someone who is not normal. The person is inhuman due to the practices they have. (Luo)

- The witch is evil and any one who does evil is a witch. From Romans 3:23. "All have sinned and fallen short of the glory of God." This shows that any person who is immoral is a witch. This practice must be avoided and feared by living a moral life. At the later stage it emerges from within a person to a visible stage (night runners). They have demonstrated some super human practices like fire comes out of their mouths. A child can never be named after a witch. (Luo)

- The witch is not just a contradiction in societal and human resources, but acts as an agent of social control where some members climb up higher on the ladder of economic success. Some people believe that if you become too rich, then you would be bewitched. (Agikuyu)

- The witch is evil and as such is avoided and feared. They have mystical powers, which transformed them into superhuman. (Luo)

- In African cultural knowledge all people have the capacity or are capable of becoming witches. The evil or immorality is within each individual and when outwardly exposed, one goes to the other extreme and becomes a witch. (Agikuyu)

- A witch is seen in African cultural knowledge as something evil. Nevertheless, there are some who use their witchcraft to help the community. These protect the weak/vulnerable ones from the harm of the other witches. (Akan)

- The witch is a person harboring ill feelings or bad thoughts against others. The immoral person is a witch. Everybody has bad thoughts against at least one person, and so everybody is a witch. (Luo)

- A witch is a person who brings bad luck to people. The witch is regarded as having "a bad eye." He/she walks/ runs around at night disturbing others. It is believed that if you marry a witch, your children will also be witches. (Luo)

- A witch is any person with the desire and potential to do evil/to harm. (Abagusii)

- The witch is the epitome of evil. Witchcraft is the worst enemy of life. To me a witch is the devil, for, in Africa, evil is personalized. Everybody is a potential witch, hence anybody can be evil and the devil is not out there but within ourselves. (Agikuyu)

- A witch is somebody who is not accepted. When someone dies, the first thing that comes to mind is that he has been bewitched and the society has a role to play to counteract the effects of the witch. (Luo)

- The witch is a representation of evil/immorality. Anyone can become a witch although some people are more inclined to being witches because of bad blood. It is important to avoid the witch and anything associated with evil lest one becomes a witch as well. (Abaluyia)

- Among the Agikuyu he was given many names (negative) such as *Murogi* (destroyer). Therefore a witch is a very destructive person and the community feared and disassociated with him/her. His fate was death. He was rolled together with a beehive to the waterfall and left to be eaten by crocodiles. (Agikuyu)

- A witch is anti-life and works against what God has created with an intention of destroying. It has no meaning in my personal, social and community life because I have never experienced the reality of witchcraft. (Agikuyu)
- Currently, I do not subscribe to the idea [of the] theme of the witch. However, in my community, the theme is the bedrock of all misfortunes in life. (Aembu)
- I, as a Christian, cannot be influenced by witchcraft in any way. However, I believe the devil uses the witch as his "messenger" to adversely affect people's lives. Witchcraft causes disunity in a person's wholeness, among the community and disrupts the social life of the community. (Akamba)
- Witchcraft is equal to evil. All people in the society have potential of committing evil including you and myself. Thus, anyone can be a witch. If I offend someone, I have bewitched him/her. Because of this, God is likely to punish me. So witchcraft/evil is a vicious circle. (Abagusii)
- Witchcraft is not very common among the Agikuyu but is an element among the medicine men who sometimes threaten life. I don't like to take someone's property without consent. I consider this as a curse rather than a blessing. (Agikuyu)
- I think of the witch as someone who is related to evil or one who wishes to do evil against others. From this point of view, any human being could be a witch. On the other hand, there are people who have this orientation and practice it to threaten life and cause confusion and disharmony in the society. Yes, I do know that witches exist and I am curious to see a witch or find out more about witchcraft. (Agikuyu)
- A witch is the anatomy of evil, which is an act of one who runs naked at night (night runner) and carries on with some strange activities that affect the society negatively. As a committed Christian, my personal, social and community life is not affected by witchcraft. Witches are the answers to would be problems. They are tools of social control to avoid greed, over individualism and therefore control the morals of individuals as well as the community. (Luo)
- My understanding of a witch is that he/she is a person with super-natural powers capable of harassing the spirit power and causing harm or death. It has a big impact on my personal life. My parents had a mysterious death, no medical explanation was found. Death of a person still in his/her working age (employable) is abnormal and mostly caused by suspicious forces such as witchcraft. (Abagusii)
- A witch is an extreme case in the moral scale. It is anti-life and thus the ultimate perversion. It shows how morally deprived men can be. That is why witches are lynched in any community they are discovered. They were seen as a threat to social order. (Agikuyu)

- Witchcraft and man are inseparable. Witchcraft is a control component of African traditional life. Essentially, everyone is a witch or could become one any time. On this regard, you have to "watch carefully your relationship with other people in the society." I believe that the witch is an angel of the devil who keeps the work of God's angels checked. Thus, the witch will be there indefinitely. (Abaluyia)

- Most people believed that some powers in form of spirits could control/ harm them. These powers harm when incited by jealousy or wrongdoing. Most evils and calamities are associated with witchcraft. If I am having a headache, for instance, I will ask, "Who did I greet first in the morning?" (Agikuyu)

- The witch is anybody who does evil. It becomes meaningful in my life when I see people with ill intentions against me. Such people even cause the country to suffer because they have made one of the pillars of the society to suffer. (Abaluyia)

- The witch exists and is the perversion of ordinary human behavior and anybody can be seen as a witch in case of funny behavior. The "night runners" cause no harm to anyone but they just behave in a terrifying manner. There are people with 'bad eyes' called "*sihoho*" in my culture. When you eat and they watch you with a 'bad eye,' you get a stomach ache on the spot. A witch has the powers to harm others through 'remote control' but they also have the power to revoke the harm. Socially, those who believe in witchcraft cause chaos in the community. (Luo)

- Anybody with an ill motive towards a fellow human being is a witch. Anyone who harms others is a witch. Evil is personal and therefore anyone with evil tendencies is a witch. (Agikuyu)

- A personification of evil; giving evil a face. Forces of evil are present in human realities though not exclusively externalized. To me, the root of evil is to be found in human relations, which arise during the production and distribution of resources within the community. (Abaluyia)

- A witch is whoever does evil and causes harm at both the communal and individual levels. The meaning it has in my personal, social and community life is that I must avoid being a witch by living well with others. (Tutsi)

- Any bad act can be attributed to witchcraft. It has an effect therefore at both personal and communal levels. (Luo)

- A witch is an enemy of life as he is the one who disturbs the harmony in the society. The fear of being labeled a witch enforces people to conform to social norms. (Akan)

- The witch is the communal embodiment of evil. The witch has no meaning in my personal life whatsoever. (Agikuyu)

- I believe there are some people who have some kind of supernatural powers to perform acts that are hard to explain based on qualitative and/or quantitative scientific investigation. However, those powers are different from the theme of witch. Thus, although I do believe that evil spirits do exist, the idea of witches and bewitching has not much meaning in my personal, social or community life. (Tigrinya)
- If you are suspected to be a witch, you are ostracized by members of the society and people will always refer/point at you using a finger as a sign that they are ashamed of you. (Tutsi)
- Today, because of Christianity, the witch is not so much discussed but anyone who harms others is a witch. Saddam, Bush, Blair, Osama bin Laden and *Al-qaeda* are modern witches. (Abaluyia)

NON-AFRICAN RESPONDENTS   N =18
*[The respondents answered according to
their understanding of African culture.]*

[There were six non-African countries represented: America (11), Norway (3), Indonesia (1), Spain (1), Italy (1), and Poland (1). The respondents were university graduates, twelve women and six men.]

- The witch is usually any one who does evil -- that is everyone has the capacity to be one. (American)
- The witch is each one of us doing evil, living immorally. There are also some people called the "witch" because of their activities. They can cause "bad things" to happen to you or your family. (Polish)
- The witch *mchawi* is the one who acts in a perverted way e.g., runs naked at night. She is regarded as no longer human; a perversion of a human being, therefore can be killed. As the African believes evil resides with the human being, then anyone can become a witch. Therefore the warning to young children "don't do that -- you will become a witch." (American)
- The theme of the witch in African culture points to the fact that in each human heart there is the potential to do evil. This potential for evil must be owned and not allowed to have its way, but must be held in check by creative and life giving forces which are also present in the human heart. (American)
- The witch is the symbol of evil. The witch is the one who does all kinds of perverted things to the point that he or she is no longer human. The witch is symbolic of immorality. (Norwegian)
- The witch figure seems to hold in tension two aspects: The first one is the witch represents the extremes of the evil tendencies that exist in human

beings, and so reflects back to us our own potential for evil. The witch warns us of what we are capable. The second figure is that the witch is an explanation for some of the evil that has happened among us. Evil results from human actions, and someone as depraved and wicked as a witch must have caused much harm to others. (American)

- Witches are perverted human beings that have evil intentions. They are depicted in grotesque forms and are feared because they outwardly are normal but cannot be trusted because they are intrinsically evil. They embody the evil in the society, and need to be exterminated if caught, since they, by their very nature try to destroy relationships. (American)

- I have the potential within me to become a witch. Evil dwells within everyone. The problem of evil exists within the human heart. The way to get rid of evil is to kill it by getting rid of the desire lest one develops into a witch. (American)

- The witch can be any human being as we all have the capacity for evil. If we choose to constantly do evil, then we have the capacity to become a witch and to no longer be human. Evil comes from within the human heart. There is no corporate/cosmic evil because the world is not broken or evil. God made it [world], so it must be good. But we choose to do evil and that affects those around us. (American)

- The witch is a symbol of evil and immorality. Though not only a symbol, but also personification of evil. Everybody runs the risk of being a witch if they promote immorality or evil. (Norwegian)

- The witch is evil in its fullest form. We all have evil in us because evil dwells within the human heart. It is when the evil takes over completely and the person commits much evil that the person is changed (physically, spiritually and emotionally) and becomes a witch. (American)

- The witch protects pregnant women to the time they give birth. (Indonesian)

- It seems that the witch is a constant presence in all communities. We are all capable of being witches if we wish ill on others. (American)

- Evil comes from the human heart, but is not human because the more evil one practices the less human and more witch-like one will become. (American)

- The witch is you and I. It is the African answer to the problem of evil in our lives. In the African mentality, there's no evil outside the human person. There is no objective hell or heaven. Doing evil transforms you into a witch little by little, with no resemblance to a human being left [at the end]. (Spaniard)

- A witch is a person becoming immoral. All evil is located in human beings, and can turn a human being to a witch. Everyone is a potential witch because all human beings are capable of doing immoral things.

(A witch can run naked at night doing inhuman things; it is only a question of time before the person doing evil gets to this stage). (Norwegian)

- All of us humans are capable of being witches. Evil is personal and we are all capable of doing immoral things. I do agree that we are capable of our own evil thoughts and that evil can be located in our heart. However, I certainly hesitate to use the expression/notion of a witch. (American)

- Every one of us could be a witch. This was my belief even before I took a MIASMU course. In the Old Testament we read "…bad things are inside a human being not outside…" I agree completely with these words. I think that this is the meaning of freedom that God gave us. In my personal, social and community life, it means that I can be - maybe I have been once - a witch, and I can meet people who behave as witches. So I have to reset my mind and face this problem. First of all finding a reason and then work on it to find a solution. Usually, I believe that people who behave as witches are people who just are lacking in love. They are people who feel lonely, who just need love. (Italian)

EDITOR'S REFLECTIONS

In African cultures when unjustified and unexplained happenings and misfortunes frequently beguile members of a lineal family it is believed to be the work of a witch. The witch, a totally evil and perverted person, is the most hated figure in Africa, as he/she threatens the life of the family, the very life of the community. In African thought there is no cosmic principle of evil, like the devil, as taught by Christianity and Islam. Evil is personalized and comes from the hearts of evil people and unhappy ancestors. If a person dies and is believed to have been a witch, his/her name is not passed on to the newborn and is completely forgotten. To name a child after a witch is to encourage and nurture the evil tendencies that are inherent in the name. It is believed that when witches die they become malevolent evil spirits that haunt and disturb people because, as a result of their evil, they have no place in the ancestral world. Furthermore, the idea of the witch is the most powerful symbol of what not to be. Mothers often scold their children saying, "don't do this [or] you will become a witch"-*usifanye hivi, utakuwa mchawi.*

DISCUSSION QUESTIONS

1. Have you or a close relative ever been harmed and affected by a witch? Explain.
2. Is the African Witch and the Christian and Islamic Devil the same or different? Explain.
3. What do African people say is the fundamental reason for people doing evil to others and therefore becoming witches?
4. What is your personal understanding of the nature of evil?

AFRICAN ILLUSTRATION

AN INCIDENT INVOLVING A WITCH

In December 2004, a man was admitted to a local hospital in Rift Valley Province, Kenya, with serious burn wounds. It is alleged that a neighbor burnt him with hot water after he caught him performing witch-like activities in his compound. Apparently the suspected witch had been throwing objects, soil and stones at his neighbors houses and making frightening noises in the night as he ran around naked. It is said that he had been disturbing neighbors for long, and that after he was injured and hospitalized, the night running incidences had stopped. **[verbatim report of a field assistant]**.

RECOMMENDED READINGS

Ray, B.C. (1975). *African Religions: Symbol, Ritual and Community.* (pp. 150-152). New Jersey: Prentice Hall.

Bourdillon, M. (1990). *Religion and Society: A Text for Africa.* (pp. 187-219). Gweru: Mambo Press.

Shorter, A. (1998). *African Culture: An Overview.* (pp. 67-68). Nairobi: Paulines Publications Africa.

NON-AFRICAN ILLUSTRATION

DESCRIPTION OF A WITCH-LIKE PERSON
IN WESTERN SOCIETIES

In the Western Christian societies, the image of a totally perverted person is usually that of the devil, a fallen angel, who is dedicated to creating major and permanent evil and unrest in the land of the living. However, there are people who have been designated as completely and totally immoral and are seen by the society as somewhat equivalent to an African witch. These people would be serial killers or brutal dictators, people who have no redeeming merit in their lives or in their activities. And, as in African thought, mothers will at times tell their children to stop doing evil things arguing that they are acting like a devil, or that their behavior is like a devil. The sense is that if you consistently act in an unjust and an evil way you will eventually become part of the devil's community and end up with the devil forever in a place of unremitting suffering called hell.

CHAPTER XIV

Theme: **WITCHCRAFT**

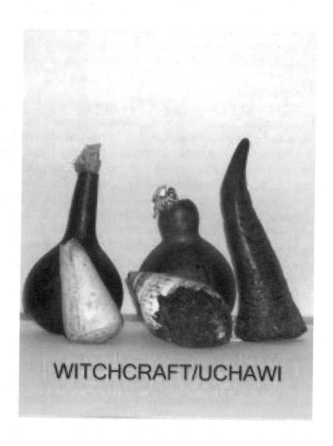

WITCHCRAFT/UCHAWI

The gourds, shells and animal horn are items used by a witch to cause harm. The gourds may contain powder, pieces of cloth, hair and nails of the intended victim.

WITCHCRAFT

Introduction

Witchcraft understood as occult practices using special objects, poisons and rituals has been part of the human condition from the beginning. There is need to know and understand unexpected difficulties, events, activities, and noises especially those happening at night. This is related to the popular belief that there are mysterious evil forces at work in the world, and these evil forces can be manipulated by rituals and incantations to achieve one's evil purpose.

Witchcraft in Africa

In Africa the craft of witches, that is their strength, techniques, skills, thus "witchcraft," is founded on the following ideas and principles. 1) All evil is personalized, nothing happens by accident, someone causes evil to happen. 2) Evil thoughts have power outside the person thinking them. They have a certain independence that can continue to harm and destroy another's health and life unless they are confronted and eliminated. 3) There is no source of evil outside the human heart and the offended wills of ancestors. A **cosmic source of evil,** as personified by the **devil** of Christianity and Islam, does not exist in African thought. 4) Evil is stopped and eliminated through appropriate rituals, charms and medicines provided by herbalists and diviners. 5) Witchcraft activities always involve people known to one another. Based on these ideas, evil is brought to bear on others through rituals, rites of passage, charms, medicines and incantations.

Witchcraft Elsewhere

In all societies worldwide there are occult activities, techniques, skills and ideas that are believed can be used to harm others, take away their good fortunes and even their lives. In the U.S. there is a yearly event called "Halloween" in which individuals dress up as witches, ghosts and goblins -- a public display of occult ideas and activities -- and go from door to door asking for sweets and gifts. The underlying idea is that if you don't respond, you will incur damages and injuries e.g., eggs or stones thrown at your windows. Also, there are no tall buildings with floors numbered thirteen, as thirteen is seen as a dangerous number and nobody would either live or work on a thirteenth floor. In the tall buildings therefore, the floor numbers skip from the twelfth to the fourteenth floor. Furthermore, many people carry good luck charms e.g., a dried rabbit's foot, a religious medal or an old coin, etc. to ward off occult/evil activity. Likewise, when things go bad, it is commonly said that it was an unlucky day, or bad luck, implying that there were occult forces at work.

Furthermore, there are activities of sending anonymous threatening letters, making anonymous phone calls, reactions to strange winds and storms especially at night, drawing threatening objects on walls near an intended victim, a mafia-style contract to kill an enemy, stories of ghosts and mysterious goings-on at night, sticking pins in a doll to harm the targeted enemy -- a Voodoo ritual, using animal parts and inscriptions to send evil to another. On Bourbon Street in New Orleans, USA there are a number of small stores that specialize in paraphernalia for magical rites involving curses, techniques to manipulate reality for evil purposes, to foretell the future, to force another to submit to sexual advances through love potions, or to enhance one's power, wealth and status in a magical way.

QUESTION

Kindly explain in detail your understanding of the theme of WITCHCRAFT. What is its contemporary meaning in your personal, social and community life?   N =73 (61 Africans, 12 non-Africans)
[Note that this question evoked some responses about the theme of Witch.]

RESPONSES COLLATED BY NINE CATEGORIES
1. *Relevance of the Theme of Witchcraft   R = 37*
2. *Definition of Witchcraft   R = 33*
3. *Consequences of Witchcraft   R = 28*
4. *How Witchcraft is Counteracted   R = 25*
5. *Witchcraft in Contemporary Society   R = 16*
6. *Where Witchcraft is Found   R = 10*
7. *How Witchcraft is Acquired   R = 6*
8. *Manifestation of Witchcraft   R = 5*
9. *Why People Practice Witchcraft   R = 3*

Other Comments   R = 22

Comments apropos to the theme "WITCH" (cf. Chapter III)
1. *Definition of a Witch   R = 18*
2. *Types of Witches   R = 2*

AFRICAN RESPONDENTS   N = 61

Relevance of the Theme of Witchcraft   (R = 29)
Has *no relevance* to me or my community (8), witchcraft is *feared* as it is the *epitome of evil* (4), it is *relevant as it is very present* in the society (2), it is considered *anti-social behavior* as it is *anti-life* (2), I have *experienced and seen* cases of witchcraft (1), the community is able to *identify* the clan or family of witches (1), it is relevant to me as I have been *bewitched* several times (1), many communities *do not like* witchcraft and they *shun away* from such activities (1), many people *fear witchcraft* and therefore there should be some truth to this theme (1), though not relevant in my life, *social pressure* can push one into *believing in it* (1), *anything bad* that happens in the community is

associated with witchcraft (1), **Luo people believe in** the existence of witchcraft and hence have witch doctors (1), it **is a habit** that **starts at a personal level** before taking root in the community (1), in Africa, an **ailment** or **death** does **not just occur but is believed to have been caused by evil spirits or bewitchment** (1), it **touches on all dimensions** of a human being (1), it is **spiritual** and it affects the **human mind, the family, society and physical well being** of the individual (1), it **challenges** an individual to be aware of his/her **bad thoughts**, which could **harm** other people and seek to **break his/her good relationship** with the family and other people in the society (1).

Definition of Witchcraft   (R = 26)

It is **willful harm** to a fellow human being or the **intention to harm** another person (4), it is an **act of evil** as **practiced by witches** (3), it is the **art of manipulating vital forces of nature for malevolent** reasons (3), it is practicing **evil or black magic** (2), it is the **ability and desire to do evil** (2), it is the **act of bewitching** which is common where reconciliation is rare   (1), it is **a craft, skill or practice and knowledge** of using some **magical powers through the devil** (1), it is the practice in which **a witch performs dubious activities with an aim of harming the victim knowingly** (1), it is the **evil that is against life and people's progress** and puts fear in the minds of people making them not to do their best in life **spiritually, psychologically and physically** (1), it is **the power** by which certain members of the community **destroy the order and balance** existing in a society (1), **connotes bad people using bad medicine** to harm others especially when used for **commercial purposes** (1), it is **the outcome of evil deeds and intentions towards a third party** (1), is an **evil spirit** that causes harm to individuals (1), refers to **whatever causes social disharmony, conflicts or misunderstandings** (1), it is **mystical power** that some **individuals have from evil spirits** which inflict pain to other people (1), it is **an evil practice carried out by witches and wizards** on people who are seen to be **progressing in the society through education, business, politics** and even having beautiful women (1), it is the **evil manifested in a thing or object** (1).

Consequences of Witchcraft   (R = 24)

Causes confusion, suspicion and hatred among relatives and the community as a whole (4), **limits** people **from doing progressive things** such as **initiation of development projects as they fear to be bewitched** (4), **causes disharmony** in the community (2), **powers of witchcraft are considered bad and wicked** (2), **people blame** their failure on witchcraft (2), it is **a threat to life** (2), witches are perceived to be **incarnates of the devil** as they carry out their duties through his evil powers (1), witches are **believed to be the cause of the death** of children and mothers during childbirth (1), causes **destruction in the community** (1), some people will not allow their **babies to eat or breastfeed**

where they suspect there is a witch [nearby] (1), witches often *cause harm to other people* (1), once a person *believes he/she has been bewitched, even if treated* he/she will always be sick until he/she gets treatment from a *traditional medicine man* (1), in my community, if one has not visited the witchdoctor, then *the community must know why he/she has not sought protection* against the witch (1), when things are going wrong in a person's life, he/she *begins to wonder who may be the cause* behind it as they suspect *witchcraft* (1).

How Witchcraft is Counteracted   (R = 18)

By *condemning* it in the society (4), by *strong belief and protection from God* for those who are Christians (3), by a *diviner through rituals* (3), by *prayers* (2), through *a herbalist* undoing the work of witchcraft (1), *ex-communicating* witches (1), *lynching* witches (1), through *healing* (1), through *exorcism* of evil spirits (1), through getting *protective medicine from traditional healers* (1).

Witchcraft in the Contemporary Society   (R = 16)

Witchcraft is *real, still exists* in different forms and *has immense effects* on the lives of people in the contemporary society (7), people *still believe that the witch is the cause of all problems* in the society (1), it is *still practiced through harming* people *using occult scientific methods* (1), it is *seen as evil* (1), there are still *cases of witches being excommunicated* from their communities (1), there are still cases of *lynching witches* in some communities just as it used to happen in the past (1), *many people, irrespective of their faith*, still believe in witchcraft and *act with fear* when certain *mysterious calamities* befall them (1), any person can *use medicine today* to harm others or as revenge on an enemy and this would be *similar to using witchcraft* (1), due to *education and Christianity*, it is now possible to find many people who appear indifferent to the question of witchcraft (1), the theme *controls social affairs* in terms of shared goods (1).

Where Witchcraft is Found   (R = 8)

In *everyone with ill intentions or thoughts* towards others (2), it has to do with *evil which is embodied in each one of us* (2), in the *eyes of the witch* (1), in the *thoughts* of the witch (1), witchcraft is found in *every society in Africa* as there is a witch in each one of these societies (1), in the *actions of a witch* (1).

How Witchcraft is Acquired   (R = 6)

By *inheriting* (3), through *buying it* from witches (2), it can be *passed on from an evil to a non-evil person* (1).

Manifestations of Witchcraft (R = 5)

Most of the events of witchcraft are *carried out by people who are related to you or know you well* (1), it is *represented by sickness, accidents, injuries and whatever causes harm* to people (1), in some communities it is *a way of life* (1), it is normally *channeled from a given source (the witch) to another party* who gets destabilized in one way or another (1), witches could *use magic to harm* people *from far away* (1).

Why People Practice Witchcraft   (R = 3)

People tend to find a reason to *perpetuate hatred* and in the process *propagate witchcraft* (1), out of *malice, revenge, jealousy and envy* (1), because of *not wanting others to surpass* them in achievement or being more recognizable than them (1).

Other Comments   (R = 14)

Propagators of *Western education and Christianity* need to take into account the *value of reconciliation if they are to manage witchcraft* (1), I have *no idea where the witches* get all these powers from (1), *evil is personalized* (1), our *daily behavior and conduct* determines whether one is a witch or not (1), beware of the witch in you for *we all are potential witches* (1), evil is with *people who do not wish others well* (1), witchcraft is *the most hated and feared theme* in the society (1), socially people do not like being associated with evil because it is *bad and destroys relationships* (1), the word *witchcraft is not commonly used in my community,* instead we use the words *onywe ogwu ojoo* which means a person with *evil medicine* or *ogwo nshi* which means *one who poisons* (1), many community members *fear and blow up incidences of witchcraft* through stories, which I have difficulty in believing because a lot of them are unreasonable (1), *my community believes witchcraft to be an Akamba practice* as they are our neighbors, and those who practice witchcraft within the community are believed to have bought it from them (1), there are *evil people around us* and they negatively affect people's lives (1), some people have the *knowledge to manipulate cosmic powers* to cause harm to others (1), *how witchcraft is done remains a secret of the practitioners* (1).

Comments Apropos to the Theme WITCH (cf. chapter III)

Definition of a Witch   (R = 16)

Is *that person who intentionally harms others* in the community (4), it is *every person who does not comply* with the *existing moral codes/norms and regulations* stipulated by the society (2), is *someone who manipulates powers* to harm others (2), is *a bad person* who has powers to bring/cause evil things to happen to others (1), is *anybody who acts in a way to curtail human happiness, success and development* (1), is *one who has evil intentions* against others (1), is anyone who *causes pain, suffering, and problems* to others *out of malice and ill motive* (1), is one who *can foretell* one's future (1), is one who *can stop a misfortune* from happening to someone (1), is one who can *make good things happen* to an individual (1), is *a normal person but his/her actions are immoral and evil* (1).

Types of Witches (R = 2)
Magic practitioners (1), *poison purveyors* (1).

NON-AFRICAN RESPONDENTS N = 12
[The respondents answered both according to their
own culture and their understanding of African culture.]

Relevance of the Theme of Witchcraft (R = 8)
Has *no relevance to me nor my community* (3), there are *some happenings that the community is not able to explain* using common sense, hence they believe in *mystical explanations such as witchcraft* (1), witchcraft is always *looked upon with awe* in the community (1), it is *relevant and has meaning in my culture* (1), it is *used as an excuse* by people who *prefer to be lazy;* they think about their mistakes or failures and seek for solutions and remedies (1), in my opinion *witchcraft cannot affect a person,* but one who believes in it is *affected psychologically* (1).

Definition of Witchcraft (R = 7)
It is something *related to both the living and spirit world* (1), it is the *act of defying God's will* (1), it is the *practice of witches* (1), it is *evil thoughts and deeds* which *lie within the human heart and actions* (1), it is the *result of power dynamics* between people choosing evil (1), it is *using forces of evil* for a particular *purpose like accumulating wealth, preserving health and destroying an enemy* (1), *according to Mbiti, witchcraft is a broad term* used to *describe many types of evil employment of mystical powers* generally in a secret fashion (1).

Consequences of Witchcraft (R = 4)
It is *often employed to bring harm to others* (1), can *affect people directly* like *poisoning a person* but the *witch cannot do anything to a person who is far away* (1), *witch trials were held hundreds of years ago in Europe* and found later to be *bogus* after *many innocent people were killed* (1), the theme of witchcraft is *present in my community*, and though it *does not directly affect the lives of people, it sometimes oppresses them* (1).

<u>How Witchcraft is Counteracted</u>   **(R = 7)**
By *avoiding relationship with a family of witches* (2), through *diviners* (1), through *herbalists* (1), by *keeping away from witches* as they could control an individual physically and could even harm him/her (1), there are *certain rituals and people* who can right the wrongs of witchcraft and get rid of the witch (1), it is *studied by all in school to prevent its recurrence* (1).

<u>Where Witchcraft is Found</u>   **(R = 2)**
Within *witches* (1), in the *heart of a person and not an outside evil agent* (1).

<u>Other Comments</u>   **(R = 8)**
I believe that *this theme is psychological* (1), I think the *term witchcraft is misused* as people have failed in their own their lives and when something wrong happens they blame others (1), in *Christian tradition* we believe that when a person sins (chooses evil) the *consequences of that choice may affect the whole body of Christ* (that is other people) and it *slows down the coming of the kingdom of God* (1), I see some *parallelism between the Christian and African* concept [of witchcraft] (1), there is *evil in the society* and it is *part of humanity* influencing individual and societal lives (1), *nobody is a hundred percent able* to live to God's will, hence *every human being is a potential witch* (1), *in every society* there are individuals who try to *resort to witchcraft* (1), witchcraft is *not a reality* that touches my individual and community history (1).

Comments Apropos to the Theme "WITCH" (cf. chapter III)

<u>Definition of a Witch</u>   **(R = 2)**
Is *a person who is immoral* and since all human beings can choose to be evil, *all are potential witches* (1), is *an old woman with green skin, a pointy black hat and waves and uses a broomstick and stirs potions* (1).

SUMMARY
Beliefs expressed regarding Witchcraft

<u>Witchcraft is</u>: *intention to do willful harm* to fellow human beings, an *act of evil* as practiced by witches, the *art of manipulating vital forces of nature for malevolent reasons, practicing* evil or black magic, the *ability and desire* to do evil, the *act of bewitching* others, a *craft, skill or practice and knowledge* of using magical powers through the *devil*, the *evil that is against life and people's progress* and *puts fear* in the minds of people causing them not to do their best *spiritually, physically and*

psychologically, the *power* by which certain members of the community *destroy the order and balance* existing in the society, *bad people using bad medicine* to harm others especially when used for commercial purposes, the *outcome of evil deeds and intentions* on a third party, an *evil spirit* that causes harm to individuals, *anything that causes social disharmony, conflicts and misunderstandings* in the community, *mystical power* which some people have from *evil spirits* which inflict pain to other people, an evil practice carried out by *witches and wizards* on people who are seen to be progressing in the society by way of *education, business and politics*, the *act of defying God's will*, *evil thoughts and deeds* which lie within the *human heart and actions*.

Relevance of the Theme of Witchcraft: gives *explanations for mysterious happenings* in the community, it is looked upon with *awe* in the community, used as an excuse by people who prefer to be lazy than think about their mistakes or failures and seek for *solutions and remedies*, it *affects those who believe in it psychologically*, is feared as it is the *epitome of evil*, an *anti-social behavior*, the community is able to identify a family of witches among them, many communities do not like it and shun away from it, it is a habit that starts at a personal level before taking root in the community, it is *spiritual and affects the human mind, family, society and the physical well being* of the people; it challenges an individual to be *aware of his/her bad thoughts* which could harm other people and seek to break his/her good relationship with the family and other people in the society.

Consequences of Witchcraft in the Community: causes *confusion, suspicion, hatred, disharmony, destruction, limits* people from doing progressive work such as initiating development projects *for the fear of being bewitched*, it is a *threat to life*, makes people *seek protective charms* to counteract the powers of the witch, it is *often employed* to harm others.

How Witchcraft is Counteracted: through *condemning the practice of witchcraft, rituals, prayers, protective charms, healing, strong belief and protection* from God for those who are Christians, by a *diviner, herbalist, excommunication, lynching, killing, exorcism* of evil spirits, *avoiding relations* with a family of witches.

Witchcraft in the Contemporary Society: still *exists in different forms* and has *immense effects* on the lives of people, *the witch* is believed to be the cause of all problems afflicting the society, practiced through harming people using *occult scientific* methods, *irrespective of the faith* many people believe in the power of witchcraft and act with fear when *mysterious or unexplained* calamities befall them, due to the influence of *Christianity and education* many people now appear indifferent to the question of witchcraft.

Where Witchcraft is Found: in *everyone* with ill intentions or thoughts towards others, *the evil embodied* in each one of us, *the eyes and thoughts* of a witch, *the witch* who is present in every community in Africa, the *heart* of a person.

How Witchcraft is Acquired: through *inheritance, buying* it from witches, *being passed on* from an evil person to a non-evil person.

Manifestations of Witchcraft: most of the events are carried out by *people related to the victim* or who know him/her very well, *mysterious sickness, accidents, injuries, sudden death,* channeled from a witch as the source to a victim, *magic*.

Why People Practice Witchcraft: to *perpetuate* hatred and *propagate* witchcraft, out of *malice, revenge, jealousy, envy, fear* of others progressing more than them.

RESPONSES FROM WORKSHEETS

[*Note that witchcraft refers to the special objects and rituals employed by perverted and evil people within the society that are believed to be effective in causing harm to others. These rituals make use of charms, hair, clothes, faecal matter, and finger nails which are a substitute for the person to be harmed, or the use of animals such as lizards, cats and snakes which are placed in one's dwelling to destroy one's life. Persons caught practicing this craft are often killed on the spot as their actions are seen as totally inhuman and without redeeming merit. Also note that some of the respondents commented on the theme Witch i.e., the practitioner.*]

❑ **Kindly explain in detail your understanding of the theme of WITCHCRAFT. What is its contemporary meaning in your personal, social and community life?**

AFRICAN RESPONDENTS   N = 61

[*There were eighteen ethnic groups represented: Luo (15), Agikuyu (13), Abaluyia (7), Akamba (6), Abagusii (3), Tutsi (3), Kategi (2), Teso (2), Aembu (1), Kipsigis (1), Baganda (1), Arusha-Meru (1), Banyankole (1), Akan (1), Ibo (1), Dinka (1), Bemba (1), and Tigrinya (1). The respondents were university graduates, seventeen women and forty-four men.*]

- This is the art of bewitching which is common where reconciliation is rare. People tend to find reason to perpetuate hatred and in the process propagate witchcraft. Efforts by western education and Christianity need to take into account the value of reconciliation. (Abaluyia)
- A witch is a bad person who has powers to bring/cause evil things to happen to others. It could be in their eyes, their thoughts or actions. I have no idea where they get all these powers from but I have met victims of witchcraft. A whole lot of things have to be done to undo the evil brought by witchcraft. Some people will go to a herbalist, a diviner or even an evangelist who would pray for them and eventually help in overcoming the evil. (Abaluyia)
- Witchcraft is the art of harming and the witch is that person who intentionally harms others in the community. It causes disharmony in the community and hatred among relatives. (Abagusii)
- Witchcraft is a threat to life. It brings confusion, suspicion and hatred in the society. In contemporary society, witchcraft is still present and has taken many forms but the fear is as strong as before. (Agikuyu)

- Witchcraft is an institution of contradicting ordinary human events for worse. Every person is a witch as long as he/she does not comply with the existing codes and regulations stipulated by the society. (Agikuyu)
- Witchcraft is represented by sickness, accidents and injuries or whatever causes the harm. In modern times, people still believe that the witch in our community causes evil. Evil is everybody who causes harm to others. (Tutsi)
- Witchcraft is a craft, skill or practice and knowledge of using some magical powers through the devil. In fact, the witches are true incarnates of the devil as they carry out the duties through his evil powers. (Luo)
- It's a way of life in my community. If you have not visited a witchdoctor, then the community must know why you have not been protected. If something bad happens to the family, then you are responsible. In the village, an occurrence like the death of children or women at birth-time is blamed on the witch. (Kategi)
- Witchcraft is the practice in which the witch performs dubious activities with an aim of harming the victim knowingly. (Akamba)
- Witchcraft is the state of being a source of evil for others. In contemporary times, witchcraft is the art of harming people using occult scientific methods. (Tutsi)
- Witchcraft is the art with destructive powers. The witch/witchcraft is taken as evil today. (Agikuyu)
- Witchcraft is the evil that is against life and people's progress. It is against progress and puts fear in the minds of people making them not do their best in life spiritually, mentally, psychologically and even physically. Once one believes that he/she is bewitched even if he/she is treated, he/she will always be sick until he/she gets a traditional medicine man to treat him/her. Some will not build a permanent house or educate children for fear of being bewitched. (Akamba)
- Witchcraft is the art of manipulating certain powers to harm others. These powers are considered bad and wicked. (Luo)
- Witchcraft is the power by which certain members of the community destroy the order and balance existing in a society. In most cases, it is passed from one member of the family to the next through inheritance. Today, we still hear cases of witches being excommunicated from their communities. In other cases, still being reported through the media, witches get lynched in line with early traditional practices. (Agikuyu)
- Witchcraft is the art of manipulating vital forces of nature for malevolent reasons i.e., harm others. Personally, I see witchcraft as the epitome of evil. (Luo)

- Witchcraft has no relevance in my contemporary life. However many people, irrespective of their faith, still believe in witchcraft and act with fear when certain mysterious calamities befall them. (Agikuyu)
- Witchcraft is the act that disrupts the well-being of the society. Anybody who acts in a way as to curtail human happiness, success and development falls into the witch category. Hence, evil is personalized. Our daily behavior and conduct determines whether one is a witch or not. Beware of the witch in you for we are all potential witches. (Agikuyu)
- A witch is an enemy of life. Any person who acts against the moral norms of the society is a witch. Therefore, everyone is a potential witch. This is the status quo even today. (Akan)
- Witchcraft is very much alive in my life. There are cases where I have experienced or seen the power of witchcraft. In my community, prominent people fear constructing big houses or to be seen with expensive property for fear of being bewitched. This is testimony to witchcraft being real and has an immense effect on the lives of the contemporary person. (Luo)
- Witchcraft has always been made to connote bad people using bad medicine to harm others. This is the case if it is used for commercial purposes. Anybody can use medicine today to harm others or as a revenge on an enemy and this would be similar to using witchcraft. (Abaluyia)
- Personally I do not care about witchcraft. In the social and community life, witchcraft has a lot of meaning. People are able to identify the family or clan of witches in the community. Evil is not out there, it is with people who do not wish others well. (Akamba)
- A witch is whoever does harm to others. It has a meaning in my personal, social and community life because it is discouraged. (Tutsi)
- Witchcraft is practicing black magic/evil magic, which is not entertained in the society. A diviner is very important in this case because he/she is there to counteract the powers of witchcraft. (Akamba)
- Witchcraft is the most hated and feared theme in my community. Without witchcraft, life can be very smooth. According to me, witchcraft limits development and holds people in a way from doing progressive things. (Akamba)
- The theme of witchcraft denotes evil-doing, an act of causing or wishing evil things to happen to someone. This is done out of malice, revenge, jealousy and even envy. Thus witchcraft to me is something evil and should be greatly condemned and this is the same meaning I have received from my social and community life. (Abagusii)
- Witchcraft is a practice done by somebody known as a witch. The witch can foretell your future, stop a misfortune from happening to you as well as making good things happen to you. The witch and witchcraft have no meaning in my personal as well as my social life. (Agikuyu)

- Witchcraft is the practice of evil. Many practitioners of witchcraft fall in to either magic or poison purveyors. The use of God-given skills malevolently disrupts social stability. We once had a neighbor (now dead) who practiced witchcraft. (Luo)

- Witchcraft is the art or outcome of evil deeds and intentions onto a third party. It is normally channeled from a given source (the witch) to the other party who often gets destabilized in one way or another. It is real and has a meaning especially in my social and community life. (Abaluyia)

- Witchcraft in the African context has to do with evil, which is embodied in each one of us. Evil is everywhere and it does affect us personally because we have a choice to choose it or choose good. Socially, people do not like being associated with evil because it is bad and it destroys relationships. (Luo)

- Witchcraft is willful harm to a fellow human being or intention to harm. This has meaning for me, for I have been bewitched several times. My community does not like witchcraft. They run away from such activities. (Luo)

- The theme of witchcraft has not had a big influence on my personal life, but at communal level. I hear various people complaining that they cannot succeed in school, or farming because someone has bewitched them. The above theme has led various people in neighboring villages not to initiate big development projects on their farms because of the fear of being bewitched. (Abaluyia)

- A witch is understood as one who is evil and with evil intention against others. A witch is seen as one who does not want the progress of others. He/ she is feared. The word witchcraft is not commonly used in my community. Rather we use the word *onywe ogwu ojoo* which means a person with evil medicine or *Ogwo nshi* which means one who poisons. (Ibo)

- Witchcraft to my understanding is surrounded by evil. This includes evil thoughts, wishes and practices. The evil spirit controls all these. In my personal life, witchcraft has no meaning, as I have not witnessed it in the community I have grown up in, which is the Agikuyu community. (Agikuyu)

- Witchcraft is an art or occupation within the society that overwhelmingly contradicts and greatly affects human life. Witches are simply people with a special skill in harming other people. However, this office/domain controls the social affairs in terms of shared goods. (Agikuyu)

- Witchcraft exists and many people fear it. I recognize witchcraft in my society. I get puzzled when I experience witchcraft. I would not allow my baby to eat or breastfeed where I know that somebody has these powers. (Luo)

- Witchcraft is to be found in every society in Africa. There is a witch in each and every one of these societies. (Kategi)
- Witchcraft is an evil spirit that causes harm to other individuals. It could be from an evil person to a non-evil person. They often tend to harm others. In my life I believe there are witches but they do not affect me as such as I believe God protects me. (Luo)
- Witchcraft has a meaning to my personal, social and community life. Most people do not like other people to surpass them in achievement, thus if you do something which makes you more recognized than them, they find a way to get rid of you. Most of the events of witchcraft are carried out by people who are related to you or people who know you well. (Akamba)
- In most African communities, an ailment or death does not just occur but is believed to be caused by bad spirits or being bewitched by a person who is not for the good of the community, hence the need for healing or chasing away those spirits. (Abaluyia)
- Witchcraft refers to whatever causes social disharmony, conflict or misunderstanding. A witch is anybody who causes pain, suffering and problems to others out of malice and ill motive. (Agikuyu)
- People who have experienced witchcraft say it is real. Many people fear it so it must have some truth. (Luo)
- For me, witchcraft creates misunderstandings among the family and because of fear that has gone into the head, socialization cannot take place in the family. There is suspicion all the time. (Baganda)
- Does not have a meaning in my personal life. In the social life, many community members fear and blow up incidents of witchcraft through stories. I have a difficulty in believing them because a lot of them are unreasonable. (Banyankole)
- It is difficult to explain what witchcraft is. It touches all dimensions of an African man and woman. Outsiders call it unscientific but for us it is spiritual and touches the human mind, the family, the society and the physical well - being of man. It is mystical power, which some individuals have from the evil spirits, which can inflict pain. Any misfortune is associated with witchcraft such as floods, inability to bear children, to find a husband or a wife. It is passed on from one generation to the next. (Teso)
- Witchcraft is feared. It is evil. It is not very relevant but social pressure can push one into believing in it. (Luo)
- In my personal life it may not have a meaning but in the community it is very active. This is because people will associate anything bad to be caused by bewitchment. (Dinka)
- The witch and the theme of witchcraft are found in every human being. Every man and woman is capable of becoming a witch. This does not have

much effect on me because I am a Christian who strongly believes in Christ. This drives my social and community life. (Teso)

- Witchcraft is the art and act of evil as practiced by witches. It is an anti-social activity for it is anti-life. Witchcraft is practiced by people who inherit it from their relatives. They are normal people but their acts are immoral and evil. (Agikuyu)

- Luo people traditionally believe in witchcraft and witchdoctors. However due to education and Christianity, it is now possible to find many people who appear indifferent to the question of witchcraft. (Luo)

- Witchcraft is rare but real. It exists in different forms. It can only be overcome by prayers or by diviners (rituals). My community projects witchcraft to be an Akamba thing (they are our neighbors). The people who practice it in my community are believed to have bought it from the Akamba. (Agikuyu)

- A witch is a person who manipulates some powers to harm others. (Luo)

- Witchcraft represents evil in the society. Anybody who could be a witch was highly discouraged and usually witches were feared. They could use magic to harm people from far away. Sometimes when things are not going on well in my life I find myself worrying about who may have caused it. (Agikuyu)

- Witchcraft is an evil practice carried out by witches and wizards on people who are seen to be progressing in the society in education, business, politics and even having beautiful women. It has a meaning in my personal, social and community life because it starts at a personal level before taking root in the community. (Kipsigis)

- Witchcraft is real and around us. There are evil people around us all the time and they negatively affect people's lives. For me as a Christian, I can seek God's protection from the evil intentions of evil people. Others go to traditional healers for protective medicine. (Abaluyia)

- Witchcraft is believed to be the source of evil and it harms life. It is in every person who has bad thoughts against others. It has a meaning in my life because it challenges me to be aware of my bad thoughts, which could harm other people. It would also break my good relationships with my family and other people in the society. (Bemba)

- A witch is a person who manipulates some powers to harm others. (Luo)

- Witchcraft is the ability and desire to do evil. (Abagusii)

- As far as I understand, witchcraft exists in reality. Some people have knowledge of how to manipulate powers (cosmic powers) to cause harm to other people. How this is done remains mysterious to many as it is the secret of the practitioners. It is a disturbing thing. (Arusha-Meru)

- Witchcraft is a craft used by witches. It does not have a meaning in my personal, social and community life because I do not practice it. (Luo)

- Witchcraft is evil manifested in a thing/object. Witchcraft can be bought or sold. It is the witches who manufacture witchcraft and sell it for evil motives. (Aembu)
- I understand witchcraft to be the act of defying God's will. It is clear that nobody is a hundred percent able to live to God's will, hence, every human being is a potential witch. I do not believe that the theme of witchcraft has a lot of meaning in my personal, social or community life. (Tigrinya)

NON-AFRICAN RESPONDENTS   N = 12
[The respondents answered both according to their own culture and their understanding of African culture.]

[There were five non-African countries represented: America (6), India (3), Italy (1), Spain (1), and Paraguay (1). The respondents were university graduates, four women and eight men.]

African Perspective

- Mbiti says that witchcraft is a broad term used to describe many types of evil employment of mystical powers generally in a secret fashion. It is often employed to bring harm to others. This is not a reality that touches my personal and communal history.   (American)

Non-African Perspective

- Witchcraft is something related to the living dead and spirit world. I believe witchcraft is psychological. There are some happenings that the community is not able to explain using common sense, hence they believe in mystical explanations. I think the term witchcraft is misused. People have failed to own their lives and when something wrong happens, they blame others. This is a big misunderstanding for people prefer to be lazy rather than think about their mistakes or failures and seek for solutions and remedies. (Italian)
- Witchcraft is the practice of witches. It is the evil thoughts and actions that lie within the human heart and deeds. It is the place of the diviners and herbalists to eliminate such evil. We do have evil in the society and we do believe it is part of humanity, influencing individual and societal lives. (American)
- Witchcraft is always looked upon with awe. People always kept a distance with the witches, because they could control you physically and could even harm you. Nobody liked to maintain any relationship with such families. Even marriage proposals would be rejected. (Indian)

- The witch is a person who is immoral and since all human beings can choose evil, all are potential witches. It seems that witchcraft is the result of power dynamics between people choosing evil. In the Christian tradition, we believe that when a person sins (chooses evil) the consequences of that choice may affect the whole body of Christ (that is other people) and it slows down the coming of the kingdom of God. I see some parallelism between these two concepts. When we go to confession, which is a rite, we receive the grace we need from God through the sacrifice of Jesus Christ, to continue pursuing our good and the good of others in life. (Spaniard)
- This does not apply in my culture. (American)
- Witchcraft has no role in my community. (American)
- By witchcraft I would mean using the forces of evil for a particular purpose like accumulating wealth, preserving health or destroying an enemy. In every society there are individuals who try to resort to witchcraft. (Indian)
- In my opinion witchcraft cannot affect a person, but one who believes in it is affected psychologically. Witchcraft can affect people directly like poisoning a person, but the witch cannot do anything to a person who is away or far. (Indian)
- Witchcraft is done by the witch. It is from the heart of the person not an outside evil agent. There are certain rituals and people who can right the wrongs of witchcraft and who can get rid of the witch. This does have a meaning in my culture. Witch trials were held hundreds of years ago in Europe and found later to be bogus after many innocent people were killed. This is studied by all in school so that it does not happen again. (American)
- It means an old woman with green skin and a pointy black hat who waves and uses a broomstick and stirs potions. (American)
- In my community, the theme of witchcraft is there but that does not affect the life of the people but only sometimes oppresses them. (Paraguayan)

EDITOR'S REFLECTIONS

In Africa, things and events such as sudden death, being struck by lightning, and strange illnesses do not just happen. There has to be someone who has caused them to happen because all reality is personalized. The theme of witchcraft therefore still continues to influence the lives of local people. In Kenya, for example, the local media continues to report news on witches and witchcraft on a daily basis. Indeed, there is often news of suspected witches being lynched in different parts of the country.

In October 2004, there were strong reactions to witch hunting sessions by a diviner at the coastal city of Mombasa, Kenya, an event widely publicized in the local media. The residents of Miritini area said they had called in the diviner to flush out the witches who were responsible for underdevelopment in the area. The residents further claimed that there had been incidences of mysterious events, including death, which were attributed to witchcraft. Those who counteract witches and their witchcraft, namely diviners, are seen as "doctors" able to overcome witches, hence the term "witch-doctor."

DISCUSSION QUESTIONS

1. In many communities in Africa, it is said that the worst thing a person can do is practice witchcraft. Why is this so?
2. Have you or a person known to you ever encountered witchcraft or ever been bewitched? Explain
3. Are the Western occult practices and the African witchcraft activities different or the same? Explain
4. Do you personally protect yourself against witchcraft by having special charms? Explain.

AFRICAN ILLUSTRATION

FEAR OF WITCHCRAFT

A Christian father who had worked as a catechist in a Catholic parish and had publicly taken a stand against all witchcraft activities and practices, still felt it necessary to instruct his children that they should bury their fingernails and hair clippings for fear that a witch could use these to harm them personally. (Fingernails and hair are perceived as sources of life as they continue to grow after a person is deceased -- seen in disinterred bodies).

RECOMMENDED READINGS

Magesa, L. (1998) *African Religion: The Moral Traditions of Abundant Life.* (pp. 165-174). Nairobi: Paulines Publications.

Idowu, B.E. (1973). *African Traditional Religion: A Definition.* (pp. 173, 175-178). New York: Orbis Books.

Zuesse, E.M. (1979). *Ritual Cosmos.* (pp. 223-237). Athens, Ohio: Ohio University Press.

NON-AFRICAN ILLUSTRATION

WITCHCRAFT TYPE OBJECTS FROM A WESTERN PERSPECTIVE

In the western world many things are used by people to protect themselves from possible evils that are present in the local environment. For example, Christian people wear medals and use crucifixes and religious garb in order to protect themselves from potential evils coming from the outside world.

In the USA during the Second World War, young sailors and soldiers on leave would visit primary schools telling of their experiences during wartime.

In one case, a young sailor related how he had been under attack and a bullet aimed for his heart struck the religious medal that his mother had given him before he went into the service; the bullet was deflected and it saved his life. As far as he was concerned it was the power of the religious medal that saved his life.

The reason for the use of protecting **things,** not only in the Western world but worldwide, is that human life is always in process and one never knows from one moment to another what will happen. The use of protecting **things** are like sentries set out in order that when something happens, whether for good or evil, there is a ready interpretation and response to the happening.

CHAPTER XV
Theme: DEATH

DEATH/KIFO

The carving is a universal representation of death in the form of a skull and crossbones.

DEATH

Introduction

Worldwide, physical and biological death is the same. However, the meaning of death and the rituals surrounding it vary from culture to culture.

Death in Africa

The African belief that the death of an elder is the birth of a baby indicates that death is a rite of passage where life is transmitted to a newly-born infant. This is illustrated by a Luo ritual in which one is both born and buried on the skin of an ox. Even the idea of the living dead, the saint-like elderly and recently deceased, shows that physical death in Africa is only the first stage in the process of dying -- one is never completely dead until one's name has been forgotten. Up to that time a person is seen as socially, emotionally and functionally alive through their things, children, wives, relatives, but especially through those who bear their names. Moreover, death is never seen as a natural event, even in the case of an elderly person, although in such a case there is not the anxiety that would be caused by an untimely death. Care must be taken, therefore, that the evil causing the death be confronted and cut off, so that it doesn't continue to take people's lives. Ritual, medicines and charms are employed to ensure that the evil that caused the death is overcome and chased away from the living. The Luo people employ a custom called "teng'o buru" by means of which the young men and adults, dressed in traditional warrior garb and driving their livestock before them, chase "death" from the homestead of the deceased to a deserted place where "death" is cursed and rendered harmless.

Death Worldwide

In some of earliest human settlements dug up by anthropologist, there is evidence that special care was taken in the burial of the dead -- an indication that death is a central theme in human existence. In fact, Becker (1973) in his book The Denial of Death argues that the issue of mortality is the most basic, fundamental and influential aspect of human existence, more than sexuality, self-preservation, power and social influence.

Evidence for his argument is seen in all the myriad, expensive and complicated rites and rituals surrounding the dead and dying. For example, in Katmandu, Nepal there are hostels for those of Hindu faith built along the Bamaputra Rive r where the dying are brought as they are close to death. The proper way to die is to be placed in the river holding onto the tail of a cow as you take your last breath. This rite is an expression of the Hindu belief in the reincarnation of a person, even in an animal form. Ancient Egyptians built the fabulous world-renown pyramids as burial chambers and placed the embalmed bodies of the dead deep within, surrounded with all the paraphernalia needed to live a human life on the other side of the world. In the Western world, bodies of the dead are routinely embalmed, dressed in new clothes, placed in a wooden or metal coffin and displayed in a parlor or chapel for at least three days before being buried. At the burial site the coffin is lowered into a cement box and sealed before filling up the grave with dirt. Some analysts relate the embalming to that of the Egyptians, saying that it is a "denial of death" ritual. Likewise, the day of viewing the body, which is dressed and made up as if the person were still alive, is a ritual to stop time, allowing the living to accept the fact that the person is truly dead. At the places of burial, grave markers made of metal or stone inscribed with a person's name and age are set as reminders and memorials to the dead. Some wealthy families go to the length of building elaborate burial chambers, called mausoleums, out of marble and granite where their loved ones are buried.

Some of the Western burial practices have been adopted by African communities as the proper way to be buried. For example, among the Luo speaking communities in North Mara Tanzania, burial societies have been started where they guarantee the members that their dead will be buried in wooden boxes. Prior to this the dead were sewn up in a white cloth, in imitation of Muslim burial rites, and earlier, traditionally, sewn up in an ox skin before being buried.

For Christians, death is never really accepted, except in the cases of the old and feeble, but it is tolerated as the passage into eternal happiness and bliss with God. Also, there is the expectation of resurrection of the body, and reunion with all one's friends and relatives who have passed away. Those without faith, the atheists, see death as the final and total despoliation of all that made them to be human beings-- an event expressing the absurdity of human life itself.

QUESTION

Kindly explain in detail your understanding of the theme of DEATH. Does it have any meaning in your personal, social and community life? N = 63 (53 Africans, 10 non-Africans)

RESPONSES COLLATED BY TEN CATEGORIES
1. *Relevance of the Theme of Death   R = 43*
2. *People's Perception of Death   R = 31*
3. *Definition of Death and Dying   R = 17*
4. *Causes of Death   R = 13*
5. *Relations Between the Living and the Dead   R = 12*
6. *Effects of Death   R = 11*
7. *Death in the Contemporary Society   R = 9*
8. *References to Death   R = 5*
9. *Nature of Death   R = 4*

10. *Where People Go When They Die   R = 1*
Other Comments   R = 20

AFRICAN RESPONDENTS   N = 53

Relevance of the Theme of Death   (R = 34)

It is *a rite of passage leading to the spiritual world* (10), it *signifies a transformation* and a beginning of a new life in the spiritual world with ancestors (7), if a person was *of good character* in this world, *he/she becomes an ancestor*, but if *he/she was bad he/she becomes a ghost* (3), the *cause of death determines* the *burial site and rituals* (2), it is a *continuation of life* together with the ancestors in the next world (2), it is through death that *one joins the spiritual world* and thus *is closer to God* (2), for *Christians death signifies the beginning of a glorious life* with God in eternity (1), it is *a transmission of life* to the *newborn infants* (1), it *evokes feelings of humility and expectations of a good life thereafter* (1), in African culture, *there is no death and dying* as *every death indicates a new life through naming* as a rite of passage (1), one is *considered dead when no child is named after him/her* (1), *the beginning and the end of a person on earth* is death (1), *gives meaning* to the *belief in the living dead* (1), death and dying are rites of passage, which *involve three phases: separation, incorporation and transition* (1).

People's Perception of Death   (R = 31)

It is an *inevitable process of life* that every person has to go through as *we are all predestined to die* (6), death is *the end of breathing and not the end of life* as there is life after death (5), death is *not always welcome* (3), it is *a phenomena that is not liked by people* (2), death is seen as *an evil hand* that takes people from the living world (1), death is perceived to be *a very painful experience* (1), it is perceived with a lot of *fear and pessimism* (1), though it is a must for everybody, it is *very difficult to accept and appreciate it* (1), death is considered as only being the *separation of the body from the spirit* (1), it is seen as *a great loss to the community* (1), among the Abaluyia people it is believed that *when one dies, he/she goes to a place of rest* (1), when *good people die* they go to a place of rest and *do not come back to haunt* their relatives (1), it *ushers people to a better life* (1), there is always *a cause* for death (1), death is *an annihilation* (1), it is the *physical body that dies while the spiritual body*, which is more important *moves on to the next world* (1), it is regarded as *a bad omen* (1), I look at death as *a period of rest* before the *coming of Jesus Christ* (1), death and dying is *feared by all except those who are yet to be born* (1).

Definition of Death   (R = 15)

It is when one *ceases to breathe* (3), is the *move from the physical to the spiritual world* (3), it is the *separation* of people who die physically from those who are living but they are *still together in spirit* (2), it is the *process of coming from living and going to the stage of the living dead* (1), it is *a rite of passage* which *ensures the transformation of human beings to the living dead and ancestors* thereafter (1), *death* is the *termination of earthly life*, while *dying is a passage* from earthly life to spiritual life (1), it is *losing the physical body and living in another state of life* where the dead become close to spiritual entities (1), is when the *physical body ceases to function* and it is buried (1), it is *a transition* in which one passes to another level of life and *has strong influence over the living* (1), is a *total and permanent disappearance* from ordinary life (1).

Causes of Death   (R = 8)

A *fellow human being* (3), caused by *natural circumstances* (1), caused by *sickness* (1), as a result of *an accident* (1), it is caused by *witchcraft* (1), *evil spirits* (1).

Relations Between the Living and the Dead   (R = 10)

The *living accord a lot of respect* to the dead so as *to avoid disturbances or harm* (3), the *dead are buried in the compound* as they are *believed to be watching over the living* (2), the *living remember the dead through nominal reincarnation* (2), the *dead are believed to have a strong influence over the living* (1), how *one lives on earth will affect his/her attitude in death* (1), the *living have to perform rituals* for the dead (1).

Effects of Death   (R= 11)

Unites a family and the whole community *in grief* (3), it *has devastating effects* on the family and the community (2), it *separates* people from their loved ones (1), death and dying keep the *population of people in check* (1), *leads to children being brought up in foster homes* (1), during *mourning it is a sad occasion* for the bereaved (1), *raises the question of inheritance and the care of the deceased's family* (1), *death of a young member* is considered a great loss to the community (1).

Death in the Contemporary Society   (R = 9)

Since I have been *living in the city, I have lost the communal aspect of sharing grief* with the other people who are not my relatives (1), *death is* understood to be *a consequence of sin* and therefore the *dead await judgment* (1), *dying is still considered a strange event* in the life of human beings (1), people *still name the newborn after their departed relatives* to ensure that they are remembered (1), death and dying is a theme that is still *viewed with a lot of suspicion* in the society (1), death is seen as *a normal and inevitable occurrence* (1), it is seen as *something that exists in the remote future* (1), it is *caused by some people out of carelessness* (1), it is *a punishment* for people's bad deeds (1).

References to Death   (R = 5)
Departing the earth (1), *going ahead* (1), being *defeated in battle* (1), an *extinguished lamp* (1), *resting* (1).

Nature of Death   (R = 4)
It is *something beyond our control* (1), the death of a young child was *not considered normal* as it was believed to have been *caused either by evil or an evil person* (1), those who die will never be seen again but only their *memories are with the living* (1), dying is a *process that never ends* (1).

Other Comments   (R= 9)
Muslims share the same view with Christians that death is not the final stage but it is a starting point, *a fact that is proven by the presence of spirits* (1), a person who has *hope in life after death, dies in dignity* and with the hope that this is not the end (1), there are *several stages* that one has to go through *before getting to the spirit world* (1), among the Agikuyu, there are *no mourning rituals but there is cleansing after death* (1), *death is only a feeling of emotional loss* which is personalized to whoever is affected (1), for some people what matters is *whether they will be ready when their time for dying comes*, if they will have *accomplished* what they should, and whether *they will be remembered* for their contribution in the community (1), I do not fear death since *I already have a lineage and sons who will carry on my name* (1), after death there is always a need to *cleanse the community and chase* the evil spirits away (1), in my community *people fear death* and they feel that it is one thing that God is unfair with, yet on the other hand they see it as a good omen as when *a person dies a child is named after him/her* and that the name then will continue (1).

NON-AFRICAN RESPONDENTS N = 10
[The respondents answered both according to their
own cultures and their understanding of African culture.]

Relevance of the Theme of Death   (R = 9)
The local society and community *join in grieving and celebration of the life of the departed* (1), for us *death signifies the end of life* (1), it is *a very central reality* in the life of my family since we lost a younger sister when she was eighteen years old (1), it *signifies the passage into a deeper and fuller life with God* (1), I see a *close connection* between life and death (1), when a

person dies, family, friends and relatives *gather to grieve for and celebrate the life of the deceased* (1), friends bring food and sometimes *money for a fund or scholarship in the name of the deceased* (1), leads to the *African concept of nominal reincarnation* as the semi-dead person continues to live on in the body of a newborn member of the family (1), *death and dying are two unhappy and inescapable realities* that bring human life to an end forever (1).

Definition of Death   (R = 2)
It is an *end in this life (world)* and *a new beginning in the next life,* a life with Christ and God (1), death and dying are *natural occurrences of the cosmic plan* that mark the end of an earthly life to open a way for a new form of *spiritual life -- eternal life* (1).

Causes of Death   (R = 5)
Natural causes (2), as a result of *a curse* (1), as a *form of punishment* (1), it is *fixed* by the creator himself (1).

Relations Between the Living and the Dead   (R = 2)
I believe that the dead person is *not far from us* and is living among us (1), we *meet the dead through dreams* and they give us messages (I have experienced this) (1).

Where People Go When They Die   (R = 1)
We go to *heaven* when we die (1).

Other Comments   (R = 11)
I fear *slow dying and death* (1), as a Christian I believe I have been *granted eternal life* (1), to me *death is quite near and I comfortably call it sister death* echoing the words of St. Francis *"in pain I know God is waiting for me and so are all our beloved ones who intercede for us the living"* (1), I *appreciate the African concept of death as a rite of passage* as a new birth into new life (1), people are *afraid of death and dying* that in many ways they *deny it is a reality* (1), to me as a Christian death can be beautiful as St. Francis' prayer says *"it is in dying that we are born into eternal life"* (1), since we *do not know what time we can expect death*, we need to be prepared to face it by being stainless when the call comes, thus we should all *try to lead a pure life* (1), my Christian belief is that *our charge is to love others and to serve God* by loving and serving others (1), in African cultures, there are *rituals and rites that surround death and dying,* which have to be done correctly (1), in the African context, *death does not fully occur until one has been forgotten* (1), death and dying are two themes whose meaning is *quite mysterious,* sometimes less understood and at other times less appreciated by people (1).

SUMMARY
Beliefs expressed regarding death and dying

<u>Death is:</u> when *one ceases to breathe*, the move from *physical to the spiritual world*, the process of *coming from the world of the living and going to the spiritual world*, *a rite of passage* which ensures the *transformation of human beings to the living dead*, *death* is the *termination of earthly life* while *dying is a passage* from earthly life to spiritual life, *losing the physical body* and living in another state of life where the dead become close to spiritual entities, *when the physical body ceases to function and it is buried*, a *transition* in which one passes to *another level of life* and has strong influence over the living, a *beginning in the next life* with Christ and God, *a natural occurrence of the cosmic plan* that marks the end of earthly life to open a way for a new form of spiritual life – eternal life.

<u>Relevance of the Theme of Death:</u> it is a *rite of passage* leading to the spiritual world, a *step to ancestorhood*, a *continuation of life* together with the ancestors in the next world, a *transmission of life* to newborn infants, it *signifies a transformation and a beginning* of a new life in the spiritual world with ancestors, the *beginning* of a glorious new life with God in eternity, *evokes* feelings of humility and expectations of a good life thereafter, *gives meaning* to the belief of the stage of the *living dead*, in African culture *there is no death and dying as every death indicates a new life* through naming as a rite of passage.

<u>People's Perception of Death:</u> it is *an inevitable process* of life that every person has to go through as we are all *predestined* to die, *very painful, a bad omen,* the *end of breathing* and *not the end of life* as there is *life after death*, a *phenomena* that is *not liked* by people, *an evil hand* that takes people from the living world, the *separation of the spirit from the body, difficult* to accept or appreciate, perceived with a lot of *fear and pessimism.*

<u>Effects of Death:</u> *unites* a family and the whole community in grief, *has devastating* effects on the family and the community, *separates* people from their loved ones, *helps to keep* the population of people in check, leads to *children* being brought up in *foster homes,* raises questions of *inheritance and the care* of the deceased's family, the death of *young member* is considered a great loss to the community.

<u>The Relations Between the Living and the Dead:</u> the living *accord* the dead a lot of respect so as to avoid disturbances or harm from them, *remember* the dead through nominal reincarnation, have to *perform* rituals for the dead, the dead are *believed to be watching over* the living, *have a strong influence* over the living, *communicate* to the living through dreams.

Death in the Contemporary Society: people living in the urban areas have *lost the communal aspect* of sharing in grief unlike those in the rural areas, it is seen *as a consequence* of sin, a *normal and inevitable* occurrence, something that exists in *the remote future*, as a *punishment* for people's bad deeds, viewed with a lot of *suspicion*, people *name* the newborn after the dead.

Causes of Death: *a fellow human being, natural circumstances, sickness, an accident, witchcraft, evil spirits,* it is a form of *punishment, fixed* by the Creator.

References to Death: *departing the earth, going ahead, defeated in the battle, an extinguished lamp, resting.*

Nature of Death: it is something *beyond our control*, the death of a *young child is not normal*, those who die will *never* be seen again but only *their memories* are with the living, *dying* is a process that never ends.

RESPONSES FROM WORKSHEETS

[*Note that death in Africa is a rite of passage, a transition, rather than a final state, as human life is recycled through the newly born. In death there are three phases: separation, incorporation and transition. Death is a separation from the earthly life and people, incorporation into the ancestral community, and transition back to the living community by way of nominal reincarnation . . . The way a person lived on earth will affect his/her status at death.*]

❑   **Kindly explain in detail your understanding of the theme of DEATH. Does it have any meaning in your personal, social and community life?**

AFRICAN RESPONDENTS   N = 53

[*There were seventeen ethnic groups of Africa represented: Agikuyu (13), Luo (11), Abaluyia (6), Akamba (3), Abagusii (3), Tutsi (3), Aembu (2), Teso (2), Kategi (2), Banyankole (1), Bemba (1), Kipsigis (1), Ibo (1), Baganda (1), Akan (1), Tigrinya (1), and Dinka (1). The respondents were university graduates, fourteen women and thirty-nine men.*]

- Death is something beyond our control. The death of a young child was not considered normal. People associated it with evil. They believed someone evil must have caused it. (Agikuyu)
- Death is a rite of passage just as initiation and birth. Death is the separation of people who die physically from those who are living but still together in spirit. Those who are dead will never be seen again but only their memories will be living with those living. Yes, death has a meaning in my personal, social and community life. (Agikuyu)
- Death is not an end to life but a transition/rite of passage that enables one to enter a new stage in life. (Abagusii)
- Death and dying is a process in life, which each person has to go through. It is the process of coming from living and going to the next stage of the living dead. Death is seen as an evil hand that takes people from the living world. Death affects the whole community. (Akamba)
- There was a reason for death. The cause of death determined where one would be buried. (Akamba)
- Death and dying are stages before the spirit world. It has a personal meaning because I know I will certainly pass that way. Death and dying evoke feelings of humility and wishing for a good life i.e., one that has inspiration for others. (Luo)
- Death and dying has a meaning to me. It means to me the continuation of life together with the ancestors in the spiritual world. (Luo)

- Death is a very painful experience and it separates people from their beloved ones. Though it is not liked by people it is a rite of passage into another world. It also transmits life into newly born infants. (Bemba)
- Death is when one ceases to breathe. The theme has a meaning in my personal, social and community life by how and when it occurs. It brings us together as one family. (Luo)
- Death and dying checks the population and leads to a vicious cycle in life. This is because there is no death and dying in African culture because every death indicates a new life through naming as a rite of passage. (Kipsigis)
- The theme is a rite of passage to the spiritual world. By dying the Agikuyu wishes the person a happy journey and stay in the far lands. Though there is cleansing, the people do not have mourning rituals. It is only a feeling of emotional loss which is personalized to whoever is affected. (Agikuyu)
- Death is devastating in all ways for the family and for the community. Death has made me grow up as a foster child in my uncle's household with my maternal grandparents. (Banyankole)
- Death is a reality though not always welcome. We shall all die some day, as this is part of human existence. For me what matters is, will I be ready to die when that time comes? Will I have accomplished what I should? Will the community I live in remember anything I did for them? Since I have been living in the city I have almost forgotten the communal aspect of sharing grief with the other people who are not my relatives. (Abaluyia)
- Death and dying are rites of passage which involve three phases: separation, incorporation and transition. The theme is relevant in my life and community life since we are all predestined to die at one time. (Aembu)
- Death is a transformation and beginning of a new life. My people believe in the communion of the living dead. For example when my father died two years ago, when we were deciding where to bury him, among the considerations of the choice of his grave was, he had to be buried within the compound for him to guard us. We mourned his passing away and grieved, yet we feel he is with us. (Ibo)
- Death is inevitable and dying is a process that is continuous in the society, which everyone has to pass through. It is a period where people experience loss and get into a sad duration of mourning. (Agikuyu)
- One is considered dead when a child is not named after him/her. I am named after my grandmother whose character I am told I really reflect. (Luo)

- Death and dying is an annihilation. It cannot be good. That is why people hate it. I lost my only sister and remained the only child of my mother. For this no person in his right mind can forgive death. (Luo)
- Death to my understanding is a passage through to the spirit world or ancestral world that acts as the mediator between the community and God the creator. (Luo)
- Dying is the beginning of a new life in a world, which is invisible but part of our own world. Members of my lineage who are related to me and who have died watch over me. (Agikuyu)
- The theme of death and dying is a rite of passage in life. To my community and me it means the completion of one's life and connotes the beginning of a new one. This is normally associated with the birth of a child. Death is perceived with a lot of fear and pessimism. (Abaluyia)
- Death and dying is the cessation of life on earth. To an African death is the passage to another world of spirits where life continues except now in a different form. That is why they buried people with some of their properties to help them start life in the next world. Death is a must for everybody but as much as we know this it becomes very difficult to accept and appreciate it. (Agikuyu)
- Death and dying is considered a passage into the world of the living dead. If he/she was good in life this person becomes an ancestor if he/she was a bad person he/she becomes a ghost. Personally I look at death as a period of rest before the coming of Jesus Christ. (Teso)
- I personally do not fear death since I already have a lineage and sons who will carry on my name. (Luo)
- Death is a transformation of the human beings into the ancestral world. The theme of death and dying is very important, as it is a rite of passage, which ensures the transformation of human beings to the living dead and the ancestors thereafter. In my community, the dead are treated with care and dignity and rituals are performed. (Agikuyu)
- Death is unpleasant but it raises the question of inheritance and care for the deceased's family. It brings in responsibility to ensure that the gap is taken care of. (Dinka)
- Death is a process of leaving the physical status for another world. One leaves for another world in the form of a spirit. It has a meaning in my personal, social and community life because it affects me whenever it happens and I have to cooperate with the bereaved ones. (Tutsi)
- After people die they join their ancestors and if he was of good character he is born back to the community. (Akamba)
- Death is the admission into life everlasting among the ancestors. Dying is a process that never ends. The dying are reborn in nominal reincarnation. Life is transformed at death, not ended. (Agikuyu)

- Death is a passage to a new life. Death is not always welcome. The death of the beloved, especially, the young is always devastating. Death affects the community and loosing a member you used to associate with in the community is painful. It affects family relations and duties. (Teso)
- Death is a rite of passage, which is inevitable. In Africa, death does not just occur. It is caused by some evil spirit. There is always a need to cleanse a community and chase them [evil spirits] away. (Abaluyia)
- Death and dying are real, feared by all except those yet to be born. (Luo)
- Death is a very sad thing in my community and here is one thing that in my culture they feel that God is unfair to them. On the other hand they feel it is a good omen because when one dies, a newborn is named after him and his name will continue. (Kategi)
- Death deprives life and leaves everybody in misery. But the beginning and the end of the person on earth is by dying. (Baganda)
- The theme of death and dying in my personal opinion is not an end; it is a physical [end] and not a spiritual one which is more important. (Tutsi)
- Death is just the real start of life to those who believe in the hereafter. It is only a separation of the body (physical) and the spirit. My fellow Muslim brothers and I share the same view with the Christians that death is not the final stage but a starting point. The presence of spirits is a clear proof and indication of this fact. (Agikuyu)
- Dying is the process of losing life. It comes through natural circumstances, sickness or accident. People also describe it as leaving us, departing, going ahead, being defeated in battle, an extinguished lamp. Death is the passage to another world. Death is a rest of some form. When death is described as going ahead of others, the implication is that we shall meet again. It is not the end of everything. (Abagusii)
- Death is the termination of earthly life; dying is a passage from earthly life to spiritual life. Through death one joins the spirit world, and thus is closer to God than the living. (Aembu)
- Death was a great loss to all communities. However, death was then understood to be a passage to serve the community in a higher capacity unless if one was unworthy to be a living dead due to his or her past deeds. (Abaluyia)
- Death is understood as losing the physical body and to live in another state of life where they [the dead] become close to the spiritual entities. In the contemporary meaning, death seems to be understood as a consequence of sin and therefore one [the dead] awaits judgment. (Akan)
- To me death is when the physical body ceases to function and it is buried. My understanding of it is a synthesis of my cultural knowledge and Christianity. Even though a person is dead and buried that is not the end

of him. There is life after death. This influences how I view death and dying. A person who has hope of life after death dies in dignity and with the hope that this is not the end. Among my people, it is believed that, after death people go to a place of rest. Good people [dead] go to rest and do not have a negative impact upon their living relatives. How one lives will affect their attitude as they die. Death ushers me to another better life. (Abaluyia)

- Death is not an end to life itself. It is a transition stage in which one passes to another level and has strong influence over the living. (Abagusii)

- Dying is still a strange event in the life of human beings. A Luo never dies; he is always killed, and in most cases, you find some neighbors being accused whenever a person dies. People are still named after their departed relatives to ensure that they are remembered. (Luo)

- Death introduces the person to the spirit world. The dead person is only absent physically but they are believed to be with us spiritually through the things and traditions they have left behind. The dead are remembered through naming them and the fact that we can still see their graves. The dead are treated with respect so that their spirits may not cause disturbance or harm the living. (Agikuyu)

- Death and dying is a theme that is always viewed with suspicion in the society. People ascribe different causes to death but mostly witchcraft is suspected to be the main cause of death. In the contemporary society death is seen as a normal and inevitable occurrence. (Agikuyu)

- Death and dying are phenomena which are not welcome. No one appreciates dying. Death is seen as something existing in the remote future. No dying person happily embraces death. (Luo)

- Death is a passage to the next world. We regard it as a bad omen. Many people are afraid of death. Although the expectation is that at one time all of us will die. (Kategi)

- Death marks the end of breathing but not the end to life. Death does not just occur, there must be a rational interpretation. Death is a reality and once one dies the community mourns and respect is accorded to the dead. (Agikuyu)

- Death is the move from physical to spiritual world. I still believe it is relevant as Christianity teaches the same way. As a Christian, death for me means going to live with God in eternity. It signifies the beginning of a glorious eternal life. (Agikuyu)

- Death is about a permanent and total disappearance from the ordinary life. It is about leaving other people on earth for another world. (Tutsi)

- No one just died. Death was caused. Today death is caused by someone too out of carelessness but also as a punishment for something bad one did. (Abaluyia)

- This is when one ends the life of being in the world or if one is separated from the living ones. It has a bigger meaning in my personal, social and community life because through it there is a social gathering and the community is united in grief. Death and dying is a challenge to one's life in the community. (Luo)
- Death and dying are two themes, whose meaning is quite mysterious, sometimes less understood, at other times less appreciated by people. For me, and for many members of my ethnic group, death and dying are natural occurrences of the cosmic plan that mark the end of an earthly life to open a way for a new form of spiritual life - - eternal life. For many others, death and dying are two unhappy and inescapable realities that bring human life to an end - - forever. (Tigrinya)

NON-AFRICAN RESPONDENTS N = 10
[The respondents answered both according to their own cultures and their understanding of African culture.]

[There were five non-African countries represented: America (5), India (2), Ireland (1), Spain (1), and Paraguay (1). The respondents were university graduates; three women and seven men.]

- I fear a slow dying and death. I see death as an end in this life (world) and a new beginning in the next life, in the life in Christ and in God. The local society and community join in this grieving and celebration of life of the departed. (Irish)
- I have lost all my ancestors. Death is an ending of life to us, not a continuation, although as a Christian I believe they have been granted eternal life. (American)
- Death is a very central reality in my life and in my family since we lost a young sister when she was eighteen. We all struggled with it. My mother still tends to see it as a "curse" or some punishment. I have grown to appreciate death as a rite of passage into deeper and fuller life with God. To me death is quite near, and I comfortably call it 'sister death' with St. Francis; in pain I know God is waiting for us and so are all our loved ones who intercede for us the living. I appreciate the African concept of death as a rite of passage, as a new birth into new life and I do see a close connection between birth and death. (Spaniard)
- I believe that the dead person is not far from us and is living among us e.g., in dreams we meet them and they give you a message. I have experienced this. (Paraguayan)

- People are afraid of death and dying to the point that in many ways they deny it is a reality. To me as a Christian, death can be very beautiful as St. Francis' prayer says "it is in dying that we are born into eternal life." (American)
- Everything that has a beginning must also have an end. It is fixed (destined) by the creator Himself. Since we do not know at what time we can expect it, we need to be prepared to face it. That would mean that we should be stainless when the call comes. Hence all try to lead a pure life. (Indian)
- After reflection my understanding of death and dying does not differ from that of the Christian idea. (Indian)
- My Christian belief is that our charge is to love others and to serve God by loving/serving others. We go to heaven when we die. (American)
- Where I come from death is death, and it is often from natural causes. Our belief is that one returns to God. In the African context, death does not fully happen until one's name has been forgotten. In the meantime, the "semi-dead" person may continue living in the body and soul of a newborn member of the family. (American)
- In African cultures there are rites and rituals that surround death and dying. These rites/rituals must be done and done correctly. In my community, there is a funeral when someone dies. Family and friends gather. Friends bring food and sometimes money for a fund or scholarship in the name of the deceased. (American)

EDITOR'S REFLECTIONS

In African cultures, there is always a reason or an explanation for the cause of death. Indeed, it is a tragedy when a young person dies, and it is believed that someone caused the death. Death of an elder, though sad, is considered more normal as it is a rite of passage to the next stage of life. At the same time, in the case of the death of a widow or widower, it is said that the dead spouse has called him/her to die.

The rituals and ceremonies often done before and after the burial rites reflect the age, sex and status of the dead person. It is also believed that the send-off accorded to a person is based on their moral standing which in turn determines his/her reception in the ancestral world. Those not accorded a good and befitting send-off, even though deserving, often hover around the living causing havoc and misfortunes.

DISCUSSION QUESTIONS

1. Discuss the statement "Africans will only die when God dies."
2. Is the death of an elderly person seen as due to the evil will and actions of another or it is due to natural causes brought on by old age?
3. Why are people with a bad reputation given a normal burial even though their name will not be given to the newly born and they will pass out of memory, therefore out of existence?
4. What has been your personal experience dealing with death? Explain.

AFRICAN ILLUSTRATION

DEATH OF THE YOUNG IS NEVER DUE TO NORMAL CAUSES

A young Catholic Wakini man with a wife and two small children, died of an unknown causes while on a trip. He was returned to his homestead for burial. As they were filling in the grave, a hollow reed about five feet long was put in his ear and then the grave was filled up. The tip of the reed protruded about six inches from the ground. When the missionary conducting the burial asked the people the reason for the reed, they said it was for communication with him to find out who it was that had caused his death.

RECOMMENDED READINGS

Mbiti, J.S. (1991). *Introduction to African Religion.* Nairobi: (pp. 116-130). East African Educational Publishers.

Zahan. D. (1979). *The Religion, Spirituality and Thought of Traditional Africa.* (pp. 36-52). Chicago: The University of Chicago Press.

Jahn, J. (1990). *Muntu: African Culture and the Western World.* (pp. 105-114). New York: Grove Weidenfeld.

NON-AFRICAN ILLUSTRATION

UNTIMELY DEATH FROM A WESTERN PERSPECTIVE

An untimely death in the Western world is never seen as accidental. There is always some need to understand why a person's life was snuffed out while they were still in their youth, and had not reached their full potential. At a recent funeral of a young man who was killed in a tragic road accident, the mother was inconsolable. She was concerned that his death was due to something she had done wrong, and that it was a punishment from God. . . Popular Christianity teaches that we do not know the reasons for untimely deaths, but eventually they will be revealed in the coming of the kingdom.

Appendix A

BELIEFS SUMMARIZED IN EACH CHAPTER

[Note that these summaries articulate in a systematic manner the beliefs of African religion which are entwined and embedded in African cultural knowledge, giving that knowledge a special sacral and personal dimension. These summaries can be used as a text for teaching African religion's contemporary beliefs and spirituality.]

CREATOR GOD
(TRANSCENDENT PRINCIPLE OF REALITY)

<u>God is</u>: the *creator*, a *supernatural being, provider, controller, protector, owner of everything, all knowing* and *eternal*. God is a *unifier, caregiver, omnipresent, omnipotent*, a *pure spirit, sustainer, immortal and beyond comprehension.*

<u>God is Known by</u>: *blessings to people, punishment meted out, key moments of life, manifestation* through nature and the *names* given to God.

<u>Human Being's Responsibilities towards God:</u> *revering, respecting, obeying, and fearing God.* They are to continue *God's work of creation through reproduction*, live a *God-centered life, not to question nor call upon God unnecessarily.*

<u>God is Approached through:</u> *worship* and *prayer, sacrifices, offerings, rituals, intermediaries,* and by going to God's *sacred dwelling places.*

ANCESTORS
(FOREBEARERS)

<u>Ancestors are:</u> *great-grandparents* from whom we *are descended* who *physically departed long ago,* we *cannot remember their physical appearance* though they are *still present in spirit form* and we *remember them through naming* the *newborn* after them, *departed lineage members, spirits of our forefathers* who lived *good and ethical lives,* and were *respected members* of the society who passed on to be near the *creator God.*

<u>Role of Ancestors in the Community:</u> to *protect* the living, give *identity, bless* people, are *moral guardians, intermediaries between God, people and other spiritual beings, owners of land, property and vital resources, source of life, role models* and *custodians of culture.*

<u>Relevance of the Theme of Ancestors:</u> *influence* people's lives, are the *source of life* in the community, still have a *stake* in the physical world, help people understand that *physical death* is only a transition to the next world, that life is *recycled,* and echoes the *belief in the communion of*

saints in the sense that they are part of the church of God's people. People still use their *names, get their personality and character* from them.

People's Responsibilities towards Ancestors: *appease* them through *sacrifices, offerings,* and *libations,* live according to the *customs* and *moral standards* set by the ancestors, *respect them, name newborn children* after them, hold *memorials* to *honor* them, *revere* and *include* them in ceremonies and to *speak well* of them.

Characteristics of Ancestors: they are *closer to God* in the hierarchy of power, lived *good lives* while on earth, *died at a mature age, must have sired children, respectable, holy, demand attention* from the living, their *names and spirits* continue to live on in their descendants, and are *immortal.*

Where Ancestors Reside: in people through *nominal reincarnation,* are *ever present* in the society, and in *special places.*

Communication Between Ancestors and the Living: through *dreams, diviners* and *young children.*

LIVING DEAD
(RECENTLY DECEASED)

Living Dead are: *people who died recently* whom we were attached to in life and *their memories are still fresh in people's minds.* They are *members of the lineal family* who *died recently* and *children have not been named after them, memories of their good works and qualities still remain with the living,* and *their children and property are still around us.*

Characteristics of Living Dead: are *in spirit form, respectable, benevolent, have children and property,* are *similar to Christian saints,* were *pious* while alive, of *reputable moral standards, outstanding leadership qualities,* and were *buried with respect.* They can demand that the *newborn be named* after them. They can *cause loss and misfortunes* when their demands are not met, can *curse* the living, and influence *social order and disorder.*

Role of Living Dead in the Society: to *intercede* for the living, *influence the decisions* of the living, apportion *blessings and property,* acts as a *link* between the *living, the dead and the spiritual world.* They are the *guardians* and *protectors* of the living, and the *cultural guardians.* They give *solutions to* crises in life, *control personal, social and communal* life.

Responsibilities of Humanity towards Living Dead: to *name the newborn* after them, *respect, emulate, honor and revere* them, offer them *sacrifices* and *pour for them libations to appease* them. People are to *consult them, avoid* what they do not like, *redress wrongs and evils* to restore *social order, pray* for them and *cherish their memories.*

Significance of the Theme of Living Dead: it shows *the link between* the *past, and present through naming*, shows that *death is a passage leading* to the *life beyond*, shows that *the spirits of the dead are still living*, and *symbolizes* the beginning of a *new life.* The theme helps *individuals believe that they will meet the departed in a future life,* signifies the *integration of the spirit of the deceased* into the living ancestral community, and shows that *the end of physical life is not the end of existence.*

Impact of the Theme of Living Dead on the Living: makes people a*ware of their duty* towards the dead, *ensure* that *correct burial rites and rituals* are carried out in accordance with the traditions. It *inspires good living,* helps people have an easier *understanding of the after life.*

Communication Between the Living and Living Dead: *dreams, thoughts, prayer,* and through *direct speech* when the living ask for help or advice.

NOMINAL REINCARNATION
(LIFE AFTER DEATH)

Nominal Reincarnation is: the *ritual transmission* of life from the dead to the living. It is the *belief that the spirit* and *personality of a dead person* lives on through a *newborn.* It is the *remembrance of the dead ancestors* by giving their names to the next generation, the dead coming back to life through the newborn, is when a *newborn embodies* the spirit of the ancestor after whom it has been named, the *coming back to life of an ancestor* through naming a child after him/her, *recycling of human life* and giving it to a newborn child, the *birth and ritual transmission of life* from one stage of development to another, the *process in which the life and spirit of a highly respected elderly person whether living or recently dead is transferred to a newborn*, is the process of *recycling human character,* and the naming of a newborn *to occupy a place in the lineage.*

Impact of the theme of nominal reincarnation: *explains the resemblance of people* to their ancestors, affects the way people *live socially,* a *newborn gets to be named after a recently deceased person,* makes people *strive to leave behind a good memory after their death,* and it gives a person the *motivation* to *remain strong in character* like the person he/she is named after.

Relevance of the theme of nominal reincarnation: emphasizes the need to *recycle life*, is a *reminder* that there is *life after death,* implies that *life is cyclical,* through nominal reincarnation life is *passed on from one generation to another,* life is given to a newborn child as *a gift from the ancestral community,* it is the *naming custom* that unites *the living* with the *ancestors,* it is to *honor, respect, and to let the spirits of the ancestors* continue living among us.

AFRICAN LINEAGE
(FAMILY STRUCTURES)

The Lineage is: *the continuity of life, tracing one's origin to the great forefathers, enhancement of life through procreation,* and represents *the interconnection between the dead, the living and the yet to be born.* It is the *lifeblood* of a person, the *continuation* of the *family line,* and the *life* energy of a person.

A Person's Responsibilities in the Lineage Includes: to *marry, bearing children* to continue the lineage, *knowing his/her family tree,* and to see the *forefathers as the guides and models* of the present life.

The Lineage Gives a Person: an *identity, legitimacy, links him/her to the living and ancestral community, determines values, rituals and behavior of the members*, through *naming, initiation, and marriage.*

A Person is Incorporated into the Lineage through: *naming, patrilineal descent, marriage, blood ties, clan membership, matrilineal descent* and by *going through all rites of passage.*

LEADERSHIP
(POLITICAL AND SOCIAL)

Leadership is: *a state* given or accorded to an individual as a result of their *outstanding character* in the society. It is the *trust bestowed* on a person to act on behalf of others, a person's ability to *lead others,* act as *a guide, protector, advisor, judge and facilitator* because of his/her wisdom.

A Leader is: a person chosen from a group because *of particular outstanding qualities,* a person with the *ability to execute on behalf of the people,* has *authority* from God, a *caretaker, specialist and guide of the people,* a person in charge of making decisions on behalf of others in a *social situation.*

Types of Leaders: *community leaders, heads of families, clan leaders, priests, teachers, local government officials, parents, diviners, chiefs and the eldest child in the family.*

The Characteristics of a Leader are: is a *role model, morally upright,* has *outstanding and exemplary character, wise, responsible, respectable, charismatic, authoritative, an expert in various fields, a specialist, articulate, understanding, reconciler, a good listener, development conscious, reliable, just to all, patient, advanced in age* and *allows for dialogue with other people.*

The Role of a Leader in the Society: is a *moral guardian, enhances community welfare,* acts as a *judge* and *arbitrator,* is a *representative of the people, guides, protects, leads and counsels people.* The leader is *an overseer* and *spokesperson* of the people.

The Significance of the Theme of Leadership is: helps to *maintain order, and unity* in the society, and *control chaos* in the society. It is a sign of *good leadership qualities* in a person. A leader is the *symbol of authority, unity, good governance and good life in the society, symbolic representative of the group,* is a *link* between *human beings, spirits and God.*

A Person Becomes a Leader through: *appointment, election, training, inheritance, grooming, being born in a lineage of leaders,* and by *having special characteristics and qualities.*

 Responsibilities of People towards Leaders are: to *respect, obey and pray for leaders.*

Leaders Today are: *self-seekers* at the expense of the society, *looting* the resources of their countries in Africa, *bosses rather than servants* of the people, *dictatorial, and unjust. Political leadership* has taken over the center stage from *cultural* leadership. *Wealth, popularity and the ability to meet certain* goals are the determinants of leadership today.

ADULTHOOD AND ELDERHOOD
(MATURITY AND WISDOM)

Definition of Adulthood and Elderhood: it is *the partaking or awarding* of responsibilities and duties to an individual, family and the community, it is the recognition that one is aged enough and *has the required* knowledge to perform responsibilities of an adult or elder, *a process* which makes a person *a full and mature member of the community* with various duties and rights that accompany it, *the introduction of an individual* to adult life through various ceremonies, *the process of recognizing* that one has reached an age of *dependability and responsibility*, to be able to *transmit life through marriage*.

Relevance of Adulthood: means that *one is accepted and empowered* as an adult and a responsible member of the community, is an *occasion for education* on community *norms and values*, *incorporates* a person into the community, *sanctions* a person to *marry and procreate, confers* upon a person an *identity* as part of a group in the community, acts as *a moral guide*, gives rise to *community leaders, gives* a person *the right to own property*, to be *involved in decision making, to protect the community,* gives certain *privileges as well as duties,* is an *indication* of reaching an age worthy of respect in the community.

Characteristics of Elders: they are *custodians of wisdom, consultants* on matters of the community as they have long experience in life and community affairs, *advanced in age, highly respected, always consulted* to give *wise counsel* to the younger generation, they have *high moral values, high personal achievements, authority* over other members of the community, *wisdom and knowledge* of life in the community, *married and have children beyond the teen years*, they can *discern and advise* from what they have learnt in life, *must be totally trustworthy*.

Signs of Adulthood: *circumcision, building a hut, marrying, a change* in one's *behavior,* giving out of *symbolic objects, things and animals, incisions,* going through *all rites of passage.*

Responsibilities of adults: *mature behavior, maintain peace and harmony* in the community, *participate actively* in the community functions as an adult.

Definition of Elderhood: is a *status* where one is looked upon for *guidance and leadership,* the move from being a *married normal community member* with limited responsibilities and authority to one with *broader community responsibilities with more authority.*

BRIDEWEALTH
(MARRIAGE GIFTS)

Bridewealth is: a *token of appreciation to the parents of the bride* in recognition for raising and caring for their daughter, *offering compensation* for the role played by the girl before getting married, *money, property or labor* given to the family of the bride to show appreciation, *a token* given to build a new relationship between the families of the man and the woman who come together because of marriage, *the exchange of valuables* to formalize a marriage as a rite of passage, *a price paid by the groom's family or clan* to the *bride's family or clan, the exchange of gifts* between the families of the bride and the groom with the groom's *family first giving* their token of appreciation, *a public proclamation* by a man to a woman's parents that she is *legally married* in his community, *products or items* given in a marriage to *cement* the relationship between a *married couple, an agreement* for an everlasting friendship between both families, *legal formal identity that customary marriage* has taken place, *a token* from the groom's family as a way of legalizing the marriage and *initiating a relationship between the two families.*

Relevance of Bridewealth: it legitimizes the *marriage, children born in the marriage, children's claim to inheritance, the family, sex* within marriage, *gives the wife the right* to inherit the husband's property, *the right to be* buried at her husband's home, *facilitates* the redistribution of wealth in the community, *acts as a seal as well as security* for the marriage, *strengthens* relationships between the two families, *enhances* the public stature of the marriage, *confers respect* upon the couple, serves as a *token of appreciation* to the woman's family, *unites* the man and woman's family, makes one *acceptable* to the family he/she is marrying into, is a *bonding* factor in marriage, gives the *husband the right* to bury his wife in his land, is a way of *ensuring* the continuity of the family, a *sign of goodwill, a reminder to the bride* that she is in the family of the man permanently.

What Bridewealth Symbolizes: *love and appreciation* for both the bride and the groom, *the groom values the bride* and will take good care of her, a *sign of commitment,* the wife has *been accepted into* the family and community that she is marrying into.

Consequences of Failure to Pay Bridewealth: the marriage is considered *illegitimate*, if a woman dies before the payment of bridewealth the husband *will not be allowed to bury her on his land,* unless he pays the required amount in full, the *woman is taken back* to her father's homestead to be buried and *the man loses claim over the children,* children lose *claim and right of inheritance* from their father's community, the woman *does not feel secure* in the marriage as well as the husband's community, the union *has no legal binding.*

People Involved in the Payment of Bridewealth: the *families* of the bride and the groom, *all members of the family* who contribute towards the payment of bridewealth, *the whole community.*

Bridewealth in the Contemporary Society: has become *commercialized, an avenue for* getting rich quickly, *a personal commitment* rather than a family or community affair, it is *slowly dying off* in the urban centers as cohabiting becomes more prevalent, *seen as a form of payment* for the bride, the commercial aspect has *overshadowed* the moral dimension that our forefathers attached to it, its meaning has been *watered down* by the money economy, *still seen as an appreciation* to the bride's family and therefore relevant in a marriage, has been *abused* as a result of *materialism and formal education.*

MARRIAGE
(MARITAL UNIONS)

Marriage is: the *union* of *two people of opposite sex* for the *purpose of procreation and companionship*, an institution in which *a mature couple unites* with the aim of *propagating their lineage*, union of a man and a woman who *through love* decide to live together as husband and wife, a *formal agreement* between *a man and a woman* in front of witnesses making them husband and wife, a *socially accepted union* between a man and a woman/women, a *rite* that unites members of two lineages to *cement kinship ties*, a *social relationship of two adults of opposite sex* who make an *emotional and legal commitment* underscored by *group sanctions* to live together as husband and wife with the *aim of raising children.*

Relevance of Marriage: *sustains* the lineage, brings *order* in the community, *unites* families, clans and communities, is *the basis* of a person's social and community life, *a condition* for *elderhood*, *legitimizes* children born of the union, helps in *propagating the family name and reincarnation* of its members, *the couple acquires new social responsibilities*, gives the *offspring an identity*.

Significance of Marriage: is *God's way of uniting humanity* and ensuring the *continuity of life*, an *institution* through which the *human race is preserved*, the only way *life is passed on legally, continuation of life* through bearing children, a *sacramental bond* that is life long, a *binding institution* for different families, clans and communities, a *bond* that brings two people together so that they may serve *God and a family* through their relationship, the *foundation* of a family, a *ritual* that confirms one as an *adult* and *tests one's capability in leadership*; marks the *rite of passage* from youth to adulthood, *defines* the *socially accepted way for procreation and sexual gratification* amongst spouses.

Elements of Marriage: is a *community* event, between two people of *opposite sex*, usually *cemented* by payment of *bridewealth, deeply rooted* in *traditional* setting, a *sacred* institution, a continuation of a *couple's love*, an *expectation* of the society that each person must marry after attaining the *right age*, it must be *legitimized, children* are important and normally expected, *traditional ceremonies* are done to bless the marriage.

Why People get Married: for *procreation, social recognition, companionship, propagation of the family name*, to *avoid social stigma, fulfill* a community *obligation.*

Marriage Today: is on the *decline* as indicated by the prevalence of *single parent families, divorces, neglected children, challenges from the socio-economic* point of view, is *not respected* nor considered so *worthy*, is still *relevant despite the setbacks* facing it, is for *convenience,* in the form of *'come-we stay,'* takes place *with or without the consent of the wider families*, may or may not be *legalized.*

POLYGYNY
(MANY WIVES)

Polygyny is: the *practice of having more than one wife, the marriage* of many women by *one man simultaneously*, having more than one wife in *a legally binding* arrangement especially with the *approval of the community, marrying as many wives* as one can be able to feed and take good care of, marrying more than one wife in a *legally organized and recognized* ceremony, having more than one wife *according to the dictates of the culture and sanctioned* by the community.

Relevance of Polygyny: was a *symbol of wealth*, considered an *economic achievement,* vital in *widening* the kinship network, necessitated by the *high mortality* rate of the males, a way of *ensuring the continuity* of the lineage especially in cases where the first marriage was childless, to *perpetuate* the lineage, *enlarge* the progeny, *increase the number* of male offspring in the lineage, an *indicator of* a higher social status, *good* *leadership and management* of the family, for *labor* through the children, *security in old age,* helped in *spacing* the children, *redistribution of wealth* in the community, *reducing infidelity*, gives rise to *interaction* of many clans and communities, *unity* between families, clans and communities, provided a *help-mate and companion* to the wife.

Who Sanctions Polygyny: it is legally sanctioned by the *culture of the community in which it takes place, the society.*

Polygyny in the Contemporary Society: it is *still relevant*, has *reduced* due to social and economic challenges, should be discouraged as it *promotes promiscuity* by unsatisfied spouses, should be looked at anew and *understood in the present day context*, seen as *risky* because of the HIV/AIDS scourge, not accepted as it is *uneconomical and exploitative,* many men *keep concubines* without the consent of their wives, in the rural set-up *polygynous men are still respected* as the practice is welcome and encouraged.

Challenges to Polygyny Today: *harsh* economic conditions, *Christianity, HIV/AIDS, gender sensitization* programs, *feminist* movements that portray it as negative and discriminative towards women, erosion of *cultural beliefs, scarcity of land, globalization, formal education, population control* campaigns, *Western culture, capitalism,* the *inflation* of bridewealth costs.

HERBALISTS
(MEDICAL PRACTITIONERS)

Herbalists are: *special people* in the community who *understand diseases* and can treat them using *herbs, have good knowledge of using herbs for treatment and in performing cultural ceremonies, medicine men, diviners, rainmakers, African doctors, ritual experts,* those *consulted* and heal sickness using *traditional methods* of healing, who have *skills in identifying medicine* and treating some *specific diseases*, who can *read* people's illnesses and treat them using *traditional medicine, experts* in the community who have a thorough knowledge in understanding a number of diseases and providing *the right treatment* using traditional medicine, those with *special gifts* to treat illnesses.

Characteristics of Herbalists: they *use locally available and natural* herbs, *diagnose and cure* illnesses and misfortunes, are *highly respected, ritual experts, spiritual directors,* have *exceptional skills* in healing, *good diagnostic* skills, *supernatural powers, cultural knowledge* regarding sickness, keep the *combination of their medicines a secret* so as to maintain its sacredness, *pass down the knowledge* of their practice to their children through *training*, offer their services *freely* to all, they may *invoke mystic* powers as part of the treatment, *know well the properties* of their medicines through knowledge **accumulated** through generations, most of them **do not possess written** knowledge of their profession.

Role of Herbalists in the Community: *treat* physical as well as psychological diseases, **sustain life** through curing, keep the society **healthy, treat and guide** people in the community, *relieve* pain and suffering caused by *evil spirits, recommend* treatment based on the diagnosis, are *African pharmacists, mediators* between human beings, the spiritual world and creator God.

Relevance of the Theme of Herbalists: to *explain* the ability of bio-diversity in medicine, **influence** people's lives, *cure* people. They **heal** taking into account that the individual belongs to a family and a community, **provide** for vertical healing in relation to the ancestors and horizontal healing in relation to the community, **embody knowledge** that is passed on from one generation to the next, **make use** of healing methods that form part of the accumulated wisdom of a people.

How One Becomes a Herbalist: through **inheritance, apprenticeship, training, power from God.**

Unique Qualities of Herbalists: they *treat* some diseases that modern medicine is not able to, have **cheaper rates** in comparison to modern medical establishments, most of them are **credible, combine spiritual powers as well as knowledge** of herbs to treat the sick, their **medicines are effective with few side effects.**

Types of Herbalists: *medicine men, rainmakers, diviners.*

Herbalists Today: are **physicians and nurses, practitioners** of alternative medicine, **social workers and psychologists, counselors, influential** in the society today, somewhat **overlooked** despite the fact that they played a big role in the society before the advent of modern medicine, like **chemists** for they deal with diagnosis and administering medicine to the sick, **people who are well-educated** in botany and the use of herbal extracts to treat chronic ailments especially where Western medicine has failed, some are **commercially oriented.**

DIVINER
(SPIRITUAL DIRECTORS)

A Diviner is: a *person,* who is **gifted** by God to **counteract the forces of evil, unravel** the **mysteries** of people's lives, is a **link** between the **living,** the **spirit world** and **God.** He/she uses his/her **powers** for the **betterment** of the **community,** is a **priest, leader, and spiritual director** of African religion, and can **identify** a **problem** and provide a **solution** for it. A person regarded as a diviner is a **friend** of the **community** as he/she is **involved** in **all aspects** of the **community, knowledgeable** in many fields, **promotes life,** and is a **ritual expert.**

Role of a Diviner in the Society Includes: *mediates* between *people, the spirit world and God.* He/she *restores harmony* in the society, *predicts* the future, *reverses* the harm caused by witches, *harmonizes* the happening of events in the society, *exorcizes* evil spirits, performs *rituals and rites, reverses* the harm caused by the witch, and offers *advice.* He/she is the *moral guardian, a religious leader,* and a *healer.*

Characteristics of a Diviner Include: he/she is a *leader, an elder, a ritual expert,* at times he/she is *a rainmaker, a herbalist* and is considered a *holy person.* The diviner *promotes life,* relates to the *living* in physical form and to the *ancestors* in *spirit form.*

Relevance of the Theme of Diviner: it shows the *mediatory role* played by the diviner between the people, ancestors and God, he/she occupies a central position in Africa today, it offers a way of knowing the *hidden truth,* and through them *healing* is accomplished.

People Seek the Services of a Diviner: when *in need of healing, times of problems, seeking intervention,* and in *extreme and unexplainable circumstances.*

A Person Becomes a Diviner: through *inheritance, training or is born with the skills.*

Diviner in the Modern Society is: *Jesus, a priest, a pastor, and any religious leader.*

WITCH
(NATURE OF EVIL)

A Witch is: a *human being* who is *totally evil, immoral, untrustworthy, who runs naked at night, has superhuman and mystical powers* and *does not live in accordance with societal rules.*

A Witch's Activities Include: to *harm* people, *bring misfortunes, calamities, disharmony, to threaten life,* and is often associated with a *black cat.*

A Witch is Controlled through: *painful killing, ostracizing him/her* from the society, by the witch being encouraged to *lead a moral life,* by the *witchdoctor (diviner)* through *cleansing ceremonies* and by *punishment.* The practices of witches are discouraged by *denunciation,* and by *not naming a newborn after a witch.*

A Person can Become a Witch through: *doing evil to others, failing to control the evil that emanates from the heart, marrying into a family of witches, being born in a family of witches, having bad blood, a result of a curse,* and by *being used by the devil* to adversely affect other people's lives.

Other Effects of a Witch Include: at times *controls* the morals of individuals and the community, sometimes *helps to solve difficult problems, helps* some members of the society to *climb up the ladder of success,* and *can be engaged to counteract the power of other witches.*

WITCHCRAFT
(MALEVOLENT CHARMS AND RITUALS)

Witchcraft is: an *act of evil* as practiced by witches, the *art of manipulating vital forces of nature for malevolent reasons, practicing* evil or black magic, the *ability and desire* to do evil, the *act of bewitching* others, a *craft, skill or practice and knowledge* of using magical powers through the *devil*, the *evil that is against life and people's progress* and *puts fear* in the minds of people causing them not to do their best *spiritually, physically and psychologically,* the *power* by which certain members of the community *destroy the order and balance* existing in the society, *bad people using bad medicine* to harm others especially when used for commercial purposes, the *outcome of evil deeds and intentions* on a third party, an *evil spirit* that causes harm to individuals, *anything that causes social disharmony, conflicts and misunderstandings* in the community, *mystical power* which some people have from *evil spirits* which inflict pain to other people, an evil practice carried out by *witches and wizards* on people who are seen to be progressing in the society by way of *education, business and politics*, the *act of defying God's will, evil thoughts and deeds* which lie within the *human heart and actions, intention to do willful harm* to fellow human beings.

Relevance of the Theme of Witchcraft*: gives explanations for mysterious happenings in the community, it is looked upon with awe in the community, used as an excuse by people who prefer to be lazy than think about their mistakes or failures and seek for solutions and remedies, it affects those who believe in it psychologically, is feared as it is the epitome of evil, an anti-social behavior, the community is able to identify a family of witches among them, many communities do not like it and shun away from it, it is a habit that starts at a personal level before taking root in the community, it is spiritual and affects the human mind, family, society and the physical well being of the people; it challenges an individual to be aware of his/her bad thoughts which could harm other people and seek to break his/her good relationship with the family and other people in the society.*

Consequences of Witchcraft in the Community: causes *confusion, suspicion, hatred, disharmony, destruction, limits* people from doing progressive work such as initiating development projects *for the fear of being bewitched*, it is a *threat to life*, makes people *seek protective charms* to counteract the powers of the witch, it is *often employed* to harm others.

How Witchcraft is Counteracted: through *condemning the practice of witchcraft, rituals, prayers, protective charms, healing, strong belief and protection* from God for those who are Christians, by a *diviner, herbalist,* *excommunication, lynching, killing, exorcism* of evil spirits, *avoiding relations* with a family of witches.

Where Witchcraft is Found: in *everyone* with ill intentions or thoughts towards others, *the evil embodied* in each one of us, *the eyes and thoughts* of a witch, *the witch* who is present in every community in Africa, the *heart* of a person.

How Witchcraft is Acquired: through *inheritance, buying* it from witches, *being passed on* from an evil person to a non-evil person.

Manifestations of Witchcraft: most of the events are carried out by *people related to the victim* or who know him/her very well, *mysterious sickness, accidents, injuries, sudden death,* channeled from a witch as the source to a victim, *magic.*

Why People Practice Witchcraft: to *perpetuate* hatred and *propagate* witchcraft, out of *malice, revenge, jealousy, envy, fear* of others progressing more than them.

Witchcraft in the Contemporary Society: still *exists in different forms* and has *immense effects* on the lives of people, *the witch* is believed to be the cause of all problems afflicting the society, practiced through harming people using *occult scientific* methods, *irrespective of the faith* many people believe in the power of witchcraft and act with fear when *mysterious or unexplained* calamities befall them, due to the influence of *Christianity and education* many people now appear indifferent to the question of witchcraft.

DEATH
(CESSATION OF LIFE)

Death is: when *one ceases to breathe*, the move from *physical to the spiritual world*, the process of *coming from the world of the living and going to the spiritual world, a rite of passage* which ensures the *transformation of human beings to the living dead, death* is the *termination of earthly life* while *dying is a passage* from earthly life to spiritual life, *losing the physical body* and living in another state of life where the dead become close to spiritual entities, *when the physical body ceases to function and it is buried*, a *transition* in which one passes to *another level of life* and has strong influence over the living, *a natural occurrence of the cosmic plan* that marks the end of earthly life to open a way for a new form of spiritual life – eternal life.

Relevance of the Theme of Death: it is a *rite of passage* leading to the spiritual world, a *step to ancestorhood*, a *continuation of life* together with the ancestors in the next world, a *transmission of life* to newborn infants, it *signifies a transformation and a beginning* of a new life in the spiritual world with ancestors, the *beginning* of a glorious new life with God in eternity, *evokes* feelings of humility and expectations of a good life thereafter, *gives meaning* to the belief of the stage of the *living dead*, in African culture *there is no death and dying as every death indicates a new life* through naming as a rite of passage.

People's Perception of Death: it is *an inevitable process* of life that every person has to go through as we are all *predestined* to die, *very painful, a bad omen,* the *end of breathing* and *not the end of life* as there is *life after death*, a *phenomena* that is *not liked* by people, *an evil hand* that takes people from the living world, the *separation of the spirit from the body, difficult* to accept or appreciate, perceived with a lot of *fear and pessimism.*

Effects of Death: *unites* a family and the whole community in grief, *has devastating* effects on the family and the community, *separates* people from their loved ones, *helps to keep* the population of people in check, leads to *children* being brought up in *foster homes,* raises questions of *inheritance and the care* of the deceased's family, the death of *young member* is considered a great loss to the community.

The Relations Between the Living and the Dead: the living *accord* the dead a lot of respect so as to avoid disturbances or harm from them, *remember* the dead through nominal reincarnation, have to *perform* rituals for the dead, the dead are *believed to be watching over* the living, *have a strong influence* over the living, *communicate* to the living through dreams.

Causes of Death: *a fellow human being, natural circumstances, sickness, an accident, witchcraft, evil spirits,* it is a form of *punishment, fixed* by the Creator.

References to Death: *departing the earth, going ahead, defeated in the battle, an extinguished lamp, resting.*

Nature of Death: it is something *beyond our control*, the death of a *young child is not normal*, those who die will *never* be seen again but only *their memories* are with the living, *dying* is a process that never ends.

Death in the Contemporary Society: people living in the urban areas have *lost the communal aspect* of sharing in grief unlike those in the rural areas, a *beginning in the next life* with Christ and God, it is seen *as a consequence* of sin, a *normal and inevitable* occurrence, something that exists in *the remote future*, as a *punishment* for people's bad deeds, viewed with a lot of *suspicion*, people *name* the newborn after the dead.

Appendix B
RESPONDENTS BY NATIONALITY AND ETHNIC GROUPS

African Respondents by Nationality and Ethnic Groups

Kenya
- Abagusii
- Abaluhyia
- Aembu
- Agikuyu
- Akamba
- Akan
- Kategi
- Kipsigis
- Luo
- Nubian
- Teso

Tanzania
- Arusha-Meru

Uganda
- Baganda
- Banyankole

Zambia
- Bemba

Sudan
- Dinka

Nigeria
- Ibo

Eritrea
- Tigrinya

Rwanda & Burundi
- Tutsi

Non-African Respondents by Nationality

- American
- Indian
- Indonesian
- Irish
- Italian
- Norwegian
- Paraguayan
- Polish
- Spaniard

Appendix C

SELECTED BIBLIOGRAPHY

Ayisi, E.O. (1972). *An Introduction to the Study of African Culture.* London: Heinemann.

Ayyitey, G.B.N(1999). *Africa in Chaos.* New York: St. Martin's Griffin.

Becker, E. (1973). *The Denial of Death.* New York: The Free Press.

Boas, F. (1963). *The Mind of Primitive Man.* New York: Collier Books.

Bourdillon, M. (1990). *Religion and Society: A Text for Africa.* Harare: Mambo Press.

Brown, D.E. (1991). *Human Universals.* California: McGraw-Hill.

Burke, J. (2001). *Towards the Inculturation of Religious Life in Africa: A Case Study and Reflection Guide.* Nairobi: Paulines Publications Africa.

Geertz, C. (1973). *The Interpretation of Cultures.* New York: Basic Books.

Van Gennep, A. (1960). *The Rites of Passage.* Chicago: University of Chicago Press.

Gyekye, K. (1996). *African Cultural Values: An Introduction.* Philadelphia: Sankofa Publishing Company.

Hastings, A. (1973). *Christian Marriage in Africa.* London: SPCK.

Hillman, E. (1975) *Polygamy Reconsidered: African Plural Marriage and the Christian Churches.* New York: Orbis Books.

Idowu. E.B. (1975). *African Traditional Religion: A Definition.* New York: Orbis Books.

Jahn, J. (1990). *Muntu: African Culture and the Western World.* New York: Grove Weidenfeld.

Kirwen, M.C. (1987). *The Missionary and the Diviner.* New York: Orbis Books.

Kokwaro, J.O. (1993). *Medicinal Plants of East Africa.* Nairobi: Kenya Literature Bureau.

Kroeber, A.L. (1952). *The Nature of Culture.* Chicago: University of Chicago Press.

Lehman, A.C. & Myers, J.E. (1985). *Magic, Witchcraft and Religion.* Mountain view, California: Mayfield Publishing Company.

Magesa, L. (2004). *Anatomy of Inculturation: Transforming the Church in Africa.* New York: Orbis Books.

_____. (1998). *African Religion: The Moral Traditions of Abundant Life.* Nairobi: Paulines Publications Africa.

Mailu, D.G. (1988). *Our Kind of Polygamy.* Nairobi: Heinemann Kenya.

Mazrui, A. (1986). *The Africans: A Triple Heritage.* London: BBC Publications.

Mbiti, J.S. (1991). *Introduction to African Religion.* Nairobi: East African Educational Publishers.

_____. (1975). *Concepts of God in Africa*. Southampton: The Camelot Press Ltd.

_____. (1969). *African Religions and Philosophy*. Nairobi: East African Educational Publishers.

Mpagi, P.W. (2002). *African Christian Theology in the Contemporary Context*. Kisubi: Marianum Publishing Company Limited.

Nyamwaya, D. & Parkin, D. (Eds.). (1987). *Transformations of African Marriage*. Manchester: International African Institute.

Olupona, J.K. (1993). *African Traditional Religions in Contemporary Societies*. New York: Paragon House.

Paris, P. (1995). *The Spirituality of African Peoples: The Search for a Common Moral Discourse*. Minneapolis: Fortress Press.

Parratt, J (Ed.) (1987). *A Reader in African Christian Theology*. London: SPCK.

Pemberton, C. (2003). *Circle Thinking: African Women Theologians in Dialogue with the West*. Leiden: Koninklike Brill.

Ray, B.C. (1975). *African Religions: Symbol, Ritual and Community*. New Jersey: Prentice Hall.

Russell, B. H. (1988). *Research Methods in Cultural Anthropology*. London: Sage Publication.

Schreiter, R. (1975). *Constructing Local Theologies*. New York: Orbis Books

Shorter, A. (1998). *African Culture, An Overview: Socio-Cultural Anthropology*. Nairobi: Paulines Publications Africa.

Spradley, J. (1980). *Participant Observation*. New York: Holt Rinehart & Winston.

Stocking, G.W. (1968). *Race, Culture, and Evolution: Essays in the History of Anthropology*. New York: Free Press.

Swantz, L. (1990). *The Medicine Man Among the Zaramo of Dar Es Salaam*. Dar Es Salaam: Dar Es Salaam University Press.

Tylor, E.B. (1891). *Primitive Culture: Researches into the Development of Mythology, Philosophy, Religion, Language, Art, and Custom*. 3rd Ed., rev. Vol. I. London: Murray.

Wissler, C. (1923). *Man and Culture*. New York: Crowell Company.

Zahan, D. (1979). *The Religion, Spirituality and Thought of Traditional Africa*. Chicago: University of Chicago Press.

Zuesse, E. (1979). *Ritual Cosmos*. Athens: Ohio University Press.